anabaptist
theology
IN FACE OF
Postmodernity

The C. Henry Smith series is edited by J. Denny Weaver. As will likely be true of many future books in the CHS series, Volumes 1 and 2 are being published by Pandora Press U.S. and copublished by Herald Press in cooperation with Bluffton College and Mennonite Historical Society. Bluffton College, in consultation with the publishers, is primarily responsible for content of the studies.

1. Anabaptists and Postmodernity
   Edited by Susan Biesecker-Mast and Gerald Biesecker-Mast, 2000
2. Anabaptist Theology in Face of Postmodernity: A Proposal for the Third Millennium
   By J. Denny Weaver, 2000

anabaptist theology IN FACE OF

A Proposal for the Third Millennium

J. Denny Weaver

Foreword by Glen Stassen

The C. Henry Smith Series

Volume 2

Pandora Press U.S.
Telford, Pennsylvania

Copublished with
Herald Press
Scottdale, Pennsylvania

Pandora Press U.S. orders, information, reprint permissions:
pandoraus@netreach.net
1-215-723-9125
126 Klingerman Road, Telford PA 18969
www.PandoraPressUS.com

Library of Congress Cataloguing-in-Publication Data
Weaver, J. Denny, 1941-
  Anabaptist theology in face of postmodernity : a proposal for the third
millennium / J. Denny Weaver.
     p. cm. — (C. Henry Smith series ; v. 2)
  Includes bibliographical references and index.
  ISBN 0-9665021-4-0 (alk. paper)
     1. Mennonites—Doctrines. 2. Anabaptists—Doctrines. 3. Postmodernism—
Re ligious aspcts—Christianity. I. Title. II. Series
BX8121.2 .W43 2000
230'.97—dc21
                                                                    00-057126

11 10 09 08 07 06 05 04 03 02 01 00   10 9 8 7 6 5 4 3 2 1

To the memory of
Elizabeth Hope Weaver,
who was like a cool breeze on a hot day

CONTENTS

FOREWORD

All Christians should learn from Denny Weaver's argument, not just persons in the Anabaptist tradition. In our postmodern time, credibility is won not by making a claim to universal philosophical truth, but by demonstrating what difference Christian faith makes in the laboratory of history. In that laboratory, the Anabaptist tradition has demonstrated that it makes a difference and does witness to the way of Jesus Christ.

That witness also gives us guidance for understanding the meaning of the atonement. All Christians know Jesus died for our sins. But ask how his death took care of our sins, and you are likely to get a puzzled look. Weaver demonstrates, I think beyond dispute, that historically, Anabaptist interpretation of the atonement has emphasized that Jesus' own way of faithfulness was crucial to the effectiveness of his atoning death. Likewise, following Jesus' way is a key part of our participating in the benefits of his death for us.

The classic Christus Victor theory of the atonement, interpreted with attention to the way of Jesus in the Gospels—the way Jesus followed in winning victory over the powers of evil, violence, and death—holds more promise than other classic theories of the atonement for Anabaptist faithfulness, and Gospel faithfulness. Through Jesus' life, death, *and* resurrection, God overcame the powers of evil, violence, and death. In his ministry, his teaching, his love, his nonviolence, Jesus confronted the powers. They amassed their forces against him, and crucified him, but he stayed faithful to God, and God faithfully gave him the victory. We participate in the victory through faith that includes following his way, as part of the church community where the victory is won.

The Christus Victor understanding emphasizes that the church is intrinsic to the gospel; salvation is not only an event for scattered individuals. This, too, is an important Anabaptist theme. And, I would add, a theme for many sixteenth century Anabaptists, and now for many "new Mennonites" is the Christus Victor understanding that crucial for the Victory of Jesus is the work of the Holy Spirit, empowering and sanctifying (see the book of Acts and the letters of Paul).

Weaver also demonstrates that most historical Mennonites adopted, from other Christians of the time, a *substitutionary/satisfaction understanding of the atonement* which overlooks these essential Anabaptist themes: the faithful way of Jesus Christ, nonviolence, and the community of the church. Therefore Mennonites began the work of modifying the satisfaction theory to incorporate these classic Anabaptist themes. Carrying that work of correction to its logical conclusion will lead us to adopt the Christus Victor rather than satisfaction view of atonement.

The Christus Victor understanding is at least as "classic" and as biblical as the satisfaction theory. It is strongly affirmed in the Gospels, in the Book of Revelation—and in the letters of Paul, especially 1 and 2 Thessalonians, 1 Corinthians, and Romans. Furthermore, it was taught by the early church fathers, especially Irenaeus. It came to be known as "the classic theory," or "the patristic theory," and was also taught by Martin Luther in the Reformation, and Bishop Gustaf Aulén in the twentieth century.[1] It was taught as well by John Howard Yoder,[2] whose growing influence makes his thought, in my judgment, almost a classic already.

In his book *Keeping Salvation Ethical*, Weaver affirmed that the classic creeds do witness to truth that is essential to Jesus. Similarly, one can affirm that the satisfaction theory, if modified, does have biblical and experiential basis, and does pay attention to Jesus' suffering on the cross. But the same is true of the Christus Victor theory, which emphasizes the life of Jesus, Jesus' submission to the cross, *and* the resurrection. It can readily incorporate the truth in the satisfaction theory.

This is not relativism. The criterion for testing the truth of an understanding of the atonement or any other doctrine is, says Weaver, "a criterion accessible to all, namely the narrative of Jesus" (p. 69)."If Jesus Christ is our foundation, then it is Jesus' story and the 'politics of Jesus'—not the shape of a national ethos or fourth- and fifth-century creedal formulas—that should determine the contour of our theological agenda" (p. 47). Here, I believe, is the witness for our time, which looks for credibility in lives that follow Jesus Christ. We need to do the rich exegesis of the gospel story to develop the meaning more fully, and to give thanks to God for what God has done and is now doing in Christ!

—*Glen Stassen, Lewis Smedes Professor of Christian Ethics*
Fuller Theological Seminary
Pasadena, California

AUTHOR'S PREFACE

An ongoing agenda item and two conversations converged to bring this book into focus. The agenda item was my enduring pursuit of the following questions: whether the peace churches (or Anabaptists and Mennonites as a peace church) have or ought to have a specific perspective on theology, and whether a stance shaped by peace church assumptions might produce a different view of classic questions from that of the majority Christian tradition. My work assumes that the answer to both questions is yes.

In one way or another these questions have been integral to my theologizing since the first theology course I taught as a newly minted Ph.D. some twenty-five years ago. In light of these continuing questions, in my mind this book is really about peace theology.

The first conversation that helped to shape this volume occurs on a continuing and sometimes daily basis with Gerald and Susan Biesecker-Mast. From them I learned that my theologizing reflected postmodernity but without my acknowledgment of it. Even before they became my colleagues at Bluffton College, Sue and Gerald introduced me to the idea of postmodernity, and to both the promise and the dangers that it holds for an Anabaptist, Mennonite peace church approach to theology. Their influence on this book is great.

A second important conversation occurred about two years ago with John Howard Yoder. John helped to focus my understanding of the real but unacknowledged assumption operating behind all twentieth-century Mennonite theologizing. All this theologizing, he said, assumed the existence of a theology-in-general without acknowledging either this assumption or that significant differences existed concerning the shape and composition of the supposed general theology. This assumption drove twentieth-century Mennonite efforts to engender theology that simultaneously built on and was distinct from the supposed general theology of mainstream Protestant orthodoxy.

The intersection of these two conversations with my ongoing theological quest produced an energized mixture. Out of this the chapters of the book emerged as a multifaceted depiction of Anabaptist theology in face of postmodernity. The term *Anabaptist* in the title acknowledges that the book brings sixteenth- and nineteenth-century theologizing into the conversation alongside more recent perspectives.

A number of people read and responded to portions of this manuscript at some stage of preparation. Those whose names I recall include Rachel Reesor, Gerald Schlabach, William Trollinger, John Kampen, Venice Haynes, Loren Johns, Dwight Hopkins, James Cone, Karen Baker-Fletcher, Garth Kasimu Baker-Fletcher, Will Coleman, Howard Wiley, Alain Epp Weaver, Sonia Weaver, Thomas Heilke, Abraham Friesen, and L. L. Hartzler. Jeff Gundy's reading of the entire manuscript proved very helpful. Susan Biesecker-Mast and Gerald Biesecker-Mast diligently responded to the complete manuscript with important suggestions for nuancing the discussion of postmodernity. I am grateful to Anna Diller who did most of the work of compiling the index.

I am very thankful for all these contributions of time, good faith, and counsel, even on those occasions when I ran the risk of not accepting a suggestion. I apologize for those whose names I may have overlooked.

It was a pleasure to work with Michael King of Pandora Press U.S., who played two different roles in the production of this book. At the request of the C. Henry Smith Series editor, Michael played the role of series editor for the evaluation stage. He solicited independent evaluation and orchestrated the process of blind review to determine whether the manuscript met the prescribed criteria for inclusion in the series. When the review process returned a strong recommendation for publication in the series, Michael then began functioning as publisher. In that role his contributions included suggestions for both form and content, as well as warm support for the series in which this book appears. I am very grateful to Lee Snyder and John Kampen, the president and dean of Bluffton College, whose development of the C. Henry Smith Series makes this book possible.

But books do not live on academic and institutional contributions alone. This one would not exist without the inspiration and support of my wife, Mary, who remains peaceful both despite and because of this writing.

Finally, I want to acknowledge a special contribution to this book that has peace at its heart. Thoughts of my niece Elizabeth Hope Weaver; her parents, Gary Alvin and Susan Lee Weaver; and her brother Christopher John Weaver frequently inspired my thoughts during the writing of this manuscript. Elizabeth Hope was truly a peaceful person. She died in a traffic accident early in March 1996 at age twenty-two. The response of her parents and brother to the tragic and overwhelming circumstances of that accident modeled peace and revealed where Elizabeth learned to be peaceful. May the intent of this manuscript be worthy of her memory and of the lived expressions of peace embodied by Elizabeth Hope Weaver's family.

—J. Denny Weaver
Bluffton College
Bluffton, Ohio

INTRODUCTION

Mennonites began exploring systematic theology as a genre only in the 1980s. Opening this exploration posed new questions and choices.

What would a theology for Mennonites look like? Is there a difference between theology for Mennonites as Christians and theology for Mennonites as a peace church? Does this theological project draw on resources from inside the Anabaptist heritage and Mennonite tradition, from outside, or from both? How does a theology for the peace church relate to and compare with other Christian theology or theologies? What is the vantage point from which to judge whether the resulting theology has integrity and credibility, and whether it is appropriate for Anabaptist-Mennonites as a peace church?

Because these are postmodern questions, Anabaptist theology at the start of the third millennium is theology standing in face of postmodernity. While the following answers to these questions draw on sources from Anabaptist and Mennonite historical traditions, the conclusions apply to anyone who seeks to take Christian faith seriously in the contemporary world.

POSTMODERNITY AND THE DEMISE OF CHRISTENDOM

Although this book is not about postmodernity, it is a postmodern book. The idea of postmodernity has generated much discussion, as one might judge from the thirty-seven presentations of an August 1998 conference at Bluffton College on "Anabaptists and

Postmodernity."[1] These papers reveal no consensus among Mennonites about how to define and understand postmodernity. Neither is there consensus about postmodernity in the various intellectual worlds beyond Mennonites. Even in the absence of a definition, however, we can still identify certain characteristics of postmodernity that are relevant for the here.

In the realm of theology postmodernity corresponds to the demise of Christendom. The roots of Christendom reach back to the fourth century, when emperor Constantine legalized Christianity. Under Christendom the assumption prevailed that there was one general theological Truth for all Christians, or one generally recognizable set of answers. These answers were purveyed by the one church that encompassed the entire social order.

Working in uneasy tandem, sometimes in tension, religious and political authorities watched over that church. Over the centuries church and civil rulers struggled with one other for ultimate authority. Theological disagreements were assumed to be in-house arguments about the nature of the one faith for the one church.

With the emergence of the Eastern schism of 1054 C.E., then with the Reformation of the sixteenth century, competing visions of the church developed. Each claimed to be the true church that should be established and sustained by the civil authorities that ruled the social order. Amid these sometimes bitter conflicts about the identity of the one faith to be established, however, there was little questioning of the assumption that there was one faith for the entire social order. Among the alternatives that emerged from the Reformation, only the several Anabaptist movements rejected the solidarity of church and state, or church and the social order.

This rejection of the state church was not a completely new concept, however. Anabaptists stood in an ancient line of groups such as Donatists, Albigensians, Waldensians, and Czech Brethren, who, while not organically related, had in common the idea of rejecting some element of Constantinianism.

The idea that there is (or ought to be) one faith that encompasses the entire social order has continued in a different form in the United States. As John Howard Yoder and others have demonstrated, civil religion and public Protestantism of the United States are a continuation of the Constantinian synthesis and the church that identifies with the social order.[2] The Christendom idea remains alive and well in the United States in the belief that the U.S. is (or ought to be) a Christian nation, even if most people do not recognize or ignore the continuity with medieval Christendom and the Constantinian synthesis.

As head of this Christian nation, one of the president's roles is that of high priest. He functions as a symbol of the nation's morality in a way not expected of members of Congress or other government officials. An example of this is the virtually required mention by the White House of the minister who prays with the president before major military operations are undertaken.

Bill Clinton was clearly acting as high priest, with the nation as his congregation, when he used a national prayer breakfast as the setting in which to confess his sin of infidelity. The president asked for forgiveness of all those he had offended and suggested that his actions of confession and asking forgiveness could be an example for the nation.

Another sign of the priestly role of the U.S. president is the move that began with Jimmy Carter for candidates to announce that they are born again and that their lives are going much better since they have invited God into their hearts.

The new element in this fusion of theological truth, church, and social order has been the erosion of the assumption that there is one truth to discover. In the latter half of the twentieth century, this assumption came under increasingly intense challenge.

The loss or abandonment of the assumption about a prevailing truth, whether Christian or philosophical and rational, is a characteristic of postmodernity. Some people decry Christendom's demise as secularization, a charge raised in some form since the Enlightenment. Others have welcomed the openness to new truths it appears to offer.

The demise of the idea of one truth has occurred in two stages.

A popular introduction to postmodernity by Bluffton College professor Susan Biesecker-Mast, which partly summarizes Stephen Toulmin's narrative of the emergence of modernity, highlights the role of the Enlightenment.[3] Seventeenth-century Europe went through the Thirty Years War between Protestants and Catholics. It was called a war about religion, "caused by the passions of clashing religious commitments."[4]

Enlightenment philosophers reasoned that such wars could be avoided in the future if people could set aside their religious convictions. Governments could be built and decisions made on rational principles accessible to everyone. If individuals could "subordinate their individual interests to the common good or negotiate those interests rationally, then they could govern themselves (through a nation-state) both freely and peacefully."[5]

The idea that the one, commonly shared truth would emerge from presumed universal philosophy (thus bringing enlightenment) has come to be called modernity.

However, basing decisions on supposedly universal, rational principles did not attain the hoped-for result. Rather than eliminating wars, this merely shifted the apparent foundation of the principles on which wars were fought. Rather than fighting to defend religiously based national principles, nations now fought about philosophically grounded, supposedly universal principles such as the "democratic way of life" or "justice, freedom, and sovereignty."

"Enlightenment's reason, then, did not end war. Instead 'reason' became the reason to fight 'good' wars."[6]

This shift from a religious to a philosophical foundation for truth provided a variation in the search for the one truth. Enlightenment, the assertion of a supposedly universal philosophical foundation for truth, was thus in no way the abandonment of the idea that there was one truth. Rather, it was a shift from sources inside the church to sources outside the church as the presumed basis for identifying and sustaining the one truth for which everyone was seeking. Postmodernity is the recent term of choice to characterize the abandonment of this philosophy as the presumed foundation for universal truth.

Biesecker-Mast also describes the relativism and individualism frequently mentioned as characteristics of postmodernity. As many Americans lose confidence in Christian faith and as reason proves a shaky foundation from which to govern, people are turning increasingly to themselves and to their own stories for meaning and identity.

With ethnic traditions and ancestral histories forgotten, identity now comes from the malls, where people can buy clothing, music, and other accessories to create their own culture and identities. With the loss of an idea of a larger story and little understanding of global relationships, people lack coherent schemes for evaluating their stories in comparison with others. Many of the students in my classes can say, virtually in four-part harmony, "What's right for me may not be right for you; rather, the important thing is that we make up our minds for ourselves." Biesecker-Mast describes this postmodern U.S. outlook as "no good reasons, no shared meaning, too much work, and endless consumption."[7]

The postmodern doubt about the possibility of identifying one universal truth encompasses both religious truth and philosophical truth.[8] This questioning constitutes the larger social context, external to the Mennonite churches, when we discuss the question of what a theology for Mennonites as a peace church should look like.

This context both offers a opportunity and poses a significant challenge to the project of Mennonite theology. With Christendom's theology and Enlightenment's philosophical claims removed from the pedestal of generalness or universality, the views of some small religious traditions, particularly Mennonites, have begun to attain visibility and a new level of credibility. When it is recognized that every faith and every tradition has roots in a particular context, then no particular theology is accorded a universally recognized, a priori status as the correct one. If the debate is fair, the supposedly lesser theological traditions have no greater burden of proof than that which rests on the previously presumed general tradition.

With specific reference to Christendom and Anabaptism, the postmodern condition means that the theological traditions which emerged from the church of the Constantinian synthesis and continued in the Protestant Reformation—the so-called mainline denominations—now appear as particular traditions. As such, they would not necessarily have a favored place over the several Anabaptist movements that dissented from Christendom's fusion of church and state.

A particular theology for Mennonites as a peace church can now assert its version of truth on a logically equal footing with the theology of Christendom. The context of postmodernity thus offers Mennonites an opportunity virtually unprecedented since the early church: a chance to articulate and receive a hearing for a theology shaped specifically by the nonviolence of Jesus.

At the same time, it is important to point out that this claim to equal footing exists only in an abstract sense. Christendom theologians often presume some kind of a priori privilege, even if Mennonite theologians claim equal footing.

Christendom exercises a two-fold hegemony, both theologically and practically. Its advocates often do (even if they should not) set the terms of the discussion and the questions to answer, and Christendom surrounds us with the thought that pervades all our efforts at theologizing. The advent of postmodernity has not, therefore, made it easy for Mennonite theology to assume an equal voice in the discussion.

What it does mean is that an opening now exists for Anabaptist Mennonite theology. Mennonite theologians speaking from a particular Mennonite assumption cannot presume that others will listen merely because postmodernity has called reason into question and pointed out the particularity of all traditions. Nonetheless, there is an opening if arguments are made persuasively.

This opportunity also presents a serious challenge. It holds up the specter of unbounded relativism in which each particular theology is assumed valid for a particular group, but is also assumed to have no validity beyond its particular group. In the face of this apparent relativity, we must recall that Christian faith makes ultimate claims about Jesus Christ. A theology for Mennonites shaped by Jesus' nonviolent story is a theology that confesses the ultimate truth of Jesus Christ.

The fact that truth is particular does not mean that it has no ultimate or universal meaning. It is not a contradiction to say that particular truth has ultimate or universal meaning. Rather, it means to recognize the particular foundation of those universal claims, and to acknowledge that there is no other universally recognized location from which to prove the truth of the claims. There is no "place" beyond Jesus Christ to which one can appeal to validate the ultimate truth of Jesus Christ. One can confess the ultimate meaning of particular claims but one cannot prove those claims by appeal to supposedly universally recognizable foundations.

The way to assert truth that one cannot validate by supposed universal foundations is to choose to live a life shaped by that truth, even when others oppose it. The most profound demonstration that Jesus truly is the Lord when there is no proof, as John Howard Yoder wrote, is that we would want to follow him when we do not have to. That puts us in the same category as Jesus' first disciples: "We don't have to [follow him], as they [the disciples] didn't then."[9]

Within that context, if we are aware of the danger it poses, the pluralism that comprises one characteristic of what today we call postmodernity can be an ally. We can be tactical allies with those who deconstruct "deceptive orthodox claims to logically coercive certainty," or with those who use "liberation language to dismantle the alliance of church with privilege."[10]

INTERNAL CONTEXTS FOR MENNONITE THEOLOGY

Postmodernity without a universally provable ultimate truth comprises the widest external context in which to reflect on the project to develop a theology for Mennonites. However, there are other factors as well, some more internal, which also propel the project to develop a theology for Mennonites.

While Mennonites did not make use of the idea of systematic theology before the 1980s, it was not that they had done no prior theologizing. Rather they had done their theologizing under different categories and nomenclature. Daniel Kauffman, whose three volumes of theology defined the thinking for several generations of the Mennonite Church, wrote about Mennonite theology as doctrines of the Bible.[11]

A quarter century later, the biblical focus still prevailed, as indicated in the subtitle of John C. Wenger's *Introduction to Theology*: "An interpretation of the doctrinal content of Scripture, written to strengthen a childlike faith in Christ."[12] Two decades further along, presenting a quite different theology, E. G. Kaufman was still doing theology for Mennonites as an explication of Christian themes, rather than as a statement of systematic theology.[13]

Harold S. Bender promulgated another way of purveying theology for Mennonites. Although his theology always aligned itself with classic orthodoxy, Bender early in his career was considered something of a liberal in his context. Because the new Goshen College president feared that his theological views might not be acceptable to the constituency, Bender's first appointment at the school was to teach history. This appointment contributed to an interest in Mennonite history that Bender had already begun cultivating in Europe. He began to develop a vigorous program of research and publication in Anabaptist and Mennonite studies at Goshen College.[14]

Historical studies thus became Bender's primary mode of theological inquiry, and he defined Mennonite theology via Anabaptist history. In other words, Bender provided a theological and ethical program for the modern Mennonite Church by describing what the Anabaptist founding fathers had believed. Reflecting neo-orthodoxy's depiction of a homogeneous Reformation theology that was neither liberal nor fundamentalist, Bender described a pure, sixteenth-century Anabaptism[15] that modern Mennonites could emulate. Bender's "The Anabaptist Vision" became its defining symbol.[16]

Recent scholarship on Anabaptism, with its description of diverse origins and a pluralistic movement, renders that methodology problematic.[17] One cannot very well cite the Anabaptist theological perspective when there is not one normative Anabaptist movement.

The modern awareness that theology involves more than citing Scripture, as well as the demise of Bender's Anabaptist Vision as a defining statement of contemporary Mennonite identity, are two cultural factors in the turn toward discussion of a systematic Mennonite theology. According to an informal survey, the first conference sanctioned by denominational institutions specifically on systematic theology for Mennonites occurred in 1983 at what is now the Associated Mennonite Biblical Seminary.[18] Theology as a discipline accepted by Mennonites is not yet twenty years old.

The shift to theology has not been easy. In his *Systematic Theology*, Mennonite Gordon Kaufman acknowledged Anabaptist origins for some of his positions, described the "nonresistance of God," and suggested that the church should have a "nonresistant stance" like that of Jesus.[19] However, Kaufman's historicist methodology and perspective on issues such as the resurrection of Jesus are likely what prevented this first modern systematic theology by a Mennonite from becoming a central player in Mennonite theological discussions. C. Norman Kraus's *Jesus Christ Our Lord*[20] appeared as the logical, neo-orthodox successor to Wenger's *Introduction to Theology*. But although *Jesus Christ Our Lord* was published by the largest Mennonite press, the somewhat tumultuous response it received showed that systematic theology for Mennonites still stood on shaky ground.[21] Mennonite writers, who discussed theology from positions in Mennonite schools, either continued to do so while looking over their shoulders at administrators made nervous by potential constituency reaction or chose not to publish their cutting edge views.

In the 1990s, theology finally emerged as a discipline whose time had come for Mennonites. *Conrad Grebel Review*, which began publication in 1983, has given voice to much of the discussion of Mennonite theology. *Mennonite Quarterly Review* has also published numerous articles on theology. Perhaps one of the clearest indications that theology for Mennonites and by Mennonites has come of age is that there are disagreements—even sharp ones—about the focus and the contours of a theology for Mennonites. The debate is such that in the short space of a decade, it is already possible to identify clear options and differing methodologies and schools of thought.[22]

In less than two decades several full theologies have appeared, offering an array of approaches but each claiming to include, to represent, or to make use of perspectives from the Mennonite peace tradition. In addition to Kraus's books, these include Thomas Finger's two-volume *Christian Theology in Eschatological Perspective*,[23] Daniel Liechty's *Theology in Postliberal Perspective*,[24] and *In Face of Mystery* by Gordon Kaufman.[25] To these should be added A. James Reimer's works, which argue that a theology for Mennonites should build on classic orthodoxy,[26] and my own suggestions toward a theology for the peace church,[27] which motivates this book and is sketched in chapter 6. However one regards any particular argument, the plethora of theologies and of discussions about theology that have arisen among Mennonites in less than twenty years is striking.

CLASSIC ORTHODOXY OR A DISTINCT MENNONITE THEOLOGY?

Postmodernity confronts the contemporary peace church, and in particular Mennonites and other Anabaptist groups, with new questions and choices about theological directions. One formulation of the choice is to ask whether Mennonites as a peace church either already have, or should develop, a distinctive theology that reflects their particular historical tradition.

A number of scholars have suggested that the future direction of theology for Mennonites lies in identification with and building on the foundation of classic orthodoxy. Those who advocate this direction point out, correctly, that Mennonites have not had an explicit tradition of systematic theology, and that the minimal theological record that exists shows a Mennonite theology identified with and built on classic orthodoxy. Chapters 3, 4, and 5 in this book will assess some of this borrowing of traditional theology. For those who emphasize the supposed orthodox legacy in Mennonite theologizing, it seems almost self-evident that a comprehensive theology for Mennonites should be built on the orthodox core that is already apparent in the Mennonite tradition.

In contrast to this position, however, I believe that Mennonites do have a distinct, if not completely unique, theological tradition. While observations of the history of Mennonite theology do indeed show appeals to classic formulations, careful analysis also reveals that assumptions about nonviolence and believers church ecclesiology have shaped Mennonite views on the classic questions of theology. Consequently, past Mennonite theology is not merely a restatement of classic orthodoxy. A different direction is indicated. The chapters to follow thus argue in different ways that Mennonites as a peace church should develop that distinctiveness into a particular theology for the peace church which, rather than building on classic orthodoxy, will pose important alternatives to it.

The Place of Peace

Emanating from the first choice is a second decision to be made about future theological directions. This choice concerns the place of peace, nonviolence, and believers church ecclesiology in a theology for the peace church.

Do assumptions about nonviolence and believers church ecclesiology shape a theology for Mennonites as a peace church that is distinct from theology produced by the Christendom traditions? Is peace an issue which Mennonites should allow to separate them from other Christians? These are not trivial issues in an increasingly secular world where Christians are a minority religion.

Some peace church adherents believe that one should not allow commitment to one issue, such as the rejection of violence, to further fragment an already fractious Christian church and Christian tradition. Not allowing peace to separate us from other Christians does not mean abandoning a commitment to nonviolence by Mennonites, the argument goes. It just means that we will not make it a test issue which would hinder linkages and fellowship across denominational boundaries or prevent an otherwise earnest seeker from joining a Mennonite congregation.

I believe that such a view, however well intentioned, is actually a declaration that nonviolence and the rejection of the sword are not intrinsic to the teaching and example of Jesus. Further, I believe that it is precisely at the point of rejecting violence that the reign of God made visible in Jesus is most distinct from the prevailing social order. In a variety of ways the following pages exhibit the potential impact of making nonviolence and believers church ecclesiology intrinsic dimensions of theological equation.

Grounds for Universality

A third way to conceptualize the choices among these theological approaches concerns the fashion in which a theology for Mennonites can claim universality.

Is a theology for Mennonites universal, as some have argued, because it builds on and is in agreement with the older and supposedly wider theology that Western Christendom has presumed to be universal? Or, as has already been suggested above, should a theology for Mennonites make a different confession of universality? The question is whether one discusses the nature of universal truth from a stance in the majority tradition of Western Christendom, or from an alternative stance for which rejection of violence is an intrinsic dimension of the gospel of Jesus Christ.

This way of posing the choice is most clearly a postmodern question. To argue that the universal meaning of theology for Mennonites depends on identity with the supposedly wider and time-honored theology of Christendom is to reject the postmodern realization that every theological tradition is particular, including the formulations of classic orthodoxy. Conversely, it is clearly a postmodern stance to point out the particularity of classic theology and to confess a truth with universal intent from the particular perspective of the Anabaptist peace church tradition that can critique Christendom's violence-accommodating theology.

These ways of visualizing the choice of direction for Mennonite theologizing intersect and complement each other. These choices are driven by "push" factors, or impulses from within the Anabaptist, peace church tradition, and by "pull" factors, or options opened up by postmodernity and awareness of the demise of Christendom.

TOWARD A POSTMODERN THEOLOGY FOR A PEACE CHURCH

The chapters to follow all reflect both the push and pull: the external condition of postmodernity and the internal drive to identify the future faithful direction of Mennonites as a peace church. These impulses arrive at the same point of discussion, albeit coming from different directions.

Chapter 1 considers the question of a theology for Mennonites as a function of the significant differences in cultural ethos that exist between Canada and the United States. The United States has a monolithic civil religion and emphasizes the image of a melting pot, while Canada lacks a corresponding civil religion and has a cultural mosaic.

These differences have pushed Mennonite theology in different directions in the two countries. Nonetheless, theologians in both nations face different versions of the same temptation: namely, to allow the church to become fused with the social order. Chapter 1 argues that the best way to avoid this temptation is not to build on orthodox theology, which originated in such a fusion of church and society, but to develop a theology that clearly distinguishes the church from the social order.

Chapter 2 surveys Mennonite efforts in the twentieth century to find a foundational, general core of doctrines shared with all Christians. The analysis shows that while Mennonites of fundamentalist, evangelical, and liberal stripes alike assumed that there was a general theological core to which Mennonites added their theological distinctives, they had quite different assumptions about what that theology-in-general looked like. In response, I suggest abandonment of the idea of a theology-in-general, and development of a theology that reflects specific Mennonite peace and justice concerns.

Chapter 3 focuses on nineteenth-century Mennonite theologizing. Using atonement as the indicator doctrine, the analysis shows that while the nineteenth-century writers all professed atonement views that would identify them with classic, evangelical positions, to describe them as evangelical on the basis of a shared doctrine does not fathom the true character of nineteenth-century Mennonite theology and ethics. Instead, the true continuation of their intent in postmodern configuration would be a theology specifically shaped by assumptions of nonviolence and believers church ecclesiology.

Chapters 2 and 3 examine materials in which Anabaptist and Mennonite writers clearly adopted and used traditional, mainline theology. A number of contemporary Mennonite scholars appeal to such writings to argue that contemporary Mennonites should affirm classic creeds and traditional theology. Chapter 4 provides a three-fold response to such arguments.

First, the chapter uses examples from both sixteenth-century Anabaptist theology and more recent Mennonite writings to show that contemporary assumptions alway influence how we read historical sources. Interpreting this material is much more a matter of applying present-day assumptions than of simply reading the truth off the surface of the historic sources. Second, the chapter explains how the context of persecution, followed by other recent factors, has prevented Anabaptists and Mennonites from having the leisure to consider new theological directions until virtually the present time. Finally, the essay concludes that history is not destiny—that decisions in earlier generations do not obligate us to similar choices today.

Chapter 5 outlines some specific suggestions on the shape of a postmodern theology for Mennonites as a peace church and conversation with Christendom theology, as well as examples of black and womanist theology. The discussion summarizes how my critique of classic Christology and atonement formulas was anticipated and paralleled by James H. Cone.

In my critique, which developed quite independent of Cone's, I argue that the abstract categories of Nicaea-Chalcedon and Anselmian atonement accommodated the sword. Cone shows how they accommodate slavery and racism. In response, each of us advocates a historicized version of *Christus Victor* atonement imagery.

This discussion continues with reflections on *My Sister, My Brother* by Karen Baker-Fletcher and Garth Kasimu Baker-Fletcher, who represent second-generation black and womanist theology.

Engaging Mennonite theology with black theology has several implications for future Mennonite theologizing. For one, it demonstrates that Mennonites are not alone in rethinking their theology in light of postmodernity. For another, it lays bare the extent to which peace and justice concerns have not been intrinsic to Mennonite theology , and strongly points to the need for Mennonites to develop a theology specifically shaped by peace church ethical concerns. Finally, these observations indicate a previously unrecognized avenue for potentially fruitful ecumenical conversations.

The last item in the book is an essay concerning some theological implications that emerge from consideration of ecclesiological ambiguity in Harold S. Bender's *The Anabaptist Vision*,[28] a work that continues to have a great deal of influence even today. Bender wrote that Anabaptists both built on the vision of Martin Luther and John Calvin and posed an alternative to it, and that Anabaptists both rejected the ecclesiology of Christendom and accepted Christendom's theology.

While Bender wrote to distinguish Anabaptists, some recent writers have appealed to Anabaptist Vision to blend Anabaptists into mainline Protestantism. The essay suggests that the ambiguity of ecclesiology in Anabaptist Vision should be resolved on the side of developing alternatives to the theology of Christendom. In this argument, the essay takes a quite different path to reach the same conclusion as do the earlier chapters of the book.

anabaptist theology
IN FACE OF
Postmodernity

ONE

MENNONITE THEOLOGY IN FACE OF CANADIAN AND U.S. SOCIETY[1]

NATIONAL SIMILARITIES AND DIFFERENCES

The United States and Canada share a great deal, starting with the longest demilitarized border in the world. Citizens pass freely and easily from one nation to the other. Both countries claim English as their dominant language.

Canadians and Americans watch many of the same movies and television programs, and they follow baseball, basketball, and hockey teams in the same professional leagues. When their supposedly dominant national hockey teams fell far short of expectations in the 1998 Winter Olympic Games, people on both sides of the border felt similar embarrassment.

However, such similarities can easily blind us to the major differences of cultural ethos and national identity between Canada and the United States. It is my thesis that theologizing in both the United States and Canada has been profoundly marked by the national character in our respective nations. In this chapter I will sketch some of these differences, then suggest how they have been reflected in one slice of Mennonite theologizing in the United States. This analysis will provide the basis for suggestions about the implications of national differences for the future of Mennonite theologizing, as well as for the very identity of Mennonite churches in both nations.

33

Two National Characters[2]

The United States has a civil religion that presents itself as hegemonic or all encompassing, and the nation considers itself a melting pot of cultures. Canada lacks a unifying civil religion, and rather than having a cultural melting pot, it describes itself as a cultural mosaic. These differences are profound and say much about the character of the two nations.

Make no mistake about it. The civil religion that exists in the United States is indeed a religion. Postmodernity's insight about the particularity of all theology can highlight civil religion's specifically U.S. context, as well as the symbiotic relationship between this faith and what Catherine Albanese called "public Protestantism."[3] Acknowledging the particular character of these supposedly general theological phenomena sheds new light on the relationship of Mennonite theology to supposed general Protestant theology and to a supposed generally religious national ethos.

Is Mennonite theology a subcategory of a larger or wider, generally religious national identity? Or should Mennonite theology pose a particular theological witness over against the particular theological witness of the supposedly general national theologies? As will become clear in what follows, to pose the questions in this way already reflects a U.S. rather than a Canadian context. Since these questions and answers take on different forms in the United States and Canada, comparing the two national cultures is highly significant for contemplating the continuing development of theology for Mennonites in a postmodern world.

U.S. Civil Religion

Civil religion in the United States consists of a "set of sacred persons, events, beliefs, rituals, and symbols quite distinct from those of the denominations."[4] These sacred connotations are derived from a founding myth and imbue the nation with a divine identity and agenda.

According to the myth, oppressed peoples from Europe came to America seeking freedom, which was then forged in the Revolutionary War. The righteousness of this war was anchored, as the Declaration of Independence put it, in "a firm Reliance on the Protection of Divine Providence." This founding myth serves as the story of every

American, including all immigrants, who learn that their newly acquired freedom is founded on George Washington's defeat of the evil British.

This story conveys a specific point—that war is the basis for freedom and that without war there will not be freedom. The curriculum of public schools and many private schools teach the link between freedom and violence very effectively. When I ask students in my classes what would have happened had there been no war in the 1770s, they frequently answer, "We wouldn't have our freedom," or "I guess that we would still be oppressed by the British."

Likewise, deeply entrenched in the public mentality is the notion that if the nation is to "do something" about Saddam Hussein, Somalia, Libya, Serbia, terrorism, crime, or drugs, effective action implies the use of guns or bombs. In the public mind, violence and freedom are tightly bound together. Public ceremonies on patriotic holidays, with politicians of all stripes clamoring to participate and be seen, consistently reinforce the link.

Civil religion portrays its version of religion in primarily civil or secular terms. The unaware do not even recognize it as a religion. The God of civil religion is referred to in rather vague, distant terms: Supreme Being, Supreme Judge, and so on. My favorite example comes from Richard Nixon's address at a Billy Graham crusade. Nixon looked directly into the television camera and reverently confessed that the basis of his strength to carry out the awesome duties of the presidency came from his great faith in "Something Else."

Such vague references to God in civil religion both allow and expect every religious group and denomination to include itself as a lesser subcategory under the umbrella of the higher national civil religion. When this happens, each denomination becomes a particular representation of the national religion. The presence of U.S. flags in churches symbolizes this representation and union. These are churches which frequently assume that institutions of the sociopolitical order are the appropriate institutions through which to express Christian social concern. Christians of this orientation assume and often express the idea that one serves God by serving the nation. This is a modern American continuation of Christendom.

U.S. civil religion lifts a specific political philosophy (democracy) and a specific economic philosophy (capitalism) to the level of ultimate, unquestioned belief. Alongside these social doctrines stand a number of individual rights that are also given ultimate—that is, in-alienable, by right of birth—significance. These include freedoms of speech, press, assembly, and so on. The ultimacy of these social and individual beliefs is shown by the nation's willingness to invoke the supreme sanction—death—on nations which threaten these beliefs.

Public Protestantism

Alongside civil religion is the religious entity that Catherine Albanese has called public Protestantism. In contrast to civil religion, which uses nonreligious language, public Protestantism is specifically religious. It consists of the shared beliefs and practices derived from the majority Protestant traditions that together give the United States a publicly (if unofficially) Protestant character.

Public Protestantism operates under the conditions of religious liberty, democratic equality, and separation of church and state. Its denominations, which preserve their particular teachings, nonetheless consider themselves part of a larger Protestant and American whole. These denominations are supported by voluntary contributions and voluntary membership.

Due to the influence of revivalism and the frontier experience, public Protestantism tends toward reductionism—an inclination to prune religion to the bare essentials and to promote a simple gospel. It also has an ahistorical character that locates the most important be-ginnings in North America and discounts European Christian origins and the continuation of theology inherited from Europe.

In continuity with its Puritan origins, public Protestantism has a strong moral component. Moral issues—slavery and temperance in the nineteenth century, abortion, homosexuality and "Hollywood morality" today, become the test of public life.

Over the past three decades, Catholics in the United States have increasingly changed to incorporate the views characterized here as public Protestantism.

The voluntary character of public Protestantism obscures the fact that, despite the explicit separation of church and state, it stands as the unofficial but real dominant public religion. As such, it is a quasi-es-tablished church. Separation of church and state exists in the sense that the Unitd States Congress does not approve the liturgy and the hymnbook worshipers use on Sunday. However, the United States is an overtly religious society with a public Protestantism that complements the national civil religion.

Public Protestantism comes in both liberal and conservative versions. The recent rise of the religious right is really a shift from liberal (or ecumenical) to evangelical voices as the dominant ones in defining the public religion of the nation.

As John H. Yoder, John A. Lapp, and others have shown, civil religion and public Protestantism continue the Constantinian synthesis that identifies the church with the social order.[5] A brief sketch of the linkage starts with the observation that the magisterial Protestants of the sixteenth century continued the established church of medieval Christendom. The change brought by the Reformation was that the political authorities now had to choose which among the competing faiths was the one to establish. The Puritans left England because parliament and king established the wrong religion; they settled New England with the intent of establishing the correct one.

When the church was disestablished at the federal level after the Revolution of 1776 and by states in the early nineteenth century, the response of the religious majority was to Christianize America voluntarily.[6] The nineteenth-century revival movement, along with the development of missionary societies, Bible and tract societies, YMCAs, and a host of other nineteenth-century parachurch organizations, had that purpose in mind. The idea that the United States is (or ought to be) a "Christian nation" remains current. It is pursued with considerable vigor, even if the continuity with medieval Christendom and the Constantinian synthesis is not always recognized or acknowledged.

The U.S. Melting Pot

Along with its civil religion, the ethos of the United States also functions as a melting pot of cultures. Academics today criticize this idea, and the terminology has disappeared from its once prominent place in school curricula, to be replaced by *cultural mosaic*. Yet the melting pot image continues to function in the popular imagination. This concept assumes individuals will lose, abandon, or at least subdue their original ethnic identity and adopt an American national identity. According to this view, the growth of the United States is the story of how people lose old identities to adopt a new, superior one.

The melting pot that produces the new identity is the necessary complement to civil religion; as people's old identities fade, they can assume a new identity from the American story. People who refuse to blend in appear somewhat less than good Americans. Peace churches and their members appear in that light when they refuse to melt into the national acceptance of violence, particularly in times of war.[7] People who cannot blend in for other reasons, such as skin color, also experience discrimination.

The melting pot exerts pressure on any entity—including ethnic religious traditions like Mennonites—to give up something of its particularity to join America. To retain a particular identity is to resist the melting pot, which means to hold oneself apart from the norm. This is a zero-sum game: when one side gains, the other side loses. Much of the controversy about and resistance to multiculturalism in the United States is a debate about the extent to which particular cultures may pose an alternative to, or should be subsumed under, the dominant culture defined by civil religion and the melting pot.

Canada: Story of Many Peoples

Most of this picture changes when the scene shifts to Canada.[8] Canada is the story of many peoples, not one people. Therefore Canada has neither a unifying civil religion nor a melting pot.

In the United States, freedom was supposedly forged out of war, which gave it new and revolutionary connotations. English Canada, by contrast, developed in evolutionary fashion from English colonialism, and Canadian independence brought an actual decline in world prestige, as Canada no longer belonged to a worldwide empire. Furthermore, the war that made Quebec a part of British North America in the eighteenth century was a defeat for the French Canadians. A recurrent issue in much of the last 150 years of Canada's history has been the struggle to reach some kind of accommodation with the defeated Quebecois. These multiple stories mean that Canada lacks a unifying national myth and the attendant civil religion so pervasive just across the border in the United States.

The Canadian Mosaic

Neither does Canada have a melting pot. In contrast to the United States, Canada sees itself as a cultural mosaic, a multiethnic society in which each separate cultural or ethnic entity is allowed—

even encouraged—to keep and practice its particular identity. This is not a zero-sum game; one can simultaneously be a good Canadian and cultivate a particular cultural identity.

The Canadian government gives monies in support of various ethnic groups. Mennonites, who are clearly perceived as a religious group in the United States, are seen in Canada as a German-Russian ethnic tradition and therefore have received government funds for study conferences, the publication of books on Mennonite identity, and the operation of Mennonite schools. A new, federated Mennonite university in Winnipeg has received significant government assistance.

The Canadian Temptation

The cultural mosaic that supports Mennonite ethnic groups in Canada seems like a safe haven when compared with civil religion and the U.S. melting pot, which relentlessly erode Mennonite beliefs and commitments. Yet the Canadian context also presents a powerful temptation. The supportive ethos of Canada poses the temptation to become comfortable with the government and to lose sight of the distinction between the church and the surrounding society. Because the state does not challenge them, Mennonites in Canada are tempted to forget that the world is not like the church. Time will tell whether the temptation presented by the Canadian or the American environment poses the more lethal threat to the faithfulness of the peace church.

The Canadian ideal of a harmonious cultural mosaic does have its problems and sometimes breaks down in practice. In 1980 and again in 1995, rising tides of nationalist sentiment in Quebec culminated in referendums on the question of separation from English Canada. Each time the issue was defeated, though the 1995 vote was decided by an exceedingly thin margin.

There has been a great deal of discussion about what, if anything, the ten provinces have in common that can hold them together as a country. In the United States, a war was fought in the 1860s to preserve the union against secession. By contrast, it is conceivable, if not yet probable, that Canada would accept some kind of secession by Quebec, if decided on by majority vote of Quebecois.

In addition to the perception of French Canada that it receives insufficient recognition from English Canada, Canadian government policies toward Native peoples constitute another failure in the practice of the mosaic. Governmental policy has been to pressure Natives to abandon rather than to preserve their ethnic heritage, and to replace their traditions with language, cultural, and vocational patterns adopted from European civilization.

THEOLOGY AND NATIONAL CHARACTER: THE UNITED STATES

What has been the impact of these two national cultures and national environments? How have they affected theologizing in the Swiss-German and Dutch-Russian Mennonite traditions of the Mennonite Church and of the General Conference Mennonite Church?

The discussion calls for consideration of two questions. First, how has each national ethos shaped theology produced in it, and how might theologizing by Mennonites reflect the national ethos in which the theology was produced? Second, how might a Mennonite steeped in one of these national cultures perceive theology shaped in the other? I trust that the necessarily subjective and speculative nature of the observations will not obscure the importance of the issues.

Over the past century, Mennonites have displayed a schizophrenic attitude toward the United States and its religious culture. On one hand, Mennonites have resisted civil religion and the melting pot. On the other, they have wanted to affirm and be part of public Protestantism and the national society.

Claiming a Place in the U.S. Scene

Historically classified with the outsiders, Mennonites at the turn of the twenty-first century increasingly want to belong, and being accepted seems quite possible under the umbrella of civil religion and public Protestantism. After all, the principles of freedom of religion, separation of church and state, democratic equality, voluntary faith, and voluntary church membership all resonate with historic free church beliefs. In fact, adherents of public Protestantism have credited Anabaptists with rediscovering for the modern era the ideas of freedom of religion and separation of church and state.[9] For their part, Mennonite writers have also claimed that credit and have used it to claim a place for Mennonites in the U.S. scene.

Over the years a variety of church leaders made explicit efforts to put Mennonites into the national culture. Thus, in his address "Spirit of Progress" at the dedication of Elkhart Institute in 1896, Mennonite Church leader John S. Coffman gave several examples to show that the United States was beginning to accept teachings on peace that Anabaptists and other dissenters "have contended through all the Christian age."[10] General Conference scholar C. H. Wedel wrote that many Mennonite principles were validated in America, including recognition of "the rights of all men" and that the relationship to God takes precedence over all civic responsibilities, which means that Mennonites have been a good influence in their society.[11]

General Conference historian C. Henry Smith described his thrill at discovering that he had a wrong perception of Mennonites. They were not an "obscure, peculiar people" characterized as "good, honest, and thrifty . . . but with little influence in the world," as he had feared. Instead "they were pioneers in the rise of religious toleration" and were "the source of the ideas of religious toleration from which the separatism of our own Pilgrim Fathers later developed."[12]

In his Anabaptist Vision, Mennonite Church historian and church leader Harold S. Bender wrote: "There can be no question but that the great principles of freedom of conscience, separation of church and state, and voluntarism in religion, so basic to American Protestantism and so essential to democracy, ultimately are derived from the Anabaptists of the Reformation period."[13]

In attitudes toward relief service, Mennonites have even mirrored civil religion's faith in war and violence as the basis of American freedoms. As James Juhnke describes it, the first workers who went out under the auspices of the Mennonite Relief Commission were called "our first expedition," which echoed the military nomenclature of the "American Expeditionary Forces." When Mennonites petitioned the government for relief from military service, they sometimes described their relief and benevolence programs as "Our Substitution for War." While Mennonites also found deeper motivation for benevolence in the Bible and in Anabaptist-Mennonite history, echoes of military imagery pointed toward desire for a place in the American nation.[14]

Resisting Civil Religion and the Melting Pot

On the other hand, when American civil religion places the nation under God, the implication is that the United States is God's people. From a Mennonite perspective, it appears that civil religion has substituted a national political entity for God's people and that civil religion is blasphemy. Thus Mennonites have resisted U.S. civil religion and the allure of the melting pot, a resistance based on both ethnicity and theology. Mennonites have maintained a story that challenges the great American story at its most deep-seated points, namely faith in violence and its usurping of the status of God's people. In resisting these beliefs, Mennonites have sensed themselves to be somewhat un-American.

One of my early memories is of being a self-consciously Mennonite kindergartner in a school attended by no other Mennonites. I felt very uneasy about having to stand and recite the Pledge of Allegiance to the flag of the United States of America. I do not recall discussing the flag salute with my parents, nor did they suggest that I ought to abstain from the pledge. But I was acutely aware that I was supposed to be nonresistant and that "church boys" did not go into the army. Somehow this pledge about allegiance and God and the United States seemed like a ritual that did not belong to me.

That was in 1947, before Harold Bender's Anabaptist Vision became the mantra of a distinct Mennonite identity.[15] Both Bender's Anabaptist Vision and its continuation in John H. Yoder's delineation of free church ecclesiology (in contrast to a supposedly fallen "Constantinian" ecclesiology) express an un-American Mennonite ecclesiology against the backdrop of U.S. civil religion and public Protestantism.

For the first half of the twentieth century, this resistance to and distinction from American society was maintained with ideas like "nonconformity to the world" and "separation from the world," reinforced by German language or distinctive "plain" dress. Civil religion and the melting pot have exerted relentless pressure on Mennonites to give up something of Mennonite identity, either as the price of entering the mainstream of American culture or to reach out and attract persons from the mainstream without causing them undue discomfort.

In this zero-sum game when American identity gains, Mennonite identity loses. With German language and plain dress all but gone, the primary focus of compromise has now shifted to peace theology and the traditional commitment to nonviolence.

Ambivalence in Mennonite Theologizing

Twentieth-century Mennonite theologizing reflected an ambivalent, almost schizophrenic attitude toward the wider Protestant theology that is subsumed in public Protestantism and civil religion. Most discussions of theology by Mennonites focused on two categories, namely doctrines shared with wider Protestantism and those doctrines or practices that make Mennonites distinct. With such a theology, it was possible to be part of Protestantism yet also to be distinct from it.

The doctrines shared with mainstream Protestantism included the classic doctrines on Christology, the Trinity, and atonement. Distinctly Mennonite doctrines included nonresistance, as well as other primarily ethical issues such as separation, nonconformity, and the distinctly Mennonite practices of the ordinances. One can trace fundamentalist, conservative, and evangelical versions of these two lists in the twentieth century, beginning with John Horsch and such names as Daniel Kauffman, Harold S. Bender, John C. Wenger, and Ronald Sider. A progressive trajectory might include C. H. Wedel, J. E. Hartzler, and Edmund G. Kaufman.[16]

Thomas N. Finger's two-volume systematic theology[17] constitutes an evolutionary stage in the development of a Mennonite theology that is part of, as well as distinct from, the American Protestant melting pot. These volumes contain a wealth of helpful analysis across the entire range of the theological spectrum, from the early church until the present and taken from conservative as well as liberal writers. Finger's methodology is to select pieces from many traditions and weave these strands into a modern synthesis. In this synthesis one discovers many discrete elements from the traditions that contribute to public Protestantism (as well as from Catholicism) along with elements clearly taken from the Anabaptist, peace church tradition.[18]

Without being either completely one or the other, this modern synthesis both accommodates mainstream Protestantism and is distinct from it. This systematic theology seems transparently a reflection of the U.S. melting pot ethos that molds the various ethnic groups and traditions into a new American character.

John H. Yoder's ecclesiology continues and further develops Bender's Anabaptist ecclesiology as the alternative to the state church. Yoder's delineation of a "Constantinian" ecclesiology in contrast to free church ecclesiology obviously makes sense against the backdrop of

American civil religion and public Protestantism. However, Yoder also represents a watershed in the development of Mennonite theology. His analysis of Nicene-Chalcedonian Christology[19] opened the door to seeing the particular context of these formulas and their specific link to Constantinian ecclesiology,[20] the ecclesiology that continues through several revisions in the U.S. religious ethos. For the first time it became possible to see that one could interpret Christology from a specific stance in free church ecclesiology. Thus a theology for the peace church was not obligated to maintain a link with the particular formulas of the ecclesiological tradition that informs the amalgam of civil religion and public Protestantism.

Alternatives to Violence-Accommodating Formulas

My own theologizing has pushed beyond Yoder to articulate christological and atonement alternatives to the classic formulas that accommodated the sword.[21] My efforts to construct a theology for the peace church have quite clearly echoed American civil religion; if civil religion posed a monolithic edifice, then theology challenging it should do likewise.

Tracing the links from civil religion and public Protestantism in the modern era back through medieval Christendom to the Constantinian synthesis strengthened my conviction that an alternative theology is needed. The more one is conscious of civil religion's idolatrous faith in efficacious violence, the more urgent becomes the need to articulate a theology that has no place for the sword.

An alternative theology must show that nonviolence informs the entire theological program. To articulate specific alternatives to Christendom's violence-accommodating christological formulas and atonement doctrines, which attained their mature form and creedal status in the post-Constantinian church, is a logical extension of Yoder's program. Developing such alternatives is a solution to the conundrum of a peace church theology that has both built on yet stressed its difference from Christendom's supposed general theology.[22]

As will become clear below as well as in chapter 5, it is important to state that merely posing an alternative to the prevailing theological edifice is an inadequate theological foundation. While mirroring elements will be unavoidably present, it is most important to show that the theology begins as an articulation of the meaning of the story of Jesus.

Not all Mennonite theologians have agreed on the need to revise Christology and atonement. Whether one finds such efforts at reconstruction more attractive than the time-honored Mennonite efforts to simultaneously build on and be distinct from the Protestant amalgam depends in part on one's comfort level with U.S. civil religion and public Protestantism. The more comfortable one is, the more these efforts to develop a theological alternative seem narrow, prideful, and sectarian. After all, how could such a small group that originated only in the sixteenth century claim to have a comprehensive theology that challenges the much older edifice of Christendom's theology? But from a perspective that senses continuity between modern Christian America and medieval Christendom, efforts to develop an alternative theology seem like valiant attempts to prevent the bulldozer of modernity[23] from flattening all bumps in the road of civil religion and public Protestantism.

THEOLOGY AND NATIONAL CHARACTER: CANADA

It is my hunch that these theological enterprises shaped in the U.S. ethos may seem to play a different melody for persons from Canada, who listen via a receiver tuned by experience in Canada's cultural mosaic. I think that Canadians and people from the United States may hear very different music when listening to the same score.

In Canada, the various denominations and historical traditions all belong to the mosaic. Without a particular national identity grinding away relentlessly at their particular identities, religious denominations can affirm themselves as part of the Canadian scene. Absent is the sense of a zero-sum game in which accepting a national identity compromises church or religious identity; one can comfortably espouse Mennonite theology and be Canadian.[24]

Theologians in such a context have felt much less need for a comprehensive theological construction to maintain Mennonite or peace church identity. Because the identity of Mennonites in Canada has not been directly challenged by the Canadian ethos, theology has not carried the weight of Mennonite faithfulness as much as in the United States. Canadian Mennonites thus have been less constrained to seek a specific theology for Mennonites than have their churchly brothers and sisters south of the border. When imported into Canada, the alternative theology described above may seem a lot like shadow boxing—like fighting an unnecessary battle against a phantom opponent.

From a Canadian context, even more than in the United States, it may seem arrogant for a small tradition with relatively recent, sixteenth-century roots to profess a comprehensive theology that challenges all of Christendom. No piece of the mosaic is complete in and of itself. To Canadians a Mennonite alternative theology may appear as an effort for one element of the mosaic to vaunt itself triumphantly over the rest. Thus theology emanating from Bender's Anabaptist Vision, or John H. Yoder's nonConstantinian ecclesiology, or my own efforts to draw implications for Christology and atonement from Yoder's nonConstantinian ecclesiology, can sound all too proud and triumphant in a Canadian context.

It comes as no surprise, then, that Mennonite theologizing in Canada has hesitated to adopt an agenda with seemingly grandiose claims about the need to pose a specific theology for Mennonites. It is much easier or more comfortable for Canadian Mennonite theologians to see Mennonite theology as one particular emphasis to combine with others to develop a complete picture.

In the absence of civil religion and public Protestantism, and with the classic creeds affirmed by most or all Christian parts of the Canadian mosaic, it is more difficult for Mennonites to sense that Nicene-Chalcedonian Christology and Anselmian atonement belong to the violence-accommodating tradition. The effort to develop a theology that challenges Christendom's formulas runs counter to Mennonite theologians in Canada (and some in the United States) who have advocated a theology for Mennonites built on a common Christian foundation of classic or creedal orthodoxy.

BEYOND THE CANADA-U.S. DIVIDE

The differences between Canada and the United States are real, as is their potential impact on our theologizing. The temptation is to say that each ethos may require a somewhat different theology.[25] But we dare not leave the situation there. To make the shape of the national culture an intrinsic dimension of theological equation is actually a surreptitious way to enshrine a nonChristian authority (a national ethos) in a determinant role.[26]

We are left with two distinct but related questions. First, how do we avoid being determined by our national cultures, particularly when their impact will inevitably make us into two churches going in different directions? Second, if we are one church living in two nations, what is the basis of our oneness?

Many voices will suggest that the classic creedal formulas of Christendom provide the obvious common theological foundation for Mennonites in Canada and the United States. To enshrine these formulas, however, is to build on an inadequate foundation, one that has discarded those dimensions of the story of Jesus that ought to be central to the faithfulness of the peace church. If Jesus Christ is our foundation, then it is Jesus' story and the "politics of Jesus"—not the shape of a national ethos or fourth- and fifth-century creedal formulas—that should determine the contour of our theological agenda.

In anticipation of the discussion of black theology in chapter 5, it is significant to note that James H. Cone in *God of the Oppressed* uses the story of Jesus as the specific foundation for theological reformulation.[27] Cone demonstrates how the christological and atonement formulas of the Constantinian church accommodated and supported racism and slavery.

As Cone's observations show, more is at stake in a critique of these critique of these formulas than the sectarian question of whether it is appropriate for the small for the small Mennonite denomination to develop its own theology. The issue is one of competing, comprehensive theological visions and the extent to which a peace and justice agenda is a specific dimension of our theology. It is a question of whether Mennonite theology will maintain a prophetic edge toward both Canadian and U.S. societies.

In the end, the story of Jesus and not a national character or context ought to shape our theology and our most fundamental identity. Beginning with Jesus does not remove the national ethos as a factor but does make it a secondary consideration. Acknowledging its potential impact is a necessary prelude to challenging it, as well as to expressing a theology that can be understood in the two different contexts.

Given the shaping power of Canada and the United States on our theological perceptions, it is important to construct a theology that speaks to but is not dependent on either ethos. We should focus on who we are as nonviolent Christians rather than on our national identity or a theology shaped by a violence-accommodating ecclesiology that we have historically professed not to accept.

Our theology expresses our self-understanding as Christians. We need a strong theological understanding that our churchly and Christian identity transcends national borders. Without this, in light of decisions by the Mennonite Church and General Conference Mennonite Church to create two national conferences as the primary working bodies of an integrated Mennonite denomination, I have serious doubts that we will survive more than a few short years as a binational entity.

A denominational self-identity that begins with national identity will inevitably produce a theology shaped to national contours. Such a result would be, in effect, the undoing of the Anabaptist Reformation.

We do have choices about the direction of the church and the theology that will guide it. The postmodern context makes us aware of the particular character of those decisions. Will the theology that guides us into the third millennium reflect primarily a national context and fourth-century formulas that accommodate violence and affirm the social order? Or will this theology locate the church in the nonviolent story of Jesus, whose life made visible the reign of God in the world?

TWO

TWENTIETH-CENTURY MENNONITE THEOLOGY IN FACE OF PRESUMED THEOLOGY-IN-GENERAL[1]

INTRODUCTION

Mennonites have been talking seriously about theology since at least the latter decades of the nineteenth century. But they did not always call it theology.

Much of the theologizing for the Mennonite churches went on under the guise of expounding Bible doctrines or describing what sixteenth-century Anabaptists believed. Only recently, perhaps in the last two decades, have we started to become comfortable talking about theology as theology. Still more recent is the search for a Christian theology that will serve specifically for today's Mennonite churches or for the contemporary peace church.

In the previous chapter, we looked at external pressures on Mennonite theologizing, namely the impact of national ethos. The present chapter considers Mennonite theologizing around an internal agenda, namely the effort to articulate a theology for Mennonites that would provide a distinct identity for the peace church but also identify it with some version of mainstream Protestantism.

A postmodern awareness of the particular character of all theology may shed new light on Mennonite theological discussions. The argument proceeds on the basis of four assertions about Mennonite theologizing in the twentieth century. The first two establish easily recognizable but not frequently stated assumptions, while the third and fourth assertions depend on the discussion of the first two. As a response to the four assertions, the chapter concludes with a specific suggestion for refocusing and restructuring the quest for a theology that will serve the peace church. While the historical analysis focuses on subjects from the Mennonite tradition, the conclusion drawn from the analysis applies to any tradition in quest of an identity as a peace church.

Two Assertions about Mennonite Theologizing

The Larger Foundation
For most of their twentieth-century theologizing, Mennonites assumed that their theology was built on a larger or broader theological entity located outside the Mennonite tradition.

This larger theological entity contained formulations of the classic foundational doctrines of Christian theology, including but not limited to the classic formulations of the Trinity, Christology, and atonement. As such, these formulas comprised a standard program—a theology-in-general or Christianity-as-such that existed independently of particular historical contexts and particular denominations. These doctrines were assumed to be suited for and accepted by all right-thinking Christians.

The Mennonite assumption that there was a theology-in-general was parallel to that in other denominations. A given writer's relationship to the standard program, theology-in-general, was the test for determining the truth or orthodoxy of that person's theology. To deviate from the standard theology-in-general was to put oneself in the category of unorthodoxy or even heresy, whether like Arius in the fourth century, those who refused to acknowledge the Lutheran and Reformed creeds in the sixteenth century, or the twentieth-century modernists who claimed the right to reject classic doctrines which no longer made sense. It was simply assumed that Mennonites borrowed this standard theology-in-general and then built their own theology on it.

For Mennonites not to build on that theology-in-general would have seemed audacious as well as unorthodox. It would have been unthinkable that such a small, Johnny-come-lately group would have anything original to say about the classic doctrines professed for so long. If the much larger traditions of Martin Luther, Ulrich Zwingli, and John Calvin, which also began in the sixteenth century, affirmed the centuries-old creeds and confessions of Christendom, it would be indeed brash for Mennonites to assert that they had something unique to say about the classic theological questions.

Mennonite Add-Ons
What was distinct about Mennonite theology came in what Mennonites added to the standard program of theology-in-general.

This, like the preceding assertion, is virtually self-evident. For the most part, the writers specifically organized their theology into two categories: general Christian teaching, and distinct Mennonite teachings, each with its own list of beliefs. While this chapter briefly acknowledges the content of the two lists, the primary focus of the discussion is the relationship between the two. As we shall see, the interaction between the lists differs significantly from one writer to another.

FUNDAMENTALIST AND EVANGELICAL PACKAGES

John Horsch
John Horsch's assumed core of standard theology came from fundamentalism. In *The Mennonite Church and Modernism*, Horsch described this core as including seven doctrines: the Word of God equated with the Bible; Jesus as unique Son of God; supernatural birth of Jesus; expiatory death of Jesus; special Creation; innate human sinfulness; justification by faith in the atoning blood; and the need for supernatural regeneration.[2]

Later, in *Mennonites in Europe*, Horsch wrote that Anabaptists and early Mennonites agreed with the major Reformers on the fundamentals relating to original sin, justification by faith, salvation through the atoning blood of Christ, the full deity of Jesus, and the Trinity of the Godhead.[3] Differences came at the point of practice; Anabaptists believed that justification by faith should of necessity result in Christian living, which included nonresistance.[4] Other incorrect practices of the Reformers included "infant baptism, the union of church and state, the persecution of dissenters, and war."[5]

Horsch also tied the fundamentals—his standard theological core—to the classic church creeds, which he located in the New Testament. Playing off a remark from J. E. Hartzler that the transition from the Sermon on the Mount to the Nicene Creed was a "philosophical acrobatic stunt,"[6] Horsch virtually equated the creed with the fundamentals of the faith and linked it to Jesus' words in Matthew 5-7.

A number of the fundamentals, Horsch said, are either expressed or implied in the Sermon on the Mount, and the rest are taught in other parts of the Scriptures. That they are not all mentioned in the Sermon on the Mount does not detract from their authoritative value.[7]

Such comments make clear that Horsch operated with two lists: Christian doctrines and Mennonite practices. They also imply the priority of the first list over the second. Horsch eventually makes this explicit. An individual who rejected the deity of Christ, his supernatural birth, and his resurrection would not be a Christian, Horsch said, "even if he believed in the principle of nonresistance." Although some Christian supporters of World War I—what he called the "last war"— were "unenlightened or disobedient," they were still Christians. As Horsch said,

> Placing first things first we have the fundamentals of the faith and then the principles and commandments that have reference to practical life and conduct. If you deny Christ, these principles lose their importance.[8]

In Horsch's view, there was more difference between Mennonites and a modernist who believed in nonresistance than there was between Mennonites and a fundamentalist who rejected nonresistance. For Horsch, the list of Mennonite distinctives defers to the list of fundamentals.

Daniel Kauffman

Like John Horsch, Daniel Kauffman specifically organized theology into those doctrines that Mennonites shared with others and the distinctive Mennonite doctrines. While a careful comparison of Kauffman's writings would reveal their increasingly fundamentalist-like language and conceptualization, that development is secondary. What is important here is how Kauffman viewed the relationship between the Mennonite and general beliefs. Unlike Horsch, Kauffman viewed the Mennonite list as including both general and specifically Mennonite doctrines. Thus it was complete as compared to fundamentalist lists that included only general doctrines.

A 1910 list by Daniel Kauffman in *Gospel Herald*, for example, identified nine points (with some subpoints) on which "all Christian people" should be able to agree.[9] A similar list in 1916 presented a different version of the same "Christian Doctrine" in nineteen points.[10] This list included some explicitly Mennonite oriented beliefs. For example, the twelfth item on the list stated that Christian people are a "separate people from the world," and thus cannot have part in the world's "fashions, carnal strife, oaths, secret societies, or unscriptural insurance."[11]

Another Kauffman list from 1920 was offered to counter a proposed list of unifying doctrines from the church federationists. Kauffman did not consider the items on the liberal list to be inherently false. Rather, he indicated, the problem was that they promised a self-help approach to human betterment without recognizing the need to be born again. If they would emphasize the items in his list, Kauffman said, then "we might have a different opinion" of their set.[12] Such comments make clear that Kauffman considered his first list to be general theology, to which any and all right-thinking Christians should adhere.

If there were items on which all Christians should agree, in Kauffman's view, it is equally true that there were beliefs on which all Mennonites should agree. Note, for example, the chapter on "Mennonite Doctrine" in Kauffman's *The Mennonite Church and Current Issues*. After yet another Kauffman list of nineteen points that Mennonites believe "in common with all other adherents of the evangelical faith," a second list followed. This was called "Distinctive Doctrines." These included fifteen items that Mennonites believe "in common with some churches and unlike other churches." This list covered the range of practices commonly attributed to the conservative Mennonite agenda: belief in obedience to all the commandments of Christ, adult baptism, prayer veiling, footwashing, the holy kiss, separation of church and state, no participation in war or in law suits, nonswearing of oaths, nonmembership in secret societies, and more.[13]

While Kauffman called the second list "Mennonite doctrine," he considered it more than that. "In reality," Kauffman said, "it is *Bible*

Doctrine, for [the points] are all taught in the Word of God."[14] In other words, Kauffman's formulation was really one list consisting of subgroups.

A similar understanding of the relationship of the Mennonite list to the list of general doctrines, supposedly accepted by all right-thinking Christians, appeared in two of Kauffman's *Gospel Herald* editorials separated by a ten year interval. In a comment on "Unfundamental Fundamentalists," he chastised militaristic fundamentalists who attempt to discredit pacifist organizations.

The chief criticism he had of pacifists, Kauffman said, was that "they do not go far enough" on the issue of peace and war, since "they do not endorse the nonresistant doctrine in its entirety." The philosophy that compels fundamentalists to accept the doctrines of immediate creation, absolute reliability of Scripture, the deity, and the virgin birth of Christ also "requires that we accept the nonresistant teachings of the gospel of Christ."[15] In its best light, then, nonresistance is actually a fundamental for all Christians, and any list of fundamentals without it is an incomplete list.

Ten years later, Kauffman classed Mennonites as fundamentalists, although on the doctrine of nonresistance they were "more nearly like the liberalists." Frequently liberals "assume the role of pacifists" and "on this point they are more scripturally fundamental than are the so-called fundamentalists who at times advocate war."[16]

Whereas Horsch gave priority to the first list, Kauffman virtually equated the lists or made them two segments of one list. The problem with the fundamentalists was not that their list of general doctrines was wrong; rather, it was too short. Mennonites had the complete set of biblical doctrines, in contrast to fundamentalists, who possessed an admirable but incomplete set. In essence, the list of specifically Mennonite fundamentals revealed that the supposed general list of beliefs held by all Christians was actually deficient.[17]

Harold S. Bender

Harold Bender's description of what Anabaptists, Mennonites, and magisterial Protestants believed also uses two lists. In *Anabaptist Vision* he wrote that Anabaptism was a "consistent evangelical Protestantism seeking to recreate without compromise the original New Testament church, the vision of Christ and the apostles."[18]

That identity with mainline Protestantism included an embrace of the core of Protestant theology. Some years before Anabaptist Vision, in describing the beliefs of North American Mennonites for the 1936 Mennonite World Conference in Amsterdam, Bender gave this Protestant summary:

> All the American Mennonite groups, without exception, stand on a platform of conservative evangelicalism in theology, being thoroughly orthodox in the great fundamental doctrines of the Christian faith such as the unity of the Godhead, the true deity of Christ, the atonement by the shedding of blood, the plenary inspiration and divine authority of the Holy Scriptures as the Word of God.[19]

Somewhat later Bender wrote that Anabaptists did not differ from the major Reformers "on such doctrines as the sole authority of the Scriptures, grace, and justification by faith, or in the classic Christian loci of doctrine."[20]

Such comments show several things. First, Bender thought in terms of a general core of doctrines--a theological given, or theology-in-general—located outside the Mennonite tradition. Second, he assumed that the validity and truth of Mennonite views on these classic Christian doctrines was vouchsafed because Mennonites had learned them, or borrowed them, from that outside source.[21] Third, the distinct Anabaptist and Mennonite identity came from additions to that central core.

But fourth, much like Daniel Kauffman, Bender considered the items on the so-called second list not mere add-ons, but integral parts of full-orbed Christian faith. Without these Anabaptist emphases, Christian faith is incomplete. Some of Bender's well-known formulations in Anabaptist Vision display that integration, as when he wrote that "the essence of Christianity [is] discipleship" and when he called the Anabaptist movement "a consistent evangelical Protestantism" and "the culmination of the Reformation."[22]

John C. Wenger

In a similar fashion, the writings of John C. Wenger, Bender's longtime colleague, friend, and supporter, portray theology for Mennonites in terms of a general core with particular Mennonite additions. Wenger followed Bender in calling Anabaptism "the logical outcome of the Protestant reformation." Wenger then divided theology of these more consistent Protestants into two primary categories: major doctrines and Mennonite emphases. On these fundamental doctrines Anabaptists agreed with Lutherans and Reformed thinkers, Wenger said, "since Anabaptism was simply a radical form of Protestantism."[23] Included in Wenger's list of major doctrines were evangelical or conservative-oriented statements on God, Jesus Christ, the Holy Spirit, sin, regeneration, holiness of life, divine grace, the church, eschatology, and inspiration of the Bible.

Wenger listed Mennonite emphases under three major headings: the Bible, the church, and the Christian life. The biblical emphases included "Bible, not theology"; "biblicism," which included ordinances and restrictions; and "New Testament finality." The church section dealt with discipleship and church discipline, while the section on the Christian life emphasized the importance of a lived faith and a church obedient to the will of God.[25]

Wenger's description of theology for Mennonites specifically divided it into two categories: an assumed general category shared with Protestantism, and a category of Mennonite emphases. As for Kauffman and Bender, however, the items on the second list were not merely add-ons. For Wenger, they were necessary to have a complete, full-orbed biblical faith.[26]

Ronald Sider

Some years ago, in an address directed primarily to a Mennonite audience, evangelical Mennonite theologian Ronald Sider depicted a theology in terms of the two categories: a set of doctrines claimed by all right-thinking Christians, whether evangelicals or Anabaptists, and a set of "emphases" associated with Anabaptism.[27] Sider's list of "central doctrines of the historic Christian creeds" included "the Trinity, the full humanity and full Deity of Jesus Christ, the atonement, the bodily resurrection." Two more doctrines supported by both evangelicals and Anabaptists were "concern for evangelism" and commitment "to the full authority of the Scriptures as the norm for faith and practice."[28] On the Anabaptist side, Sider listed four beliefs related to practice: "costly discipleship, on living the Christian life, on the church as a new society living the ethics of the kingdom (and therefore living a set of values radically different from the world), on the way of the cross as the Christian approach to violence."[29]

While Sider posed two lists, like Kauffman, Bender, and Wenger he considered them two parts of one greater whole. In the article just cited, Sider argued a twofold thesis. If evangelicals who care deeply about the first list are truly as biblical as they claim, they will also embrace the Anabaptist list; conversely, commitment to the Anabaptist list is ultimately invalid without adherence to the first list. "Orthodoxy and orthopraxy are equally important."[30] When addressing Mennonites, Sider was emphatic that the two lists, or the pairing of orthodoxy and orthopraxy, are really one: that either emphasis without the other is a truncated or rootless gospel or Christian faith.

Writing recently for a wider, generally evangelical audience, Sider offered a somewhat different understanding of the relationship of the two lists.[31] The core, on which Sider assumes all Christians agree, remained basically unchanged from the statement to a Mennonite audience.[32] Yet Sider noted that Christians differ on important as well as insignificant differences.

An example of an insignificant difference might be the use of candles in spiritual devotion. Important differences are those which clearly form the basis of denominational traditions. These might include disagreement about predestination between Presbyterians and Wesleyans or disagreement between Mennonites and "just war" Christians on whether there are exceptions to Jesus' teaching about killing.

On these important differences, Sider asserts, the denominations and local congregations need to insist that membership means acceptance of the item in question as something the denomination believes is taught in Scripture. However, Sider adds, these denominational differences ought not be allowed to obscure the underlying unity which all Christians have in "the same triune God," the confession of "the deity and humanity of Christ," and a shared "trust in salvation through Christ alone."[33] The implication is that these constitute the sine qua non of theology-in-general, whereas Mennonite belief in Jesus' rejection of the sword is outside the heart of the gospel.

Sider's description for a wide Christian audience regarding the relationship of the two lists appears to make the connection less tight than in his earlier discussion. In this second instance, the peace church focus on rejection of violence is clearly in a category of things to agree to disagree on; it is not intrinsically part of the gospel.

When addressing evangelicals at large, Sider chose to focus on the core and allow the second list to appear optional. Earlier, when addressing a primarily Mennonite audience, he appeared to say that the two lists were, in essence, one list—that evangelicals without the Anabaptist emphases were not fully biblical, while Mennonites without the general theological core lacked a valid foundation for nonviolence. In comparison with the other Mennonites noted here, the first Sider related the two lists in the same manner as Kauffman, Bender, and Wenger, while the second Sider resembled Horsch.

The discussion of these several writers reveals a significant amount of tension or ambiguity about the relationship between the assumed general theology and Mennonite distinctives. Rodney Sawatsky has used orthodoxy and orthopraxy to distinguish the content of what I have here called the two lists.[34]

The difficulty in relating the two is real. The divergent ways that Ron Sider resolved this dilemma when speaking in different contexts seem a particularly vivid illustration of this. Tension results when Mennonite theologians assume, on one hand, that Anabaptist distinctives must stand on a general Christian core, yet realize, on the other hand, that the general core lacks at least one point crucial to their Mennonite Christian identity. That point is, of course, Jesus' teaching and example of nonviolence, rejection of the sword, or love of enemies.

Clearly, the (primarily) ethical items in the second lists are specific to Mennonites and, as such, do not belong to theology-in-general that is claimed both by Mennonites and by those located outside the Mennonite tradition. Yet the second lists noted above consist of what these Mennonites all considered clear biblical commands that must be obeyed, since obedience was the essence of what it meant to be Christian. From this standpoint, the Mennonite emphases were not mere add-ons, but a part of the full gospel.

These Mennonite theologians had a sense both of agreeing with a core assumed by wider Christian tradition and claiming this core was incomplete. They did not fully resolve the tension between those two points. Their implicit evaluation of wider Christendom was that it proclaimed a partial gospel and held to an incomplete list of Christian doctrines. Mennonites could not identify with this inadequate version of Christian faith. On the other hand, Mennonites needed that wider faith of Christendom because it supplied theology-in-general on which Mennonite theology was or should be built.

PROGRESSIVE AND LIBERAL PACKAGES

Cornelius H. Wedel

The approach of beginning with a general core and adding on Mennonite distinctives was not limited to the fundamentalist, conservative, or evangelical side of the Mennonite theological spectrum. The theology of Mennonite progressives and liberals exhibited the same characteristic.

Cornelius H. Wedel, the culturally and educationally progressive first president of Bethel College in Kansas, did not make theological lists. It is clear, however, that his comprehensive theology was built around a set of Anabaptist and Mennonite beliefs and a set of beliefs shared with majority Christendom. Wedel's four-volume history of Mennonites identified the distinct Mennonite tradition in terms of *Gemeindechristentum,* or "Congregation Christendom." This was a believers church Christendom, a pacifist Christendom, posed as an alternative to state church Christendom.

In Wedel's analysis, congregation Christendom described those who maintained New Testament Christianity when the majority church became the church of the bishop in the third century and the imperial church under Constantine in the fourth century. An unbroken succession of groups retained and maintained this believers church Christendom through the centuries, right down to Wedel's own Mennonite people on the prairies.[35]

Wedel wrote a systematic theology, which exists only in manuscript form.[36] While this theology dealt quite knowledgeably with the classic formulas of Christology, the Trinity, and atonement, it did so without reference to congregation Christendom. In effect, Wedel assumed that for these classic issues, the views of Mennonites would be the same as those learned from the wider Christian tradition. Although he did not state explicitly that he divided theology into the two categories of beliefs shared with Protestantism and Mennonite distinctives, his writings reflect that division. When he wrote a history of Mennonites with a view to identifying Mennonite beliefs and practices for his church, he depicted the church in terms of a progressive version of the traditional Mennonite issues such as rejection of violence and adult baptism. When he talked about theology, however, he used the classic theological categories of Christendom, and his discussion carried the arguments from the American Protestant discussion without major impact from the Mennonite tradition.[37]

J. E. Hartzler

Progressive J. E. Hartzler posed an assumed general core in his address to the 1919 All-Mennonite Convention in Bluffton, Ohio. The core that he described had a marked liberal-leaning cast. Hartzler noted the three essentials "around which may be thrown all other essentials, or non-essentials, if such there be."[38] The three, each of which had several subpoints, were "The Fatherhood of God," "The Brotherhood of Man," and "Salvation by Faith Alone in Christ as the Divine Savior of Mankind."[39]

Speaking to Western District Mennonite Conference in 1920, Hartzler listed a core that still sounded liberal when he described the "five leading doctrines of Christian Faith around which may be thrown every other detail of the Christian Religion." These doctrines included: (1) Jesus Christ as "the Divine Son of God"; (2) the doctrine of the atonement in which "the Christian God . . . gave his Son in sacrificial death that the atonement might be provided"; (3) salvation from sin, through faith in Christ, repentance, regeneration by the Holy Spirit and adoption in the God's family; (4) the doctrine of the Holy Spirit, who reproves the world, teaches believers and comforts the saints; and (5) the doctrine of the Bible, which is inspired, "authentic and trustworthy," and the source of redemption.[40]

Hartzler's article "The Faith of Our Fathers"[41] described the Anabaptist and Mennonite additions to this liberal-leaning Protestant core. The faith of the sixteenth-century Anabaptist fathers included the following four points:

> (1) That the Bible was an open book . . . for all men . . . (2) The right of any person, under the guidance of the Holy Spirit, to freely interpret this Book for him or herself. (3) The right of every person to an individual conscience in matters of religious belief and conduct, and the personal right of dissent in matters political, social, or religious. . . . (4) Religious toleration; in other words, the right of men to differ on matters nonessential to vital faith, and yet maintain a brotherly attitude toward each other.[42]

A similar list a quarter century later added a fifth point: "complete separation of church and state."[43]

Hartzler's liberal version of the core plus Anabaptist or Mennonite emphases displayed less tension or contrast between the lists than did the formulations proposed by Mennonite fundamentalists.[44] In the article "Faith of Our Fathers," Hartzler wrote that the four Anabaptist principles "implied" his liberal core.[45] That core likewise provided glimpses, he said, of the Mennonite emphases. For example, in the section on "The Brotherhood of Mankind," Hartzler wrote that this doctrine contains

> all the elements of right living," including "service of friends and enemies, . . . the protection of life, rather than its destruction. God only has the right to end the life which He alone began. . . . Brotherhood means no war.[46]

Whereas John Horsch considered the lists separated, established the priority of one list over the other, and admitted that not all the fundamentals were in the Sermon on the Mount, Hartzler could say that the general (liberal) Protestant core was implied in the list of Mennonite distinctives, and that the liberal Protestant core contained the Mennonite emphases.

Hartzler's liberal core and distinctives are quite obviously not those of the Mennonite fundamentalists. Nonetheless, like the various fundamentalists and evangelicals, Hartzler conceptualized Mennonite theology in terms of two lists.

Edmund G. Kaufman

Edmund G. Kaufman exhibited a liberal-leaning theology that he described as "Basic Christian Convictions."[47] His book of that title begins with a discussion of the general topic of religion as the context for expounding the Christian doctrine of God. Explicitly stated Mennonite perspectives are minimal.

Kaufman used the traditional language about Jesus as divine and human and spoke of him as a mediator between God and humankind. Yet the discussion of Jesus dealt primarily with his human life. Kaufman described strengths and weaknesses for each of the three families of atonement, but his evaluation favored the moral influence theory. Sections on the Christian life did not deal with issues of pacifism and refusal of military service or with church-state relationships.

James Juhnke is correct to characterize Kaufman's theological orientation as "a Mennonite-biased Christocentric progressivism."[48]

Kaufman's list of the specific Anabaptist ideas appeared in an extended footnote of *Basic Christian Convictions*. He noted six such beliefs: (1) discipleship, (2) separation of church and state, (3) freedom of conscience, (4) adult baptism, the Lord's Supper and baptism as outward symbols of inward convictions, (5) nonparticipation in war and nonviolence, and (6) emphasis on the simple life.[49] Placement of these six concepts in a footnote does not indicate a lack of commitment to them on Kaufman's part, but it does show clearly that his theologizing operated in terms of an assumed general Christian core with specific Anabaptist or Mennonite additions.[50]

The tension between the two was unresolved and is perhaps mirrored in his life. Earlier, as a mission worker in China, he had not made the Mennonite peace witness central to the gospel proclaimed. He had supported "Christian General" Feng, who practiced mass baptisms on his army, as "an instrument in God's hand to bring order out of chaos. . . ." Nevertheless, as president of Bethel College, Kaufman remained a staunch pacifist throughout World War II.[51]

RECENT GENERAL THEOLOGY PLUS DISTINCTIVES

A. James Reimer

Although the terminology differs, some recent efforts at theologizing for Mennonites have continued in some fashion to use the idea of a theology-in-general plus distinctives. One example is found in the work of A. James Reimer. He has posed the Nicene Creed as the core of the assumed general foundation on which theology for Mennonites should build, and he has specifically rejected the suggestion from John H. Yoder[52] that peace church theology might pose some alternatives to Nicaea-Chalcedon.[53] For Reimer, Nicaea, with its culmination in trinitarian doctrine, constitutes the necessary development and statement in nonbiblical language of the essence of the New Testament's depiction of Jesus Christ.[54]

At this level, it is the classic creedal statements which assume for Reimer the a priori quality of a theology-in-general, which would be the functional equivalent of the list of general doctrines in theology of the writers noted earlier. Reimer is quite aware of the absence of explicit ethical dimensions to Nicaea, as well as to Chalcedon's formula and the doctrine of the Trinity. As Reimer has said, "the ethical gets lost" between the first and fourth or fifth centuries.[55] Since Reimer has affirmed the nonviolence of his Mennonite tradition, he recognizes, like the writers of the two lists, the need to add to the core of the presumed theology-in-general. His solution is to "retrieve the historical, narrative, and ethical content of trinitarian Christology."[56]

To preserve the biblical character of Nicaea and thus its role as the assumed theology-in-general on which Mennonites should build, Reimer distances the Nicene formula from Emperor Constantine, who proposed it at the council of Nicaea and who participated in the council's deliberations.[57] Reimer then proposes that the trinitarian orthodoxy of Nicaea is necessary to anchor "the moral claims of Jesus" in the "very nature and person of God." In particular, this moral claim includes "a nonviolent love ethic."[58]

Reimer believes that a trinitarian orthodoxy built around Nicene Christology is "the surest way of guarding against all forms of political and national idolatry (Constantinianism)."[59] For Reimer, the nonviolent love ethic, which must be added to the creedal formula which is without ethics, is the functional parallel to the list of distinctive Anabaptist or Mennonite doctrines for writers such as Daniel Kauffman, Harold S. Bender, J. C. Wenger, or Ron Sider.

If some tension appeared in the efforts of the earlier writers to hold together the two lists, a parallel tension appears in Reimer's effort. It remains unclear how the creedal formulations, which Reimer acknowledges were the end result of a process that allowed ethics to get lost and that contain no explicit ethical dimensions, now turn out to be the best foundation for ethics. Equally ambiguous is how these formulations become the buttress against Constantinianism, the political theology that legitimated a civil religion, in the very Constantinian church that initiated the fusion of church and state.[60]

In my view, Reimer does not sufficiently acknowledge that both sides in the Arian controversy sought imperial support whenever it suited their purposes. As R. P. C. Hanson wrote,

> Neither East nor West formulated any coherent theory . . . of the relation of church and state. When the state brought pressure to bear on them bishops of every theological hue complained. When it used its power to coerce their opponents, they approved."[61]

Thomas Finger

The well-known work of Thomas Finger suggests a third and quite different way to hold emphases from particular classic theologies together with peace church emphases.

Finger's approach appears to be as much a methodology as a theology. Finger collects motifs, terms, themes, or content from a great variety of historical traditions. Sometimes providing traditional terms with new definitions, other times retaining traditional definitions and content under new names, he weaves a new, modern synthesis on top of a peace church framework. The result is a theology whose bare skeleton is Anabaptist, peace church, but which also retains many characteristics of a Protestant Reformed orthodoxy flavored by Catholicism.

Finger seems to view each particular historic theology or historic tradition as, to some extent, incomplete or inadequate. Its full potential is realized or completed only in the synthesis available only to the modern observer. Or perhaps we can say that Finger's methodology is to treat the themes and doctrines of various traditions as discrete and interchangeable parts to use in building a complete theology, analogous to the way one may use interchangeable parts to customize an automobile.

Constructing an Anabaptist theology, then, is like building or customizing a car of a specific make. Begin with a recognizable frame or a chassis and motor of the wanted manufacture. Then make changes and add components from a variety of other models to arrive at a complete, unique machine. Lower and chop, import the gear box from one make, the steering mechanism from another, fenders from a third, and wheels and hub caps from still another, then garnish with custom-made hood ornament.

While this is not at all the simple two lists approach described earlier, Finger's methodology remains in that genre. It is a more sophisticated version of combining particular Anabaptist distinctives with other particular Protestant and Catholic emphases. Finger's theology gains validation from other traditions to the extent that it needs borrowings of particular pieces to fill out its own presumed incomplete outline. On the other hand, this procedure also reflects the recognition that the traditions from which the peace church or Mennonite theology achieves validation also have holes and inadequacies and that need to be filled. The result is the functional equivalent of a two list approach: fusing Anabaptist and other theology into a comprehensive, creative, customized synthesis.

Orienting the project as a whole is apparently the modern assumption that there is one identifiable and comprehensive theology, if only we can collect enough of the pieces to fill it in. Since this new theology is constructed of pieces borrowed from a variety of writers and traditions, the implication is that earlier theologies were all in some way incomplete (as opposed to complete but differently oriented), and that the modern observer is who can survey the incomplete theologies and select the parts suitable for integration.[62]

Scott Holland

Scott Holland's kind of postorthodoxy might be another approach to a Mennonite theology that begins with roots in an assumed general theology. Holland has worried that persons such as John H. Yoder and myself are "sectarian." While obviously cognizant of violence and justice issues, Holland is concerned that a proper theology for the peace church be one that embraces learnings from the world, be accessible in the world, use some of the language and concepts of American democracy, and serve the world, that is the public sphere, as well as the church.

But one must ask whether a theology that presumes to "despise middle-class culture," yet finds the voice of God in the diversity of the "public square" containing a temple where we enter "beside priests and strangers, merchants and foreigners, the leading men of the temple and the unknown woman from the far country," has exchanged Christendom's kind of territorial faith for a new version of a people of God, one defined by social location rather than faith in the risen Jesus. ("Ask not simply what God is doing in the church; ask what God is doing in the world.") It is arguable that this public theology is searching for a foundation in a supposed theology-in-general, albeit a foundation markedly different from that of any of the other writers cited thus far.[63]

TWO MORE ASSERTIONS

Lack of Consensus
Although much theologizing by Mennonites has assumed a standard core of doctrines located outside the Mennonite tradition, or in some other way

combined what were considered Anabaptist and non-Anabaptist doctrines, there has been little consensus on the identity or shape of the core or the material borrowed. Theologizing on the basis of a supposed theology-in-general has not produced consensus on the nature of that theology.

This point should be obvious from the foregoing discussion. My survey has noted several versions of the supposed theology-in-general: fundamentalist, evangelical, liberal, creedal orthodox, and more. Each of these various Mennonite theologies—or theologies for Mennonites—assumed that it was related to a theology-in-general. Each assumed some kind of a standard theological agenda from which a theology for Mennonites acquires validity.

Yet the effort to construct a theology by adding Mennonite distinctives to an assumed standard core has bypassed a crucial step. It has assumed that one can build on this core without going through the difficult process of developing a consensus about the nature of it.

This brings us to a fourth assertion.

The Hole in the Core

Theologizing on the basis of a core and Mennonite additives was motivated, at least in part, by a perceived gap or inadequacy in the received theology-in-general.

This too should be obvious from the foregoing discussion. Although in very different ways, each of the writers suggested either a list or a methodology that would combine Mennonite emphases with doctrines from some other theological tradition, whether assumed general or particular. None of the borrowed theologies made nonviolence central. In fact, to begin with an imported theology-in-general, as did all writers surveyed except Thomas Finger, was to begin with a theology that had already made nonviolence or Jesus' rejection of the sword peripheral. The tension between needing a presumed core theology-in-general and the perceived incompleteness or inadequacy of that core was never fully resolved.

A further problem is that the fused lists, or redefined or revised versions of the core, will no longer satisfy the other-than-Mennonite guardians of the supposed theology-in-general. In effect, the Mennonite second lists, or additions, demonstrate that the supposed general core was actually inadequate as a foundation. Filling in or rounding out that core with additions renders it unacceptable to those for whom it was the complete foundation.

Unless the other-than-Mennonite bearers of the supposed theology-in-general have somehow developed peace church sympathies, they will not readily accept the expanded or reshaped core that now has Jesus' rejection of the sword added to it. I suspect that the effort to retain a theology-in-general has succeeded more in enabling Mennonites to identify with some version of wider Christendom than it has produced a genuine peace theology for the Mennonite churches or has persuaded other Christians of the truth of Christian nonviolence.[64]

A PROPOSAL

These observations ought to change the form of the question about a peace church theology. If we are serious about peace, does a theology for the peace church begin with a theology based on the assumptions of another tradition (which is the case if there is a theology-in-general) or with peace church assumptions that shape theologizing?

The postmodern acknowledgement of the particularity of all theology suggests that we discard the idea that there is a theology-in-general that carries an assumed priority to which we must connect. What was treated as a theology-in-general was not really general. That should be clear when we note the labels attached to the several assumed standard programs that twentieth-century Mennonite theologies built on: John Horsch's and Daniel Kauffman's fundamental ones; the evangelical-oriented core of Harold Bender, J. C. Wenger, and Ron Sider; the progressive cores of C. H. Wedel, J. E. Hartzler, and Edmund Kaufman; Jim Reimer's Catholic orthodoxy; Tom Finger's more Reformed and evangelical orthodoxy; and Scott Holland's postmodern public theology.

These are not general theologies. Rather, each is a theology first developed in or for a specific tradition to respond to or to reflect specific needs in that tradition. When others accept those answers, they are accepting a specific tradition. Alongside those particular theologies, I suggest, it certainly ought to be possible for the peace church tradition to develop a theology that is shaped by its particular understanding of and commitment to Jesus Christ.

Acknowledging that the presumed theology-in-general is really specific theology is a freeing act. It frees us from having to accommodate a theology that does not share peace church assumptions about the centrality of nonviolence in the story of Jesus Christ.[65]

Much of theology of Western Christendom has accommodated violence and war, and has done so in such a presumed universal fashion that even peace churches barely recognize it. That accommodation is true of the several assumed general theologies which twentieth-century Mennonite theologizing attempted to build on or borrow from. If these presumed theologies-in-general had not accommodated violence, the various Mennonite writers would not be adding Mennonite lists or making other kinds of adaptations. Does the fact that violence-accommodating theology has been so widely accepted that its specific reference point is usually forgotten qualify it to be the core of a theology for the peace church? I think not.

Stated another way, if one begins with peace church assumptions, rather than with theological assumptions of the violence-accommodating established church, is it not possible that a fresh reading of the Bible might produce a different and better rendering of Christology and atonement than that which emerged from the Constantinian church? I think so.

Recognizing that there is no theology-in-general, but only specific theologies, leads to a change in understanding the nature of theological disagreement. We move from a discussion of orthodoxy versus heresy to a comparison of competing, conflicting, or alternative versions of what it means to be Christian.

To posit a theology-in-general, a core, or standard program is to assume its validity and to place the burden of proof on those who raise questions or pose any kind of alternative. On the other hand, to recognize that the received theology-in-general, of whatever stripe, is a particular theology that reflects a specific context is to change the question about the burden of proof. This burden does not disappear. When the argument is fair, however, the burden will fall equally on all parties in the discussion. An assumed theology-in-general no longer is privileged based on number of adherents or length of existence.[66]

As was pointed out in the introductory chapter, such a level playing field exists in the abstract rather than in reality. The theology-in-general of Christendom, now unmasked as a particular theology, still exercises a de facto hegemony. The size and length of its traditions provide a presumed right to define theological agenda. Nevertheless, the advent of postmodernity provides an opening for peace church advocates to make a theological case.

At this point let me state explicitly that I am not saying that persons who accommodate war and violence are not Christian. I take them at their word that they are. Precisely because I take them seriously as Christians I challenge their understanding of Christian theology, which lends itself so well to the rationalization of violence.

I recognize that there are different kinds of Christians, with differing theologies. But, I suggest, the basis for comparing these several Christian theologies or traditions is a criterion accessible to all, namely the narrative of Jesus. It is with reference to this criterion that I call for this development of a new peace church theology, rather than merely adding a couple of components or in some other way trying to salvage Christendom's violence-accommodating formulas.

I believe that this differentiation of Christian theologies with reference to the narrative of Jesus is not an exclusivist or triumphalist stance. Indeed, I suggest that it constitutes a more accessible basis for ecumenical dialogue than does the assumption that we begin from a supposed common foundation in a theology-in-general, whose character we have not agreed on and which we characterize differently (by calling it incomplete) than do the dialogue partners whose theology it actually is.

The question of violence is unavoidable. We cannot avoid a decision on whether to look at the world from the violence-accommodating perspective of the U.S. ethos or from the perspective of the violence-rejecting narrative of the peace church understanding of Jesus. Most North American Christians make the decision about violence by default; they accept the violence-accommodating world view without reflection. They do not perceive the extent to which the supposed theology-in-general of Western Christendom has accommodated and supported war and violence.

One cannot make a decision about Jesus without also making a decision, one way or another, about whether rejection of the sword was intrinsic to his life and work. The question is whether that decision is made by default or with conscious awareness of the issues and their implications. That Jesus is the norm for ethics, that Jesus' rejection of the sword is intrinsic to his life and teaching, is not a self-contained idea that is true in and of itself. It is an assumption about what one does with the Jesus we discover in the New Testament. These assumptions about Jesus as the norm of ethics and the rejection of the sword are then understood as a perspective from which to examine all the issues that Christian theology discusses.

Theology from a nonviolent perspective is theology specifically shaped by the assumption that rejection of violence is intrinsic to the reign of God as made visible in the life and teaching of Jesus. My challenge to the would-be peace church is to acknowledge very consciously and specifically that Jesus means nonviolence, then to look at our entire theological endeavor from that perspective.[67] The continuing existence of the peace churches depends on it.

THREE

NINETEENTH-CENTURY MENNONITE THEOLOGY IN FACE OF PRESUMED THEOLOGY-IN-GENERAL[1]

INTRODUCTION

Previous chapters used conversation with twentieth-century Mennonite theologizing to discuss the difference peace makes for theology and to suggest that the peace church rethink its theology in face of postmodernity. This chapter and the next take the analysis of the relationship of Mennonite and Christendom's theology into earlier centuries.

The current chapter deals with theological difference in the nineteenth century, when Mennonite theology was still largely assumed to be the received faith and before it underwent the changes that resulted from engagement with the modernist-fundamentalist controversy. Chapter 4 brings a similar agenda to the sixteenth century, the epoch of Anabaptist origins. Both chapters 3 and 4 use primarily the concept of atonement to test the relationship of Mennonite theology to presumed theology-in-general.

Atonement doctrine serves well as an indicator of mainstream and evangelical theology. It is a classic doctrine that has belonged to all Christian traditions since the beginning of Christianity.

Since the time of Anselm of Canterbury (c.1033-1109), theologians have depended predominantly, though not exclusively, on some form of satisfaction or substitutionary atonement. The moral influence theory associated with Peter Abelard (1079-1142) appeared alongside Anselmian atonement as a persistent but minority alternative.

No early church council established an authoritative position on atonement as occurred for Christology. The various churchly traditions did not reach a confessional stance on this doctrine until satisfaction or substitutionary atonement became established and recognized as a hallmark of fundamentalism and evangelicalism.[2] The absence of a longstanding authoritative, official position (at least until the recent past) makes this a significant doctrine by which to make comparisons across the boundaries of traditions and denominations, and to assess the orientation of theologians and the views that have influenced them. Since atonement may also involve issues of Christocentricism and discipleship, it is particularly suited to use in comparing historic Mennonite theology with that of other traditions. The following discussion focuses on the peace church dimensions of atonement theology and its relationship to ethics, most specifically nonresistance, for a spectrum of Amish and Mennonite writers from the latter half of the nineteenth century.

The eight writers cited represent a cross section of Amish and Mennonite ethnic and ecclesiological stances. In Jacob Stauffer (1811-55), the first Old Order Mennonite leader, we glimpse the traditionalist or conservative Mennonite orientation at the beginning of the confrontation with modernity. Speaking for the Old Order Amish, David Beiler (1786-1871) provides an Amish parallel to Stauffer.

Cornelius H. Wedel (1860-1910), who was also quoted in the previous chapter, represents the more progressive, immigrant German-Russian Mennonites from the Molotschna Colony. This group began arriving from the Ukraine in 1874 and settled primarily in central Kansas. Gerhard Wiebe (1827-1900) was the senior bishop, or *Aeltester,* of the Bergthal colony. He led a more conservative group of Russian immigrants, who settled in southern Manitoba, away from the Molotschna contingent.

John M. Brenneman (1816-1895) reflects the majority Swiss-American Mennonite tradition, whose immigrant roots in North America reach back as far as the late seventeenth century. John

Holdeman (1832-1900) abandoned that body in 1859 and formed the pietistic and somewhat revivalist Church of God in Christ, Mennonite, commonly known as the Holdeman Mennonites. The son of immigrants, Johannes Moser (1826-1908) represents the nineteenth-century Swiss immigrant tradition before it felt the full impact of various modernizing and Americanizing influences. German immigrant Heinrich Egly (1824-1890) led a revivalist schism from the Amish in 1865 to form what came to be called the Defenseless Mennonite Church.

The goal of analyzing such a cross section is to determine what is specific to a range of peace church theologizing as well as to see what is shared with other Protestants. In their context, these writers were trying to keep their theology relevant as they engaged the prevailing wisdom of the day. While they were clearly influenced by the voices of their times, their theology did not merely repeat those American voices. In their discussions, they brought crucial features of their Mennonite, peace church theology into their present. They were mindful of the differences they had from an assumed general faith shared with other Protestants, and their theologizing reflects these differences even as they used much of the idiom of U.S. evangelicalism and revivalism.

ATONEMENT: NARROW FOCUS

All eight of the named individuals assumed some form of the substitutionary, sacrificial, or satisfaction theory of atonement. That much can be stated without extensive quotes.[3] Together their writings provide a cluster of atonement images that are variations and developments of the view that is frequently identified with Anselm of Canterbury. It was Anselm's *Cur Deus Homo?* (1098)[4] that provided the first full articulation of Jesus' death as satisfaction of God's honor.

Of the eight subjects, only C. H. Wedel referred to Anselm and Abelard by name and analyzed the differences between competing theories of atonement. None of the other seven referred to Anselm nor to his theory of atonement, nor even identified his discussion of salvation with a particular atonement doctrine. Thus one can not say that these men were "Anselmian," if that term is used to mean that they knowingly accepted and advocated a version of the atonement doctrine that they developed on the basis of Anselm. However, they can be called "Anselmian" when that term is used as shorthand for the collection of satisfaction, substitutionary, and sacrificial images in contrast to moral influence and Christus Victor images.

C. H. Wedel did acknowledge the existence of multiple theories of atonement and analyzed their differences. Without identifying other views, John Holdeman also obliquely acknowledged their existence when he said that "some professors of Christ deny that Christ died in our stead, and made an offering to satisfy God and His Father, to redeem and release us from sin."[5] However, the remaining six men simply assumed that when they discussed substitution, sacrifice, or satisfaction of penalty, they were discussing salvation itself.

The difference between Wedel and the others clearly reflects the widely disparate educational levels of these men. Wedel attended the German-language Bloomfield Theological Seminary in New Jersey. J. M. Brenneman learned to read only as an adult. The remaining six were primarily self-educated after grammar school.

Despite their common orientation in a general Anselmian approach, the outlook of these writers cannot be adequately understood by characterizing their thought in terms of an atonement image. A look at the several contexts in which they mentioned atonement provides evidence that together they represent a distinct peace church theological and ecclesiological tradition in the stream of U.S. Protestantism. That common theological orientation puts Wedel in the same camp with his co-religionists, despite their differences in education and Wedel's more sophisticated argument.

The Context of Atonement

Jacob Stauffer[6]
Stauffer, the first Old Order Mennonite leader, barely mentioned atonement as a doctrine. It was his view of the church that shaped his worldview in general and his view of atonement in particular.

Jesus chose the church and made it separate from the world, Stauffer said. As a community, the church takes Jesus as its pattern and example, and each individual member follows Jesus' example. Characteristics of that church include nonresistance to evil, humility, separation from the world, and strong discipline, which includes both excommunication and shunning of sinners until they repent and adopt a new, changed life.

Above all, it is discipline that holds this church together. Stauffer referred to excommunication and shunning as the wall that protects God's people and keeps them pure.

That Stauffer lived in the world of the Bible is clearly indicated by his citation of several pages of Old Testament examples as evidence that God wants sin to be punished. He admonished the "beloved reader to test in these confused and fallen times how truly necessary it is to pay attention to the teaching of Jesus and his apostles because so many such teachings, examples and stories of Israel [being punished] are in the Old Testament."[7]

At the most general level of theological context, the death of Christ makes possible salvation in this disciplined church. However, the disciplined church also contributes to salvation. Numerous times Stauffer described discipline—specifically, excommunication and shunning—as something practiced for the salvation of immortal souls. When done out of a spirit of love and concern, shunning will shame the sinful one and bring about repentance and a bettering of life—that is, salvation. Discipline thus contributes to the salvation of immortal souls. Stauffer called the discipline of excommunication and shunning "the best medicine for the poor wounded soul, through which the fallen sinner comes to repentance, remorse, and suffering for sin, and to confession of truth."[8]

The doctrine of nonresistance[9] also belonged to the wider theological context of Stauffer's understanding of atonement. Nonresistance was more than a special Mennonite practice. In referring to the "nonresistant foundation" *(wehrlosen Grund)* of the gospel, Stauffer called the reader to notice

> how patiently the innocent lamb of God, Jesus Christ, suffered for us . . . he could have chastised all his enemies with a word and punished them with death. However, to show us a defenseless pattern and example, he suffered ridicule, shame and beating, not seeking to avenge himself but praying for his enemies and loving them until death.[10]

Thus Stauffer located the foundation of nonresistance in the redeeming act of Jesus. For that reason, nonresistance belonged integrally to the life of Jesus' followers.

David Beiler[11]

When Old Order Amish bishop David Beiler discussed salvation, his concern was twofold: the necessity of rebirth or conversion and the nature of the saved life, which follows from the saving work of Christ and constitutes the primary evidence that one is saved. All mentions of atonement in the narrow sense, that is, Jesus' substitutionary bearing of sinful humanity's deserved penalty or punishment, are a prelude to rebirth or conversion and the saved life.[12]

Two things occupy Beiler's remarks on that saved life. First, it happens only as a result of rebirth or conversion, that is, an inner, subjective component. Second, it is a life of external submission and obedience to the Word and to the teaching and example of Jesus.[13]

The new birth happens by the grace of God and through the Spirit of God. It has an experiential component that the reborn person senses as he or she becomes oriented to Christ and lives in Christ. The sinner's heart and mind are transformed so that the sinful inclinations of the flesh are overcome. The person becomes a new creature in Christ and follows obediently his commands. Like Stauffer, Beiler believed that the covering of sin and punishment achieved by Jesus' sacrificial death was one of the factors which made the new birth possible.[14]

Frequently, Beiler rolled new birth and the obedient life together into one package. It is the obedient one whom God can save, and it is only the saved, that is reborn ones, who can be and are obedient. "Thus all reborn Christians must be so minded that they follow the command of Jesus Christ in all obedience."[15]

The shape of that obedience as described by Beiler is the outlook of what would come to be called the Old Order Amish. Obviously it includes nonresistance to evil. Also important are the virtue of humility, refusal to swear oaths or use the worldly law courts to settle disputes, the practice of church discipline, and more.[16] Thus while Beiler's writing exhibited a larger role for experiential religion than did Stauffer's, Beiler otherwise kept his focus on the disciplined church and the saved life, quite parallel to the outlook of Old Order Mennonite Jacob Stauffer.

Gerhard Wiebe[17]

What shaped Wiebe's worldview and supplied the context for his apparent assumption of satisfaction atonement was his perception of a life of obedience to the commandments of God. The particular character Wiebe gave to that obedience reflected strikingly his experiences as leader of the Bergthal colony and his perception of the relationship of Bergthal to the other Mennonite colonies in Russia.

Bergthal had come into existence in 1836, as a daughter colony of Chortitza. Chortitza was the first Mennonite colony in Russia, founded in 1789 by West Prussian Mennonite immigrants from the area of Danzig. Molotschna, a second colony of West Prussian Mennonite immigrants, had been founded in 1804. For a variety of reasons, the Chortitza colony experienced much hardship in its early years, while Molotschna quickly prospered and outstripped the performance of Chortitza in various ways. As a result, Chortitza came to feel itself somewhat inferior to and even ridiculed by Molotschna.

The problem of land ownership affected both colonies. To ensure that farms would retain sufficient land to produce a livelihood, the original settlement provisions of 1789 prohibited the subdivison of farms. In effect, only one child could inherit the family homestead. There soon developed an unlucky and disgruntled majority of non-landowners, called *Anwohner*. As one way to redress the land problem, Bergthal was founded as a daughter colony of Chortitza. Stated in oversimplified terms, the founders of Bergthal came primarily from the unlucky, or *Anwohner*, of Chortitza. As the son of *Anwohner* parents who had moved to the Bergthal village of Heuboden in 1839 when he was a boy of 12, Gerhard Wiebe inherited the feelings of people who had frequently thought of themselves as second best, both as Chortitzans and *Anwohner*.

In *Ursachen und Geschichte,* Wiebe sketched conditions in Russia. He related events of the Bergthaler immigration to southern Manitoba and his leadership there, his resignation from the office of bishop, probably early in 1882,[18] and his perception of the decaying state of Mennonites as they entered the twentieth century. The little book begins and ends with calls to be obedient to the commands of God. Humility, nonresistance, and opposition to higher education characterize that obedience, with humility as the common denominator. It is hardly surprising that his humble Bergthaler appear as more obedient than the proud Mennonites in other colonies.

For Wiebe, the protection promised by God to his people depends on obedience, whether in the Old Testament or in later times.

Wiebe attributed the Bergthalers' survival of the hardships of immigration to the unity created by their obedience to the commands of God.[19] On the other hand, the scattering of the Mennonite churches to the four winds and the fragmentation of the two large congregations that remained in Russia were the result of having ceased to listen to the Word of God.[20] Such falling away might even signal the end times. Throughout, Wiebe emphasized consequences of obedience.[21]

Not surprisingly, Wiebe believed Jesus outlook was humble and unpretentious. In fact, it was Jesus' humility that led to his rejection: "Had Jesus come in pride and magnificence [*Hoffart und Pracht*], then they would have accepted him."[22] Jesus also chose humble people as his disciples. They came from "the lowliest people, namely, fishermen and also a customs collector." None came from the "advanced school" of Gamaliel, which trained its students in "arrogance and self-righteousness." Because Paul had imbibed the teaching of Gamaliel's school, he had to be called "through thunder and lightning."[23]

Nonresistance belonged indelibly to the obedient, humble life. In the opening sentence of *Ursachen und Geschichte*, Wiebe gave the saving of "our children from military service and ruin" as the reason for emigration to North America.[24] In other settings he linked nonresistance, humility, and opposition to advanced education. For example, while the change in the fourth-century church represented by Constantine was a struggle between the false bishops who followed "state laws" and the true bishops who held to "God's Word and command,"[25] the most serious fourth-century offense concerned education. The church's "biggest error" was "its building of advanced schools; for here the Word of God and human wisdom were mixed together, and through this simplicity and innocence decreased steadily. . . . So it was that after four hundred years the teaching of humility was transformed into an arrogant priesthood" which preached to please the emperor in exchange for an imperial supply of wealth.[26]

Some humble flames, such as Menno Simons, did flicker through the centuries, Wiebe said. Menno "held fast to the Lord's teaching" and was "meek and lowly."[27] Eventually Menno's legacy was carried to Poland and then to Russia. Meanwhile, nonresistance disappeared from the Mennonites in Prussia, Wiebe said, when "the rich began to let their sons study in the advanced school of Danzig, [and] from there they went to the Berlin university." They learned to dress fashionably "and bore themselves like military officers. . . . Finally our teachers were chosen from this educated group and so we ourselves planted the germ of arrogance and pride into our schools, as well as into our congregations."[28] In 1862, Wiebe said, the last nonresistant ones moved from Prussia to Russia.[29]

In these accounts, whether about the fourth-century church or the Mennonite church in Prussia, the loss was nonresistance, but education was the culprit. Prideful higher education undermined nonresistance, while humility and simplicity remained content to obey the Word of God and retain nonresistance.[30]

For Wiebe, signs of arrogance were not limited to support for education and the loss of nonresistance. Arrogant, educated ministers as well as revival preachers[31] proclaimed a repentance which touched the heart but accepted everything from the world. No doubt Wiebe had a dual meaning in mind when he wrote, "They preach repentance, but live in greatest arrogance, and try to cover up with the aura of Holy Scripture their belief that a person can go along with everything in the world, as long as his heart is not attached to it."[32] Such preachers mention only a few words about the text, Wiebe said; then to attract acclaim, they talk about the railroad, newspapers, and whatever is happening in the world.[33]

For Wiebe, things that displayed arrogance or lack of humility included ostentatious display in clothing and fashions, buggies and coaches, marriage into other confessions, standing for and holding public office, and placing money at interest.[34] Wiebe's critique of Mennonites for arrogance, education, and display applied both to the wealthy who remained behind in Russia and to the advocates of education in southern Manitoba.

Taken together, the observations in *Ursachen und Geschichte* show a worldview comprised of humility, simplicity, obedience, nonresistance, and opposition to education. However, Wiebe's comments are less a theological outlook than an understanding of the visible church. Wiebe did not defend nonresistance, humility, or opposition to education by appeals to biblical authority. Rather, the church existed as the living extension of Christ and his disciples. It was a community defined and reinforced by lifestyle rather than by an explicitly biblical and theological rationale.

Instead of appealing to biblical authority, Wiebe wanted to preserve a simple nonresistant people by opposing the outside influences which would enter via higher education. In that context, his brief references to atonement constitute an addendum to this package of the simple, obedient, nonresistant life. Arrogance belonged to the sins that were heaped on Jesus, and for which he had to undergo suffering and rejection from God. Jesus' death carried away the sin and punishment of those who violated the humble, obedient life.

This understanding of atonement deals with the legacy of sin but does not shape Wiebe's view of the obedient life. It is not a view of atonement but the visible church— humble, nonresistant, and opposed to higher education—that identifies Wiebe's outlook. One need not agree with the specifics of his worldview to observe that it is another version of lived faith and a visible church which distinguishes Mennonites from North American Protestantism.

Cornelius H. Wedel[35]

In the narrow sense of the term *atonement,* the progressive Wedel advocated substitutionary understanding. He used the terms *Stellvertretung* or *stellvertretend* (substitution, substitutionary) in describing the Old Testament sacrifices as a foreshadowing of Jesus' death. In his death Jesus bears the penalty for the sin of humankind, sin previously covered by the blood of the sacrificed animal.[36] Yet Wedel's treatment of atonement was shaped both by his roots in Mennonite tradition and a growing awareness of historical scholarship. Thus his is much more than a mere assertion of substitutionary atonement.

Wedel acknowledged that much of Anselm's treatment of atonement was correct, but argued that Anselm should have begun with the idea of atonement as necessitated by human sin rather than required to placate an offense against God's honor.[37] After identifying a modified Anselmian position as his basic approach to atonement, Wedel also sought to come to terms with Abelard. Although he believed that Abelard had a "one-sided" emphasis on the love of God and a "lax" concept of sin,[38] Wedel preserved Abelard's emphasis on love, calling it the "framework" *(Rahmen)* that surrounds the sacrificial suffering of Christ.[39] The death of Christ is a revelation of the love of God.

Like the other figures of this chapter, Wedel described and encouraged both internal and external components of faith and emphasized that the true inner faith will necessarily manifest itself externally in the way the regenerate person lives. Despite his higher level of education, the overall intent of Wedel's discussion was clearly parallel to the others. Wedel underscored such traditional Mennonite emphases as love of enemies and nonresistance to evil, avoidance of government service, avoidance of the oath, and willingness to suffer.[40]

In his view of discipleship, Wedel placed significant limits on the experiential dimensions of religion. Becoming Christian is not an instantaneous event but a lifelong process of growth, analogous to learning to play a musical instrument,[41] or to the way an initial foothold in an alien land is gradually expanded by an invader until the whole country is conquered.[42] "The formation of a perfect, holy character is a lifelong task, on which the Christian must work with great earnestness."[43] More important than an oral confession is a lived faith, a faith active in love.[44]

Thus Wedel rejected explicitly the idea of a uniform kind of conversion. Scripture does not provide particular conditions for a "mechanical path" that always allows fixing conversion on a particular day and time.[45] If one comes to that experience from a life deep in sin and without God, the awakening is usually rather spirited. Yet this "also can be done in an artificial or even feigned way" *(kann aber auch auf eine künstliche Weise gehoben und wohl auch erkünstelt werden),* as one can observe in the "so-called revival meetings of the Methodists" *(sogennanten Erweckungsversammlungen der Methodisten).*[46] Wedel emphasized that this awakening is "transitory" and not yet the culmination of conversion, though it can have validity as a turning point that marks the beginning of a lifelong process of growth in the Christian life.[47]

Wedel's brake on revivalistic forms had both family and ecclesiological dimensions. Around 1880 his father, Cornelius P. Wedel, had led a breakaway from Alexanderwohl, their congregation of Russian Mennonite immigrants established in 1874 north of Newton, Kansas. The elder Wedel founded a Mennonite Brethren congregation nearby.

Most of the family joined the father in the breakaway, while Cornelius H. stayed with the original congregation. The Mennonite Brethren, whose roots reached back to 1860 in the Russian empire, emphasized "spiritual renewal through heartfelt conversion"[48] as well as baptism by immersion (another item which Wedel rejected as a required form in *Glaubenslehre*). Thus C. H. Wedel's limitation on conversion clearly posed an alternative to the impact of the Mennonite Brethren on his own people.

Wedel also placed limits on the "soul struggle" *(Bußkampf)* of "pietistic circles." While some who are deep in sin may experience a great struggle and a sudden breakthrough, Wedel cautioned that many others do not experience that struggle and instead come to salvation in a quiet manner. He cautioned that a preoccupation with feeling can overshadow trust in the external death of Christ "for us" as the source of salvation. "Our certainty of salvation does not rest on our feelings of repentance, . . . but on simple, childlike faith in the merit of Christ."[49]

True repentance is verified neither by a stylized revivalistic conversion experience nor by a great soul struggle, but rather by the saved life one leads following conversion. In that focus on the external righteous life, the rejection of feeling as a validator, and the placing of limits on the significance of the experiential dimensions of faith, Wedel is similar to Stauffer and Beiler, and to Johannes Moser to follow.

Finally, Wedel's understanding of atonement and the relationship of experiential to external religion needs to be set in the context of his synthesis of Mennonite history in world and Christian history.

Using as a base the work of German scholars Ludwig Keller and Anna Brons, Wedel called the historic tradition to which Mennonites belonged "congregational Christendom," or *Gemeindechristentum*.[50] Wedel considered *Gemeindechristentum* a norm against which to interpret all of Christian history. It was a universal Christianity, existing continuously since Jesus had established the church until the present. In this church, the truly saved, who possessed heartfelt piety, were united by the Spirit into a community or congregation. Characteristics of this congregational form of Christianity included discipleship, apostolicity, voluntarism, progress, nonresistance, separation of church and state, freedom in religious doctrine, lay responsibility, and congregational authority.[51]

When Wedel traced the decline of the church, as it lost its congregational form and became the church of the bishop in the third century, then a state church in the fourth century, *Gemeindechristentum* was carried on in various forms by a succession of groups. Through the

centuries, Wedel said, these groups retained a New Testament understanding of the church. Waldensians, the purest medieval adherents,
passed on this understanding to the Anabaptists, who then emerged as
key sixteenth-century bearers of this believers' church Christendom,
over against both Catholic and Protestant versions of state church
Christendom. Thus Mennonites, who were and are the direct descendants of Anabaptists, belonged not to a recent tradition which had
come into existence only with the Reformation but rather to a comprehensive Christian tradition that had unbroken links all the way
back to Jesus himself.[52]

On the one hand, *Gemeindechristentum* was clearly a way to link
all of history to Wedel's own time, and to give wider meaning and focus both to individual salvation and to denominational identity. On
the other hand, it enabled Wedel to borrow from U.S. society and to
chart a way for his Mennonite people to participate in the world and
accept new elements from it without being absorbed by the world.
Any number of times, Wedel mentioned the value of the Americanizing concept of progress or expressed criticism of the conservative
Mennonite groups that objected to new ideas and new institutions.

The idea of *Gemeindechristentum* enabled Wedel to accept
progress and cultural accommodation, and to absorb some of the new
theological emphases, while maintaining essentially an orthodox direction in classic terms and preserving Mennonite emphases in the
context of the whole.[53] Despite the great discrepancies in educational
level and worldview between them, Wedel's focus on historic Mennonite descriptions of the saved life places him in the same ecclesiological
tradition as Stauffer and Beiler.

Johannes Moser[54]

Johannes Moser was minister and bishop in the Swiss Mennonite
church of Bluffton, Ohio, for the last half of the nineteenth century. For
Moser, the substitutionary death of Jesus exemplified the nonresistance
that stands at the heart of what it means to be a disciple of Jesus.

Moser intended his remarks on atonement as a statement of the
foundation on which nonresistance stands.[55] He anchored nonresistance in the affirmation that "Christ is the head of his church." Jesus
taught nonresistance to his disciples and exemplified it in his person,
thus fulfilling the law of the Old Testament. That law required retri-

bution for sin, and the wars and tribulations that God sent against wicked people constituted God's justifiable and legally necessary response. Moser believed that when the Israelites who attempted faithfulness experienced punishment, they must have developed an acute desire for one who would stop the cycle of retribution by suffering in their place. The stern law that pointed out sin thus created a strong desire for a redeemer who would bring complete forgiveness and a peaceful kingdom.[56]

In contrast to the violence and retribution of the Old Testament, the Redeemer brought another way: a fulfillment of the law and thus an end to the cycle of retribution. Grace replaced law, and peace could reign in the hearts of people, who would be free from the wrath of God and the curse of the law.[57]

The major point Moser wanted to make, that is, his primary reason for discussing atonement, was to say that the atoning act of Jesus happened *nonresistantly*. For Moser, the sacrificial atonement is inherently nonresistant. Further, any who would be followers of Jesus must be motivated and regenerated by his Spirit, the same spirit of nonresistance. "In this sense the entire context of Scripture teaches nonresistance."[58] Moser's gospel, as defined in a sacrificial view of atonement, is thus inherently a gospel of peace.

Moser emphasized both internal and external components of atonement and salvation. On the one hand, inner transformation is essential and without it no salvation exists. The sacrificial death of Christ is the foundation for this inner transformation. On the other hand, the inner life will necessarily manifest itself in external behavior. The externals do not guarantee salvation; one can conform outwardly without a corresponding inner change. However, the inner change cannot fail to produce an external manifestation, and evil works clearly show that one's heart has not been changed.[59]

Moser dealt with revivalism explicitly; he opposed it. Much like C. H. Wedel, Moser believed that the inner transformation was a lifelong process of nurture which took place in the loving embrace of the church. Many of Moser's articles have sections that deal with objection to revivalism; with the process of nurture and the patience and tolerance required by the nurturing leaders toward those growing in the faith; or with the disappointment of spiritual leaders when some fall away despite the best efforts of the shepherds.[60]

The assumption that conversion consists of a nurturing process constituted the foundation of Moser's objection to revivalism. The crisis conversion of revivalism substitutes a single event for a long journey, he believed. Further, revivalism substitutes the notoriously unreliable criterion of feeling for the visible criteria of obedience to Christ as the means of validating conversion. Moser recognized that not all persons receive the same measure of joy, and like Wedel, he rejected the emphasis on feelings as the sign of conversion.[61]

Appeal to a crisis conversion elevates some persons over others who may be striving diligently to lead a Christian life, Moser believed. Those who have experienced such a conversion become critical and suspicious of the "unconverted" who have not. At the same time, Moser expressed a clear openness to mutual acceptance of diverse religious expressions. Individual preachers and congregations could experience conversion differently yet still accept each other in love.[62]

Moser's quite explicit objections to revivalism did not arise in a vacuum. In the 1880s, the revivalist work in Bluffton of Heinrich Egly, founder of the Defenseless Mennonite Church, created an upheaval in Moser's congregation. A significant number of members joined the new Defenseless Mennonite congregation in Bluffton. Although Moser did not mention Egly by name, parts of several articles posed a response to Egly's challenge.[63] A following section deals with Egly's perspective on these developments.

These observations about Johannes Moser make clear that, like Wedel and others, he emphasized the saved, nonresistant life in a way that is not shown by simply describing his traditional atonement doctrine.

John M. Brenneman[64]

Bishop John M. Brenneman belonged to the largest body of U.S. Mennonites in the nineteenth century. Brenneman welcomed the new patterns of church life that developed among this group toward the end of the century,[65] and he was well liked by the progressives.[66] On the other hand, his emphasis on repentance, humility, new birth, and new life show that Brenneman's theology and worldview belonged much more to the previous generation.[67] Thus he "was very much a link between an older Mennonitism and a newer."[68]

Brenneman assumed the satisfaction theory of atonement but did not argue for it as opposed to other doctrinal approaches. Like the other individuals in this chapter, Brenneman stressed the regenerate life of the saved person rather than the doctrine of atonement itself.

For Brenneman, the recovery of sinful individuals from the consequences of the fall begins with repentance, which in turn depends on an awareness of sin brought on by knowledge of God's law.[69] Awareness of sin insures that repentance occurs in and through an attitude of humility and that it results in a saved life. The penitent sinner confesses these sins "in deep humility" while praying to God for forgiveness.[70]

The heart of Brenneman's idea of repentance was that it would result in a visible change in the life of the sinner. Concerning the nature of the change, his book *Pride and Humility*[71] posited humility as the cornerstone of that saved life.[72] Adam and Eve fell by pride; "Hence, pride was the first sin, and will be the last to be overcome."[73] Contemporary expressions of pride mentioned by Brenneman included deportment, highly decorated houses, pictures, fancy dress, and jewelry. True Christianity rejects these, and "is to be found only in the humble and regenerate heart."[74]

God has opposed the proud throughout divine history and will continue to do so until the judgment day, Brenneman wrote. To those who repent and humble themselves, God gives the grace that results in regeneration and the beginning of a humble and obedient life. Jesus supplied us with "an unparalleled example of humility" when he washed the disciples' feet; and his redeeming death was an act of humility. A true Christian would conform to his example.[75]

By definition, Jesus' humble example included nonparticipation in war. In a tract titled *Christianity and War*, written around the time of the Civil War, Brenneman pertinently wrote that one could never take up "the weapons of death" and at the same time consider oneself a Christian.[76]

Although its coming was not without turbulence, revivalism became accepted in the Mennonite Church of John M. Brenneman. He even preached a few revivals. Revivalism was accepted when it became clear that it could be conformed to fit in the existing congregational structure. It became the form by which each year succeeding generations of young people came to faith in the congregation.

Brenneman harnessed revivalism to serve his concern for a saved lifestyle. A revivalist conversion was not a substitute for the saved life, as Stauffer and Beiler might have feared, but marked the beginning of a life characterized by humility, nonresistance, and more. Thus Brenneman exhibited a cautious acceptance of revivalism, using it to buttress his inherited stress on a saved life produced by an internal transformation.

John Holdeman[77]

In 1859, John Holdeman abandoned the Mennonite Church represented by Brenneman to found his own traditionalist-oriented group, the "Church of God in Christ, Mennonite." Holdeman was more verbose, mechanical, and heavy-handed than the other figures in this study in stating what he believed. Yet his book *Old Ground and Foundation*, the earliest of his larger writings, shares with them the tendency to subsume the discussion of atonement under broader concerns about a genuine inner change and a focus on the saved life. Following the evolution of his thought from *Old Ground* through the *History of the Church* to his later *Mirror of Truth* shows the impact of the American environment on both his piety and theology.

Old Ground describes the foundation of faith that he believed the Mennonites of his era had abandoned. The book begins with major sections on the complex of ideas related to conversion, regeneration, and beginning the Christian life, then moved to discussion of the traditional Mennonite form of the saved life as expressed in a pure church. Holdeman's outline does not differ significantly from that of the other traditional nineteenth-century Amish and Mennonites. His disagreement concerned the intensity and rigidity of his defense of the traditional practices, rather than the practices themselves.

Theologically noteworthy is the virtual absence in *Old Ground* of an explicit articulation of a doctrine of atonement. While the book obviously assumes atonement,[78] the articulation of it is nowhere near as full as in sections of the later *History of the Church* and *Mirror of Truth*.

In *History of the Church*, some thirteen years after *Old Ground*, Holdeman's outline still reflects the received Mennonite and Amish focus on salvation history. Now, however, he makes the penal and substitutionary atonement explicit as God's answer to the fall.[79] After sufficient time under the law to demonstrate unrelenting opposition to sin, God sent Jesus to die as a sacrifice.

In *Mirror*, eighteen years after Holdeman's first book, the outline itself undergoes something of a change.[80] Rather than beginning with salvation history, the book's long initial chapter carries a much more Protestant-sounding, doctrinal title; namely, "On Belief in the Triune God—of Father, Son and Holy Spirit—and what they teach us."[81]

In this chapter, Holdeman discussed attributes of God: unchangeableness, omnipotence, goodness, and wisdom. He used some christological language reminiscent of the Nicene formula,[82] introduced other dimensions of the classical debates not always found in abstract form in historic Anabaptist and Mennonite writings (namely such concerns as pre-existence, defining the deity and the humanity of Christ), and established that the attributes of God also apply to the Son and the Holy Spirit.[83] When Holdeman shows that such divine attributes as pre-existence, compassion, righteousness, omnipotence, goodness, and wisdom apply to Jesus, these emerge from the plan of salvation described in terms of substitutionary atonement.[84]

After dealing with these questions of theology and Christology, Holdeman picks up the traditional Mennonite outline of issues of faith and practice and addresses them in the remainder of the book.

It is likely that Holdeman's restructuring of the outline of his theology reflects his adoption of a bit of the vocabulary and outlook of traditional Protestantism.[85] Additional evidence of such borrowing might be Holdeman's use of language reflective of the presuppositions of Common Sense philosophy.[86] At the same time, Holdeman's concerns in this chapter have some parallels with Menno Simons' tract "Confession of the Triune God."[87] Holdeman admired Menno greatly, and the issues mentioned could reflect his reading of Menno.[88]

As just noted, Holdeman dealt with the divine origin of Jesus on the basis of substitutionary atonement. In another context, the divine origin of Jesus served to confirm the authority of his teaching, and Holdeman's most weighty argument is to imbue a churchly practice with the authority of Christ. Acceptance of nonresistance to evil and a total rejection of any hint of involvement with government and secular authorities provide prime examples of appeal to the authority of Christ.[89]

Holdeman also integrated nonresistance into his understanding of atonement. Under the law and the old covenant, Israel was required to use capital punishment against serious offenses or "presumptuous sinners."[90] Since Israel was overcome by the Romans and therefore no longer had kingly power,[91] and because Jesus fulfilled the law in a once-for-all fashion, there is no longer any need for God's people to exercise capital punishment or secular authority. This logical and theological assertion of nonresistance dovetails with Holdeman's defense of the same points on the basis of the authority of Christ.[92] Thus for Holdeman, nonresistance was both a doctrine to be believed and an integrative principle which exerted influence on other aspects of his theology.

In the area of revivalism, Holdeman's writing also contains an element not present in the writings of any of the subjects examined thus far. Unlike them, Holdeman embraced a conversion experience much influenced by revivalism, if a revivalism short of expressions of exuberance. While the others noted the necessity of a conversion or an inner transformation or regeneration, Holdeman described his visions and his own crisis conversion in some detail.[93] The church he founded still maintains a stress on an experiential and emotional, revivalistic conversion and an intense personal piety.[94]

Holdeman accepted revivalism's crisis conversion as a mode and fused it with traditional Mennonite emphases. While other traditionalist-minded Mennonite reformers had opposed revivalism as a challenge to their way of life, Holdeman embraced it as the foundation of the traditional lifestyle. Though accepting revivalism was an innovation, he used it for a conservative purpose. Despite the observable changes in Holdeman's thought, he remained shaped by inherited Mennonite emphases, an orientation that cannot be described by categorizing his atonement theology. In fact, it would appear that his attention to atonement doctrine was evidence of departure from traditional Mennonite theologizing, rather than a sign of adherence to it.

Heinrich Egly[95]

Virtually all the articles by Heinrich Egly, a German Amish immigrant who founded the Defenseless Mennonite Church, emphasized a crisis conversion as the basis of salvation.[96] This divine action in the heart is the context in which Egly's language of atonement occurs.

While Egly nowhere spelled out a theory of atonement, he referred to Christ as Redeemer and to the need for repentance, redemption, expiation, payment for sin, and forgiveness through Jesus' blood. Egly liked to find types in the Old Testament, and he sometimes used atonement terminology in conjunction with such images as the Passover lamb.[97] The blood of the Passover lamb that saved the obedient Israelites is a type of Jesus, the true Passover lamb, whose blood redeems those who believe. While Egly does not spell out specifically the link between the Passover type and the satisfaction terminology of atonement, his principal point was that those who believe and accept this sacrifice of Christ would experience a pouring out of the Holy Spirit and a conversion, or rebirth. The new believer would receive a new heart worked in by the Spirit of Christ, or the Holy Spirit.

Conversion, Egly indicated, occurred in revivalist fashion. He believed that a convert would experience the new birth vividly, with immediate assurance of salvation and visible fruits of the Spirit.[98] A visitor to Egly's home congregation in Geneva, Indiana, noted that a conversion experience was a requirement for baptism and membership.[99]

Egly considered ministers such as C. H. Wedel or Johannes Moser to be unsaved because they believed that conversion could happen gradually as a result of nurture. In the "Autobiography," Egly said that Moser's problem was that he "had no assurance of his salvation in his heart" and called him an "instrument through which [Satan] worked against us."[100]

As is clear from earlier sections of this chapter, other Mennonite and Amish ministers considered conversion important and necessary. Egly differed from them not in emphasizing conversion but in requiring a specifically revivalist-style, crisis conversion, much as Holdeman did.[101] Most of Egly's articles reflect a fusion of this revivalist conversion with traditional Mennonite and Amish issues. There are, for example, a number of explanations to the effect that keeping the commands of Jesus depends on conversion, or the new heart created by the Holy Ghost or the Spirit of Christ.

The list of Jesus' commands begins with the requirement that sinners repent as the basis of conversion. The believer then is to receive baptism and join the people of God; participate in the ordinances of the Lord's Supper and of footwashing; and show obedience through such things as nonswearing of oaths, not holding worldly offices, nonresistance to evil, and love and prayer for enemies.[102] In fact, Egly singled out nonresistance and love as the key signs of conversion and a new heart. Since the inclinations of the natural, unconverted person are love of self, hatred of enemies, and vengeance-seeking, it is impossible to follow Jesus' command to love the enemy unless one has a new heart wrought by the Holy Spirit, or the Spirit of Christ.

> The commands of Jesus are, Matt. 5:44, "Love your enemies, bless those who curse you," . . . Dear reader, could you do that before you were truly converted? And if you cannot do it, then it is as clear as sunshine that your heart has not been recreated and renewed by God to that which his beloved Son, Jesus Christ requires of you.[103]

Love of enemies and praying for their good constitute proof of rebirth. Once again, while perhaps a bit different in tone, Egly's linking of conversion and nonresistance does not differ significantly from the views of other subjects of this essay—including Johannes Moser, whom Egly rejected as unconverted. The difference is Egly's requirement of a specific kind of conversion experience.

Thus far most of the description of Egly's theology has come from his published articles. Analysis of his unpublished "Autobiography" modifies the picture and shows changes in his outlook. In the "Autobiography," written as an elderly churchman reminiscing on his life, Egly refers to many of his preaching trips. There is an obvious emphasis on conversion; and the sequence of confession of sin, repentance, conversion, and reception of a new heart is quite clear. Rather surprisingly, however, the manuscript includes no reference to nonresistance and love of enemies as evidence of conversion. Egly seems to have evolved quite far in the direction his church would go: namely, the validation of conversion by the felt experience of rebirth,[104] rather than by a humble, nonresistant daily life as described variously by Stauffer, Beiler, Wedel, Moser, and Brenneman.[105]

The Heinrich Egly of the "Autobiography" is revivalist more than Amish and Mennonite in his theology. This change was one of the first steps in the direction of what George Marsden called "a classic case of a transformation from an Anabaptist to a fundamentalist Protestantism."[106] This description of the way that nonresistance shaped Egly's early writing, followed by observation of changes that accompanied his complete espousal of a revivalist orientation, shows once again that merely identifying Mennonite theologizing in terms of doctrines shared with Protestantism does not depict the genus of Amish and Mennonite theology.

CONCLUSION

It is obvious that these nineteenth-century writers all espoused some form of the satisfaction or substitutionary theory of atonement. If use of satisfaction or substitutionary atonement were all that we knew about the outlook of these eight Mennonite and Amish leaders, it would be legitimate to define them primarily as evangelicals and to emphasize that Mennonite theology is evangelical theology, as Harold Bender and others have suggested. And if that were all that we knew about their theology, the discussion might end there.

But we know more. The observations in this chapter show the nineteenth-century affinity for a kind of orthodoxy, but demonstrate that the driving force of theology for these writers clearly lay elsewhere. The orientation of their theology came, not from the element which they had in common with versions of U.S. Protestantism, but from the presuppositions which they inherited from their Anabaptist tradition. One overarching presupposition shared by all was the belief that commitment to Christ, that is being Christian, would inevitably and of necessity manifest itself in the way an individual lived, and that this lived expression of Christian faith was modeled on the life and teaching of Jesus. As a specific application of following Jesus' example and teaching, all agreed that nonresistance, love of enemies, and refusal of military service constituted a clear and intrinsic dimension of the saved life. In this context, it should be apparent that using an atonement doctrine shared with wider Protestantism as the basis for identifying Mennonite theology with Protestantism has the effect of moving to the periphery the central assumptions of all eight characters in this chapter.

An emphasis on revivalist or experiential conversion can either blur or sharpen the distinction between Mennonite and Protestant assumptions. When experiential conversion replaces nonviolence as evidence of saving faith, as appeared to happen with Heinrich Egly, the potential exists to allow nonviolence to slide away all together. Little difference then remains between Mennonite and Protestant theology. On the other hand, as was the case for John Brenneman and John Holdeman, revivalist or experiential conversion could be called on to reinforce such Mennonite emphases as nonviolence. In this case, the difference between Mennonite and Protestant theology is maintained or emphasized. In either of these cases, the difference was not a product of experiential religious faith itself but of the prior assumption about the location of nonviolence in the economy of atonement and salvation.

For the most part, this nineteenth-century theology was not rationalized theology, or theology developed systematically with the classic theological issues in mind. Only C. H. Wedel had formal theological education; the others simply wrote down their inherited beliefs.

In what way is this nineteenth-century theology a model or a norm for peace church theology at the beginning of the twenty-first century? Does the use of atonement images from wider Protestant theology by these nineteenth-century writers oblige us to do likewise? Is charting a different path, as earlier chapters of this book argued, a departure from or even a betrayal of these writers and the church they represented? Is their history our destiny? Chapter 5 provides responses to such questions, following analysis in chapter 4 of some sixteenth-century Anabaptist case studies.

FOUR

CHAPTER 4

MENNONITE THEOLOGY
IN FACE OF SIXTEENTH-CENTURY
ANABAPTIST THEOLOGY

INTRODUCTION

This book has worked backward through history. Chapters 1 and 2 dealt with twentieth-century discussions. Chapter 3 moved into the nineteenth century. Each chapter used analyses of a survey of writers to show both the desirability and feasibility of constructing a theology shaped by Anabaptist, peace church assumptions, rather than building on a core of doctrine inherited from classic Protestantism. This chapter now carries the argument back to the sixteenth century and the Anabaptist movement, in which today's Mennonites and a significant portion of the contemporary peace church locate their origin.

These glimpses from earlier epochs provide perspective on contemporary Mennonite theologizing. Without making idols of past formulations, it is important to understand how history impacts theology and the significance that different contexts make.

APPEALS TO THE SIXTEENTH CENTURY

There is a venerable tradition of pointing to sixteenth-century Anabaptism's acceptance of the classic creeds of Christendom. As was noted in chapter 3, in positioning Anabaptists in relation to the magisterial Reformers in his Anabaptist Vision, Harold S. Bender called Anabaptism "consistent evangelical Protestantism."[1] In another article, Bender wrote that what Anabaptists shared with Protestantism included agreement on such central doctrines of the Reformation as "the sole authority of the Scriptures, grace, and justification by faith, or in the classic Christian loci of doctrine."[2]

What Bender meant by the "classic Christian loci" had been spelled out earlier in an address to the 1936 Mennonite World Conference in Amsterdam. Bender told the delegates there that all U.S. Mennonites "were thoroughly orthodox in the great fundamental doctrines of the Christian faith such as the unity of the Godhead, the true deity of Christ, the atonement of the shedding of blood, the plenary inspiration and divine authority of the Holy Scriptures as the Word of God."[3]

Bender was certainly not alone in these assertions. John Horsch, well known for his stringent opposition to Protestant liberalism, strongly asserted the absolute orthodoxy of sixteenth-century Anabaptists; his description of their beliefs, presented through selected quotations, emphasized agreement with the classic doctrines.[4] Those ideas were echoed, if less stridently, in words of John C. Wenger[5] and Cornelius Krahn.[6]

These earlier observations have counterparts among recent scholars of a much different historical bent. Walter Klaassen wrote, "Earlier interpreters of Anabaptism saw clearly what we today often miss, and that is that the sixteenth-century Anabaptists, on the whole, accepted the ancient Christian symbols which identified orthodox Christian belief." Klaassen went on to stress Anabaptists' frequent use of the Apostles' Creed and their trinitarian orientation, an "important tenet of Anabaptism that is relevant for today." He continued, "We desperately need links to the tradition of the church which transcends the Mennonite churches," and must recognize that "our tradition was not a brand new departure but very much a part of the rest of Christianity, however much that Christianity was criticized and rejected by the sixteenth-century Anabaptists." For Klaassen, "the transcendent anchorage of a trinitarian theology is absolutely essential today" as the barrier against getting "lost in the relativities of history and our culture."[7]

C. Arnold Snyder's recent historical synthesis has similarly stressed trinitarian orientation and the roots of Anabaptist theology in the classic creeds. "Acceptance of the historical Christian *doxa* or teachings, as summarized in the ecumenical Creeds and symbols, was common to all Anabaptist movements," he writes. "The Anabaptists were orthodox in their understanding of the central elements of the faith" with the "major" exception of "Melchiorite Christology" and the "minor" exception of "anti-trinitarianism in Silesia and by some individuals in the Netherlands."[8]

In a parallel article, Snyder has observed that on the

> most basic of Christian beliefs (God, Christ, Holy Spirit, church) we find that the overwhelming majority of Anabaptists in Western Europe subscribed to the doctrines articulated in [the orthodox and ecumenical creeds of Christendom], with the significant exception of Melchiorite Christology. While the Anabaptists may not have incorporated the Creed in a liturgical way in their services, the record is clear that the principles of Christian orthodoxy formed the common background of their faith.[9]

Of course Horsch, Bender, Wenger, Krahn, Klaassen, and Snyder are correct in their observations that sixteenth-century Anabaptists generally affirmed the classic creeds and asserted their orthodoxy on classic theological issues. Obviously such data must be considered when asking what the historical record says or implies about the quest for a theology for the peace church in the era of postmodernity. Much as Bender and others did earlier, Klaassen and Snyder both posit these sixteenth-century claims as precedents that the modern Anabaptist church ought to follow.

Such appeals can appear to buttress the case that theology for the contemporary peace church should identify with and build on the classic theology of Western Christendom, which is shared by both Catholicism and magisterial, or established church, Protestantism. Without this theology, Klaassen argues, we will "get lost in the relativities of history and our culture."[10] In support of the argument, one might add that discovering this common Christian core appears to take on even more urgency at a time when Christians are a minority in the world, and, in the foreseeable future, will be a minority in North America. Seeking to develop and emphasize a specific theology for the peace church, it may seem, is not only historically invalid but also harmful to the cause of the Christian faith in the modern world.

The remainder of this chapter provides a rejoinder to such a claim. The section "Sixteenth-Century Atonement and Christology" uses several historical vignettes that raise questions about defining Anabaptist beliefs in terms of a core shared with Christendom. As these examples show, interpreting sixteenth-century Anabaptist theology does not consist merely of reading the sources accurately but involves the presuppositions that one brings to the sources. Following this historical discussion, "Innovation and Erasmian Hypothesis" puts my argument in conversation with Abraham Friesen's recent hypothesis about the Erasmian origins of sixteenth-century Anabaptism. "On Sixteenth-Century Anabaptism as 'Orthodox'" then deals with some philosophical and theological problems concerning the supposed Anabaptist core and the precedent it establishes for the modern church.

In conclusion, "Sixteenth-Century Anabaptism and the Modern Search for a Theology for Mennonites" offers an explanation why Anabaptists did not actually develop to any great extent theological potential evident in their beginnings. This explanation invites the contemporary church to pursue that task.

SIXTEENTH-CENTURY ATONEMENT AND CHRISTOLOGY

As was stated in chapter 1, I suggest that understandings of ecclesiology are related to or can have an impact on formulations of classic issues such as Christology or atonement. In other words, our picture of sixteenth-century Anabaptist theology can change markedly if we approach the subject with two assumptions. The first is that the questions debated with magisterial Reformers were considered significant and not peripheral by Anabaptists. The second assumption is that the differences which threatened the magisterial Reformers enough that they perceived a need to kill Anabaptists may have produced differences in understandings at the very heart of the gospel and theological enterprise that expressed it.

Most scholars have recognized that sixteenth-century Anabaptists did develop a new understanding of ecclesiology, as well as such emphases as discipleship and the idea of lived faith. It is reasonable to ask whether these Anabaptist perspectives might be reflected in any way in other areas, such as in understandings of the classic doctrines discussed by all Christian traditions. As the following indicates, whether one finds novelty or assertions of classic orthodoxy in sixteenth-century Anabaptist theology depends as much on presuppositions and the questions asked as it does on accurately reading the historical sources.

The examples to follow deal with a sampling of sixteenth-century writers on two themes, namely, atonement and Christology. This discussion draws on analyses originally published in relation to questions posed differently than the present one. The fact that the following makes new use of earlier results, and therefore was not developed specifically for the thesis argued in this chapter, in itself supports the thesis that defining sixteenth-century Anabaptists as orthodox in theology is not merely a matter of reading the historical record.

Bucer, Sattler, and Denck on Atonement

A comment by Martin Bucer about atonement doctrines of Michael Sattler and Hans Denck stimulated exploration of atonement images in the writing of these three men.[11] In a summary statement after the execution of Sattler, Bucer wrote that while Sattler had erred on some issues, "concerning the redemption of Christ Jesus, on which everything rests, we have not found such errors in Michael Sattler as in Denck."[12] My original analysis of the writings of the three men had a twofold focus: to determine what led Bucer to declare one heretical and the other orthodox on the work of Christ; and to see if Anabaptist assumptions in any way linked the atonement thought of Sattler and Denck and gave it a distinct orientation over against Bucer.

A reading of the sources revealed that all three individuals can be classified in terms of classic images of atonement. Both Bucer and Sattler, to the extent that we can determine, reflect an orientation historically identified with Anselm. In contrast, Denck's atonement concept fits generally in the moral influence image associated historically with Abelard

One of the concerns of Bucer, who reflected the new Reformation theology including its belief in predestination, was to show that salvation of sinful humankind depended on Christ's work entirely apart from any human contribution or participation. That concern builds on Anselmian, substitutionary atonement rather than on the moral influence theory, whose primary emphasis focuses on the sinner's response to the death of Christ. If Bucer assumed that only an Anselmian atonement image was acceptable, and that the sinner's response to Christ's death in the moral influence theory was a matter of human effort, that would explain the different evaluations Bucer gave on Sattler and Denck.

Although they differed in their understandings of atonement, all three leaders believed that faith would express itself in life. Working out of a satisfaction understanding of atonement, both Bucer and Sattler assumed that as a first step of faith, the sinner appropriated the effects of the death of Christ, which happened apart from the individual sinner. As a second step, the reception of the Holy Spirit which accompanied that step of faith would transform the sinner, and the result would be a changed life.

Denck took a different avenue into faith that expressed itself in life. He rejected the Reformation doctrine of predestination, which appeared to define salvation apart from human responsibility. Denck wanted the responsibility of the individual sinner to be engaged in salvation. For him, appropriation of the Word in every human heart was the means to affirm both the divine origin of salvation and human responsibility in a salvation that was expressed in the way one lived. Denck contrasted that lived faith with the Reformation concept of salvation, which seemed to him to define salvation apart from any response of the sinner.

Despite this disagreement, it is clear that Bucer, Sattler, and Denck all had a concept of lived faith, or faith which expressed itself in a transformed life. From another perspective, however, the two Anabaptists are linked together against Bucer. Although Sattler and Denck had quite different underlying presuppositions as well as differing atonement images, each assumed that Jesus was the norm in a way that distinguished them from Bucer.

Bucer said that the response to the work of Christ would be love and service in imitation of Christ's self-giving love. However, that love and service was expressed through "office." Since one such office was civil authority, a part of the expression of love and service as understood by Bucer was to exercise the sword of government. Thus killing at the behest of civil authority was an act of love.

I suspect that expressing love through office is linked to predestination, which Bucer and the magisterial Reformers accepted. Predestination accepts the status quo as God-ordained, and thus accepts the suggestion that vocation and office are normal contexts for loving, Christian service. In contrast, when Sattler and Denck made Christ the norm of the Christian life, they appealed to the specific example of the earthly Jesus, which appears to affirm a concept of free will. As a result, Jesus' rejection of the sword was normative for the Christian life and even applied to the sword of the magistrate. For Sattler and Denck, killing could not be a loving act, even when supposedly legitimated by civil authorities.

Although in different ways, both Sattler and Denck believed that Bucer's use of "office" was a rationalization for not following the example of Jesus. Sattler's assumption that the earthly Jesus was normative—and Sattler's rejection of predestination, if the previous premise is correct—thus gave his expression of the implications of satisfaction atonement a different slant than Bucer's, though this does not negate their agreement on the atonement image itself. Yet it is noteworthy that their assumption about the earthly Jesus linked Sattler and Denck against Bucer.

This analysis of atonement images in Bucer, Sattler, and Denck does not in itself show whether Anabaptists shared a core theological identity with Protestant Reformers and with Catholicism. That question is not solved by merely reading the sources. Similar conclusions result from an exploration of atonement images in the theology of Balthasar Hubmaier and Hans Hut.

Hubmaier and Hut on Atonement

Hubmaier and Hut engaged in significant conflict in Hubmaier's Nicholsburg.[13] The stimulus for the study of atonement in the thought of these two Anabaptists was the fifth of the Nicolsburg Articles, which Hubmaier probably formulated. In Article 5 Hubmaier accused Hut of denying the satisfaction of Christ. The specific focus of my earlier research was to determine the veracity of that claim by comparing and analyzing the images of atonement found in the writings of Hubmaier and Hut.

Careful reading of Hubmaier's corpus reveals that Hubmaier assumed a satisfaction image of atonement. Once the atoning death of Christ had taken care of the penalty of sin, Word and Spirit could then work rebirth and produce a transformed life in believers. In Hubmaier's thought, the emphasis falls on this latter element: namely, the importance of lived faith and a transformed life worked by the Spirit of God.

Hut's understanding of the work of Christ posed a marked contrast to Hubmaier's. While Hut's concept of the work of Christ does not fit in the confines of the moral influence theory, he did develop the work of Christ in such a way as to pose a direct challenge to the satisfaction theory of atonement. Whereas in Hubmaier's satisfaction theory, Christ suffers vicariously, Hut specifically rejected the idea of a vicarious or substitutionary suffering by Christ. Instead of seeing a Christ who suffered so that sinners need not, Hut used what he called the "gospel of all creatures" to show that the members of Christ participate in his suffering and suffer with him.

From observation of the natural order, Hut said, one learns that all things must suffer to attain the intended end. Thus, animals suffer at the hands of people to become food, trees suffer under the tools of woodsmen and builders to become houses, ground is worked by peasants before it can receive seeds, and so on. These examples teach that "the whole Christ suffers in all members. It is not as these scholarly Christians preach. . . . They say that as the Head, Christ carried out and fulfilled everything. But what then of the members and the whole body in which the suffering of Christ must be fulfilled."[14]

Hut thus understood lived faith as participation in the suffering of Christ, and he opposed the Reformation understanding of justification by faith. For Hut, justification by faith, and the vicarious suffering of Christ as held by Hubmaier, seem to mean that salvation happens apart from anything that the sinner did. Hut's concern was to understand the work of Christ in such a way that the sinner participated in Christ's suffering and was saved through that participation.

For Hubmaier, Jesus died in the place of all people, satisfying on their behalf a penalty owed to God. The inherently necessary element in Hubmaier's understanding is that Jesus does something—namely, performs satisfaction, which sinful human beings cannot perform for themselves. Salvation results precisely because Jesus did something that sinful humankind was incapable of accomplishing.

At the level of atonement images, the views of Hubmaier and Hut are mutually exclusive. Each depends on an appropriation of the work of Christ that the other rejects. For Hubmaier, salvation can happen because Christ accomplished something that sinners cannot. For Hut, sinners attain salvation through Jesus only when they participate in suffering along with Jesus.

At another level, however, there is something of a commonality. Both Hubmaier and Hut believe that salvation of sinners will manifest itself in the transformed life of the believer. To the extent that emphasis on a transformed life is an Anabaptist assumption, one could argue that in the atonement concepts of Hubmaier and Hut one sees the embryonic beginning of a reformulation of classic atonement images.

Hut's assumption of a lived faith is evident in his treatment of the work of Christ. To him, this meant suffering with Christ and also meant an interim nonresistance that would hold until Christ returned to give a different word. Hubmaier's newfound understanding of ecclesiology and baptism did not, however, result in a revision of the satisfaction image of atonement, just as it did not for Sattler. In fact, on this instance, Hubmaier's position would parallel Bucer's, since both of them advocated the use of the sword.

It is also true that both Denck and Hut were strongly influenced by the tradition of medieval mysticism. Quite possibly the mystical impulse of sharing in the suffering of Christ was at least as responsible as any newfound Anabaptist faith in shaping their approach to atonement.[15] These observations point to the conclusion that, at best, one can find only the mere beginning of a reformulation of atonement theology on the basis of Anabaptist understandings of church and discipleship.

From atonement, we turn now to a look at christological impulses in three Anabaptist writers and the impact of their ecclesiology and discipleship on classic theological categories.[16] As was previously noted, sixteenth-century Anabaptists inherited the definitions of Nicaea and Chalcedon, definitions that they shared with the wider Protestant Reformation as well as with Catholicism. At the same time, it is reasonable to ask whether the new ecclesiology, along with the idea of discipleship or the normativeness of Jesus' life, might be reflected in the way Anabaptists discussed Christology.

Denck on Christology

The Christology of Hans Denck reflected the tradition of medieval mysticism. His primary focus was on Christ the Word, who dwells in every human heart.[17]

Unlike Anabaptists, the Protestant Reformers of the sixteenth century accepted predestination as the necessary foundation for the doctrine of justification by faith. Denck appealed to the indwelling

Christ in his refutation of Martin Luther's teaching about predestination. With the Word, Christ, in every heart, Denck reasoned, no one could claim not to have heard the call of God. At the same time, the initiative in the call came from God, and the power to respond to the call came from the Christ within.

With this formula, Denck wanted to say that each individual chooses whether or not to come to God, but that the initiative and the power to do so remain nonetheless with God. Denck also wanted to say that the one who followed the Word within would lead a changed, righteous life; that is, a life in conformity to that Word.

Further, Denck said, a norm exists against which to measure that new, righteous life. That norm is Jesus of Nazareth. Since Jesus embodied the Word in a way that no one else ever could or did, he stands as the preeminent example of life lived under the aegis of the Word that indwells every heart. Rejection of the use of the sword is one of the most visible ways that the righteous life manifests itself.

In this outlook, Denck referred to Father, Son, and Holy Spirit. One can observe that he had a formal allegiance to and understanding of the triune God. His is not a traditional formulation of trinitarian thought, however. In fact, Denck's theological emphases were elsewhere. His interest was in refuting predestination in a way that left the salvific initiative with God yet preserved the free will of the believer. To characterize Denck's theology only in terms of traditional trinitarian thought, whether as orthodox or unorthodox, is to render secondary the challenge to Reformation theology that came from his theological outlook.

Marpeck on Christology

In contrast to Denck's stress on the Christ within, Pilgram Marpeck focused on a Jesus external to the believer. For Marpeck, it was this Jesus who was the means to knowing God the Father and the means to an inward experience of God.

At this level, Marpeck shared the beginning point of an external Jesus with Martin Luther rather than with mystical Hans Denck. In contrast to Luther, however, Marpeck assumed the normative nature of the earthly Jesus. Jesus was not only the means to knowing God the Father; he was also the norm by which believing persons oriented their conduct, including on such issues as the ceremonies of the church and the use of the sword.[18]

Thus, as with Denck, we misunderstand Marpeck's orientation if we read him only in terms of inherited traditional theology. On such points he would appear orthodox and Protestant. Yet Marpeck had a different orientation, one that does not fit precisely in orthodox Protestantism.

The Christology of Menno

Menno Simons provides yet a third example of why it is misleading to categorize Anabaptists solely on the basis of the traditional terminology. On the one hand, as has been frequently pointed out, Menno used a great deal of the traditional vocabulary. He had a trinitarian outlook, and he took pains to affirm the humanity and deity of Jesus.[19] On the other hand, Menno's Christology was certainly nonstandard, and perhaps even heretical, when judged by the definition of Chalcedon.

Menno followed the Melchiorite Anabaptist movement's "celestial flesh" Christology . Briefly stated, Menno believed that Jesus' flesh was human flesh, but it was a human flesh that Christ had brought with him from heaven. Thus the heavenly Word became flesh *in* Mary but not *of* Mary; Mary nourished Jesus' flesh, but the flesh came not from Mary but from heaven. Menno used the analogy of a field that receives seed from a sower. While the field nourishes and grows the crop, the seeds come from outside and are not of the nature of the field.

If one applies the definition of Chalcedon in strict fashion, Menno's view is unacceptable. Even though it would bleed, flesh that came from heaven is simply not genuine *human* flesh.

Menno's Christology reflected one kind of medieval misunderstanding about human reproduction; namely, that at conception, the male implanted a complete human being into the womb of the female, where it grew until ready for birth. With that model in mind, Menno believed that Jesus must have begun from the Word that entered Mary and became flesh.

Menno's intention was to define Christology in such a way as to ensure the sinlessness of Jesus while also preserving the unity of Jesus' person.[20] For Menno, emphasis on the flesh of Jesus affirmed his humanity, while the heavenly origin of the Word both affirmed Jesus' deity and preserved the unity of Jesus' person. Menno wanted to defend the sinlessness of Jesus because he believed that the church founded by Jesus was a pure church and an extension of Christ's work on earth. This church would then be separate or distinct from the social order, rather than the church of Christendom that supports the social order. Menno also described the process of conversion in the life of the sinner so that he or she is transformed in an incomplete way into the flesh of Christ: a transformation that will find its fulfillment at the return of Jesus.

Thus, while he got there by a quite different route than did Denck and Marpeck, Menno too is oriented by what can be called discipleship—the idea that the earthly life of Jesus constitutes an example and a norm for the life of Christian believers, and that the norm poses a radical witness to the social order.

In light of these brief observations how does one categorize the views of Sattler, Denck, Hubmaier, Hut, Marpeck, and Menno on atonement or Christology? Sattler and Hubmaier appear to line up with some version of the predominant satisfaction atonement image associated with Anselm, while Denck and Hut do not. Does this divide enable us to say that on the important core question of the work of Christ, Anabaptists shared the core idea with majority Christendom? Of course one could argue that persons in all Christian traditions, including all Anabaptists, believed that salvation depends on the death of Christ, but such a general category that includes everyone does not tell us much.

What about the christological and trinitarian comments of Denck, Marpeck, and Menno? Do the data show merely that these writers can be ranged variously along a spectrum from insignificant to rather suspicious versions of Protestant and Catholic orthodoxy? Do the observations about Sattler, Denck, Hubmaier, Hut, Marpeck, and Menno contribute to the conclusion that, with a couple of exceptions, all Anabaptists accepted a core of classic doctrines shared in agreement with Catholicism and magisterial Protestantism? Or do these observations indicate that Anabaptists had begun a process of rethinking the classic theology inherited from Christendom?

I suggest that such questions are not answered merely by reading the sixteenth-century sources. What the sources tell us depends on the questions we are willing to pose and the frame of reference in which we are willing to examine the data.

Standard Theology, Innovation, or Departure?

If sixteenth-century Anabaptists were entirely orthodox; if their predominant theological identity comes from Catholic and Protestant creedal theology, then later departures from orthodoxy are automatically suspect and Anabaptists cannot be innovators in theology. Reading Anabaptists with the belief that they were orthodox and did not develop new or different perspectives clearly has an impact on what one is prepared to find and to value in their thought.

I suggest that we miss the theological significance of these Anabaptists if we interpret them only in terms of their use of theological categories inherited from Christendom. At that level, Anabaptists become rather insignificant characters whose few innovations are suspicious. Positing this agreement with Christendom as the core of Anabaptist theology discounts the significance of any departures from the norm by Anabaptist theologizing. Of necessity, any uniquely Anabaptist emphases are pushed to the periphery or to the second level of importance. The particular identity of Anabaptism becomes marginal with reference to the norm of Christendom theology.

This picture changes markedly if we do not rank Anabaptists on the basis of a Christendom grid, or if agreement with Christendom is not the most important interpretive criterion. Anabaptists developed a new ecclesiology, which emerged out of a renewed emphasis on Jesus' life and teaching as normative (identified by the shorthand term *discipleship*) and from their sense that authentic faith is expressed by the life of the believing person. If one begins with these ecclesiological assumptions, then Anabaptist expressions of atonement and Christology can take on a different hue. Rather than seeing these formulations as suspicious or unsophisticated versions of orthodoxy, it is possible to interpret them as initial inclinations—the implications of which were not fully recognized—to amend the received, classic theological tradition on the basis of new learning. We neglect that possibility if our interpretation focuses only on the extent to which Anabaptists can be said to agree with theology of the church they rejected.

Of course we can read in the sixteenth-century sources that Anabaptists agreed with Catholicism and majority Protestantism on classic creedal theology. That observation, however, does not in itself tell us what to do. To assert that creedal theology is the foundation of

Anabaptist thought, that Anabaptist theology is virtually the same as Catholic and Protestant thought (with the attendant implication that disagreements are about relative degrees of sameness), and that agreement with the creeds is foundational and precedent-setting for the modern church requires an assumption about Catholic and Protestant creedal theology—namely that it is universal, catholic, or general. These terms have all been used to attempt to put this creedal theology in an unassailable position above and removed from the vagaries and the particularity of history.

If one attributes universality to the established church theology, then Anabaptism's theological legitimacy—its orthodoxy—depends on plugging into or building on that presumed universal theology. On the other hand, if the particularity of the established church theology is acknowledged, then that theology must make a case for itself and other expressions may legitimately assert their validity over against or alongside it. In that case, sixteenth-century Anabaptism as the embryonic start of a new theological direction becomes important, and the validity, the orthodoxy, of Anabaptist theology may very well depend on its departure from the received tradition.

If classic creedal theology is posited as the norm for Anabaptist theological legitimacy, there is a built-in necessity to discount novelty in Anabaptist theologizing, so as to preserve Anabaptism's legitimacy. If classic creedal theology is not given normative status, then departure from Christendom's norm may very well emerge as the most truthful orienting principle of Anabaptist theology. Indeed, Anabaptists' departures from dominant orthodoxy were important enough to die for.[21]

One can characterize Anabaptism's potential theological departure from orthodoxy as innovation or charting a new theological direction. However, the use of such terms should not be seen in a modernizing sense. Anabaptism was new only with respect to Christendom's orthodoxy. As the following section emphasizes, Anabaptists actually saw themselves as continuing a movement that had begun with Jesus and the early church. In their writings they grounded themselves in Scripture and identified with dissenters throughout history who had challenged the alliance of empire and church. While their departure from orthodoxy had a sense of being new, this newness was born of a desire to better relate the story of Jesus.

INNOVATION AND THE ERASMIAN HYPOTHESIS

Such an understanding of sixteenth-century Anabaptists finds support in Abraham Friesen's recent argument that the intellectual origins of Anabaptism are found in the writings of Erasmus.[22]

Friesen contrasted Catholic and Renaissance humanist interpretations of church history. In the epoch of the Reformation, Friesen said, Catholicism was the church of the present. It emphasized that ecclesiastical structure, theology, and liturgical practice had been refined over the centuries. Under the guidance of the Holy Spirit, the church had made explicit and brought to fruition what had previously been implicit in the Bible and in the primitive church. Consequently, the latest teachers were living in the age of greatest perfection, and their views were thus deemed the best or most authoritative.

Humanists such as Erasmus reversed that judgment. They argued that the primitive church was the purest and the apostles' interpretation of Christ's teaching the most reliable source. Consequently, they believed that the Bible was the best source book to Christianity and that the church had declined since the apostolic period.[23]

Until Erasmus, Matt. 28:19 was used by the church to show that valid baptism had to be in the name of the Trinity. This interpretation emerged from the Arian controversy in the fourth century. Working with the assumption that the apostles were the best interpreters of Jesus' commands, Erasmus developed an interpretation of this passage, the so-called great commission, that was an unprecedented departure from medieval theology. Thinking historically, Erasmus argued that by studying the example and teaching of the apostles as told in the book of Acts one could determine how and whether the apostles obeyed the great commission. Thus Erasmus linked the baptisms of Acts to the command to make disciples.

A significant dimension of Erasmus's interpretation was that the order of teaching and then baptism in Matt. 28:19 was important and was demonstrated by the apostolic practice described in Acts. Only Anabaptists followed Erasmus in this interpretation.[24]

It is at the point of implementing this interpretation that the difference emerges between Erasmus and the Anabaptists. Erasmus worked from a Platonic framework, which enabled him to issue sharp critiques of Catholic practice while remaining in the Catholic Church. In this context, Erasmus held up the teachings of Christ as the ideal or archetypes that were opposed to the ritualistic shadows of these ideals in the visible church. Erasmus sharply criticized the corrupt shadows, yet did not feel a need to separate from the Catholic church. This stance allowed Catholics to denounce Erasmus for sounding like the Anabaptists. And it frustrated Protestants, who heard the critiques of Catholicism but then saw an Erasmus unwilling to commit himself to the cause of the Reformation.[25]

According to Friesen, the radical followers of Zwingli who became the first Anabaptists had their most direct access to Erasmus's views through his *Annotations* and paraphrases of the New Testament, which were sold in Zurich in Andreas Castelberger's bookstore. In the *Annotations* Erasmus stated his ideas and concerns in straightforward fashion, without reference to his Platonic assumptions. This work may have influenced Swiss Anabaptists (and perhaps Menno Simons) in their views on baptism as well as the Lord's Supper, pacifism, and community of goods. For those who became Anabaptists, Erasmus's ideas were ones that followers of Jesus needed to implement. For the becoming Anabaptists, to believe and accept the teachings of Jesus and the apostles meant to act on them.[26]

Under the impulse of the biblical understanding of Eramus, Anabaptists adopted a new baptismal practice and set out to reconquer the earth that was unjustly claimed by the established church and territorial rulers. The result was a visible church shaped by the belief that faith should result in a transformed life. Baptism was accorded to those who accepted the gospel and manifested it in a changed life.[27]

The argument that Anabaptist theology contained the possibility of departure from orthodoxy, rather than merely affirming it, finds two specific points of support in Friesen's depiction of Anabaptist origins. First, that Anabaptists followed Erasmus in a new interpretation of Matt. 28:19 demonstrates clearly that they were willing to accept a view that diverged from the received tradition. This corroborates the argument I have advanced regarding the possibility of departing from traditional understandings. Second, the kind of departure from inherited orthodoxy that I have suggested as possible for sixteenth-century Anabaptists appears to require the approach to the Bible and church history that Friesen has described. It seems plausible that if historical circumstances had been kinder, the movement that began when Anabaptists followed the influence of Erasmus regarding infant baptism might well have been impelled to question the church's christological formulas on the basis of apostolic teaching.

Friesen noted that Anabaptists accepted Luther's theology but objected to the fact that Reformation theology was not implemented and did not lead to reform.[28] I suggest that when modern Anabaptists understand the extent to which classic creedal formulas are devoid of ethics, and thus have accommodated slavery and male dominance along with violence and the sword, they will rethink classical theology on the basis of New Testament understandings. The impulse to develop christological understandings with explicit justice dimensions is the same as that which led sixteenth-century Anabaptists to reform churchly rituals on the basis of understandings they had learned from Erasmus.

On Sixteenth-Century Anabaptists as "Orthodox"

We should not make too much of sixteenth-century Anabaptist use of classic creeds and theological terminology. Nor should the fact that they amended classic statements to make discipleship visible but did not develop fully a distinct approach to classic theological issues be taken as normative. There are a good many reasons to be hesitant about allowing a perceived orthodoxy to be a barrier to the contemporary quest for a theology for the Mennonite churches as a peace church.

To pose an Anabaptist core theology comprised of principles in agreement with all Christians, a second layer in agreement with majority Protestantism, then a third category of positions specific to Anabaptists[29] seems to impose a modern perspective on sixteenth-century Anabaptists, in two ways. As the identifying mantra of Anabaptism, the core that Snyder describes is accessible only to modern scholars: those from the late twentieth- or early twenty-first century who have access to a wide range of sixteenth-century documents. No sixteenth-century Anabaptist could or did describe the suggested core as that which unified all Anabaptists, and no sixteenth-century Anabaptist was martyred for his or her commitment to this core. The core seems very much a modern construction, not a sixteenth-century one. Indeed, early Anabaptists seemed less interested in commonalities than in differences, as was demonstrated, for example, by the Schleitheim Brotherly Union.

This core is also "modern" when that term is used to identify the epoch that precedes postmodernity. In this sense, modernity is characterized by the assumption that there is a universally accessible and uncontestable, objectively verifiable common truth, if only we could locate its foundation.[30]

Until the Enlightenment the foundation was sought in the church. Since the Enlightenment, what has been called the secularization of Western and North American society has caused a shift to seeking the foundation outside the church. What we have taken to calling postmodernity is the recognition that it is impossible to obtain an objectively verifiable, universally recognizable, uncontestable foundation of common truth.

Although alarmists have decried postmodernity as mere relativism, the strident claim misses the mark. Postmodernity does not necessarily mean abandonment of the idea of universal truth or universally true religion. Rather, it means abandoning the possibility that such truth will be readily apparent and thus accepted by anyone of right mind. Consequently, postmodernity requires development of other, more faithful and less secure ways to testify to the ultimate truth or the transcendent dimensions of religious commitment.

I suggest that to posit an Anabaptist core theology that depends on the presumed universality of Christendom's creedal theology is to work out of the assumptions of modernity. In contrast, when I have pointed out the particularity of Western creedal theology and argued that it is both thinkable and appropriate for the peace church to pose truthful alternatives, I am working out of postmodern assumptions.

A second point of rejoinder concerns description and prescription. A shift in the logic of justification has taken place when, on the one hand, the makeup of sixteenth-century Anabaptist theology is claimed to be based on mere historical description, but on the other hand, that description is then claimed to be prescriptive for the modern church. Stated another way, it is one thing to develop a comprehensive, descriptive grid on which one can locate all possible variations of sixteenth-century Anabaptist theology. It is quite a different thing to go on to say that the grid now defines what the modern church should believe.

While Snyder intends that his presentation of a sixteenth-century Anabaptist theology be neutral historical observation and not advo-

112 / ANABAPTIST THEOLOGY

cacy, presenting this description in denominational magazines as the Anabaptist theology that is the seed of today's church certainly seems to shift from description to prescription.[31] At the same time, when it is treated as merely description, the process avoids having to account for the priorities inherent in the description.

To make the descriptive prescriptive is to make normative the status quo or the dominant view. By prescribing Anabaptist theology that is identified with Christendom's theology, one in effect makes normative the dominant voices of Christendom.

The move from descriptive to prescriptive harbors the assumptions pointed out in earlier chapters about a presumed theology-in-general that carries the benefit of the doubt. The majority voices of Christendom are assumed to be the norm of truth. But as was argued previously, the postmodern context enables us to perceive the particular character of that inherited theology more clearly than did observers in previous epochs, and thus to challenge the claim to universality and presumption of truth. Against the presumption of writers such as Klaassen and Snyder of a universal core present in the classic creeds, postmodernity opens the door to constructing a theology that specifically reflects Jesus' rejection of violence and nonviolent confrontation of evil.

Making the status quo or dominant view normative puts contemporary Anabaptists in the awkward position of defending theology of the oppressors of Anabaptism. Identifying the core of Anabaptist theology with Christendom's core also asserts, or at least implies, that the differences between magisterial Reformers and Anabaptists must have been peripheral—that is, not related to the central issues of the gospel. This chapter, and in fact the entire book, disputes that view.

Even if Snyder is correct, relegating the differences to the periphery presents a huge problem: it would mean that Anabaptist martyrs died for peripheral rather than core principles. On the other side, Reformers such as Zwingli, who believed Anabaptists were undermining Christendom and had to be eliminated, must have been killing Anabaptists over minor issues.[32] That implication would be unacceptable, both to Anabaptists who were willing to face death and to magisterial Reformers who were willing to administer it. If the differences are in fact peripheral, this reveals a serious flaw in orthodox Christianity; namely, that it could not comprehend the commonalities between

Anabaptists and Reformers and thus wrongly executed people who were orthodox and not heretical.

Positing a core Anabaptist theology based on the foundation of Western Christendom raises questions about historical inevitability and the nature of God's Providence.

To require or to make normative the classic creedal statements and vocabulary involves Providence; the implication is that God necessarily worked through the historical forces that produced those creeds. In the case of the Nicene Creed and the Chalcedonian formula, requiring these formulations links God inextricably to the development of the imperial church, which developed the ecclesiology rejected by the Anabaptist movement and in which the classic creeds became the accepted standard of faith.

Requiring those creeds and formulas privileges the particular civilization and philosophical school of thought that produced them as more conducive than any other to the development of true theology. It also implies that the formulas would have been the same apart from church imperialization. That assumption seems unwarranted, given the enormity of other developments which accompanied this change in the church, as well as the fact that modern historical scholarship assumes that the shape of what is said is inextricably linked to the character and social location of the one who is speaking.[33] It is ironic that scholars who are quite willing to link human texts to social contexts when studying sixteenth-century Anabaptism seem unwilling to acknowledge the social location of classic creedal theology.

Posing the question of historical inevitability another way, one can ask whether we can envision any other statements of Christology that reflect New Testament emphases. Or, are the philosophical categories of the classic creeds the only categories and frames of reference in which we can articulate the implications of what the New Testament says about Jesus? When questions are posed in this way, it seems rather obvious that we can envision other options. This renders the classic creedal statements truthful in their context but certainly does not make them a universal foundation that must always be present.

Questions about historical inevitability also apply to the sixteenth century. As noted earlier, sixteenth-century Anabaptists can be interpreted as reflecting the embryonic stages of a new theological orientation. To anticipate the argument of the following section, there are historical reasons why sixteenth-century Anabaptists did not engage in more innovative theological reflection. Was the state church providentially destined to persecute Anabaptists to prevent them from developing new formulations that reflected their particular new theology? Is it possible to argue that Anabaptist theology would have been no different if there had been no persecution of first-generation Anabaptists and they had enjoyed the opportunity for more studied theological reflection? I think not. Indeed, it is arguable that what the Reformers were trying to shut down was the possibility of an alternative to orthodoxy.

Finally, a sense that theology and ethics ought to be integrated calls for the development of a specific theology for the peace church. In the classic theological traditions, dogmatic theology deals with the truths of Christian faith, while moral theology deals with ethics or the "oughts" of Christian faith. Spiritual theology is the response to the rational formulation of the first two.[34] Although Anabaptists would likely not recognize these distinctions, Snyder used them to assert that while "Anabaptist distinctives do not emerge in the categories of dogmatic and moral theology (as intellectual systems), they are visible enough in the area of spiritual theology." He adds that in the category of dogma, "except for the peculiarity of Melchiorite Christology, the Anabaptists were orthodox in their understanding of the central elements of the faith."[35]

The comment that Anabaptist distinctives do not emerge in dogmatic and moral theology demonstrates the problem with the classic definitions, namely that they allow for the separation of theology from ethics. That is, dogmatics or theology is what one does in one category; then one moves on to develop ethics or morality, the "oughts," on the basis of other categories. From a peace church perspective, the roots of this separation appear self-evident. It arose when the imperial church of the fourth century began treating as normative the christological formulas that contained no explicit ethical content and then soon began justifying use of the sword.[36] The location of Anabaptist distinctives in the area of spiritual theology but not in dogmatics or moral theology (which Anabaptists shared with Protestantism and Catholicism) seems clearly to reflect this separation.

Others have suggested, however, that the distinguishing mark of Anabaptists is the lived dimension of their faith. James William

McClendon, Jr. argues both that theology and ethics should be linked in an Anabaptist theology and that, in fact, ethics precedes theology. Thus in the development of a contemporary systematic theology specifically for "baptists,"[37] McClendon's first volume deals with ethics, while volume two deals with dogmatics as the working out of the commitments of ethics. Stanley Hauerwas has expressed the same relationship in this way:

> I wish to show that Christian ethics is not what one does after one gets clear on everything else, or after one has established a starting point or basis of theology; rather it is at the heart of theological task. For theology is a practical activity concerned to display how Christian convictions construe the self and the world.[38]

The distinction between dogmatics and ethics as separate genres versus seeing ethics as the practical and lived dimension of theology is crucial. It illuminates to a great extent the willingness one has to acknowledge that rejection of violence belongs intrinsically to the gospel of Jesus Christ. As has been acknowledged, ethics and particularly the rejection of violence, are not intrinsically part of the classic creedal statements. I have related that omission to the genesis of the creeds in the Constantinian and post-Constantinian church.

While the classic theological tradition has not called the rejection of the sword and violence immoral, neither has it called that rejection intrinsic to what it means to confess Jesus as Lord. One can use Hubmaier as the epitome of a comprehensive Anabaptist theology, as Snyder does,[39] if one is working in a theological tradition shaped by the assumptions that theology and ethics are fundamentally two different genres, and that Jesus' rejection of violence is not intrinsic to the gospel, but belongs in a different discussion apart from identification of the essence of Christian faith. On the other hand, in the definition of theology and its relationship to ethics as portrayed by McClendon and Hauerwas, the rejection of violence does belong intrinsically to the story of Jesus and to the good news, the gospel, about Jesus.

In this light, if Anabaptists are the tradition of lived faith, then they as much or more than any other tradition should develop a theology that elucidates their ethical commitments. In this perspective, one should be looking at sixteenth-century Anabaptists, asking where their new ethical commitment was reflected in explicit theology. In that case, the peculiar Melchiorite Christology adopted by Menno would not be merely the exception that demonstrates that Anabaptists were orthodox, but would reflect a first tentative effort to develop a wide-ranging theology that was concerned more with reflecting moral or ethical commitments than with being "orthodox."[40] If that attempt to rethink theology was cut short by harassment and persecution of Anabaptists in the sixteenth century, it remains a quest which modern Anabaptists, who now have the leisure to devote time to theological reflection, ought to begin anew.

SIXTEENTH-CENTURY ANABAPTISM AND THE PRESENT-DAY SEARCH FOR A THEOLOGY FOR MENNONITES

Although it is plausible to think sixteenth-century Anabaptists could have moved on to develop a new theological edifice, the fact remains that except for a few rudimentary steps they did not undertake the project. For the most part, on the classic issues they did retain and affirm the received tradition. So we must ask again about the significance this has for today.

Is this failure to move in itself a precedent? If Anabaptists constituted a new movement with a new ecclesiology and other new emphases, why did they not do more to develop a theology that specifically reflected their beliefs? Does their lack of development of a new theology obligate the modern church to a similar restraint or otherwise shape our own understanding of these issues? The final section of this chapter explores these questions with a view to guiding the ongoing theological work of the peace church.

Historical Factors that Discouraged Theological reflection

First, the confluence of a number of circumstances in the sixteenth century appear to have cut off any deliberations about new theological directions at an embryonic stage. Few first-generation Anabaptists were trained theologians, and among them only Balthasar Hubmaier was a doctor of theology. Thus there were few individuals with training that might incline them to ask whether their new ideas on baptism and rejection of the established church had implications for the time-honored language of the creeds.

Further, such reflection requires time and psychological space, a certain leisure for deliberation. This kind of reflection is not necessarily the top priority for persons concerned about personal survival, churchly survival, and maintaining the faith in the face of persecution. The majority of these early leaders were killed or otherwise disappeared in a very few years, having had little time for development of a theological program beyond the issues of particular dispute in the early years of the Reformation.

Along with this, Anabaptists were already under great suspicion for their deviance on sacraments, their rejection of the established church, and the charges of immorality they levied against established church and governing officials; they were not inclined to raise even more questions by posing alternatives to the classic creeds. Finally, Anabaptists had a certain suspicion of formal theology. They believed that trained theologians of the established church failed to take seriously Anabaptists' arguments on baptism, then used devious scholastic arguments to refute clear teaching of Scripture. To raise new theological questions about the classic creedal language may have seemed to Anabaptists to be precisely the kind of nit-picking of which they were suspicious.

Such reasons show, I believe, why sixteenth-century Anabaptist use of the classic creeds ought not be taken as a consciously chosen position, and why this should not serve as normative for later generations that are asking how theology should be expressed for the twenty-first century. In fact, it is precisely the Anabaptists' refusal to let appeals to orthodoxy change their convictions that offers a precedent for seeking our theological commitments, not in the creeds, but in the story of Jesus. Furthermore, the Anabaptist concern with being scriptural over being orthodox should free us to follow the norm of Jesus as established in the New Testament narrative without being limited by formulations imposed on the story.

New Opportunities for Theologizing

We live in an age very different from the sixteenth century. In contrast to early Anabaptists, we in North America do have the academic training and the inclination to ask questions, as well as the psychological space and time to reflect on and rethink the classic issues of theology.

As suggested in earlier chapters, this combination of circumstances is recent. Figuratively speaking, it was only yesterday that the theological context changed for Mennonites in a material way.

Those who emerged as second-generation Anabaptist leaders in the sixteenth century were, for the most part, not formally trained in theology, and they did not pursue university education. It was easy for Anabaptists and Mennonites to retain an inherited suspicion of formal theology and to continue allegiance to the classic creeds without systematic reflection on how these fit with other components of their belief and practice. For the most part that pattern was maintained by those who emigrated to North America; only very late in the nineteenth century did North American Mennonites begin seriously to develop higher education.

As they did so, the theological world was polarizing itself around the issues of the modernist-fundamentalist controversy. Mennonite theology was captured by that argument, with the majority of Mennonite leaders opting for the more "biblical" fundamentalists, who were themselves suspicious of formal theology. Theron F. Schlabach describes how Daniel Kauffman in 1910 wrote a series of articles that would have charted a "third ground" for Mennonites between fundamentalism and liberalism. But Schlabach concluded, "in Kauffman and in other church leaders, seeds of Fundamentalism took root while those others lay quite dormant."[41]

One legacy of the modernist-fundamentalist debate was that some types of Mennonite intellectual and theological development were put on hold for much of the century. According to biographer Albert Keim, Harold Bender opted for historical rather than biblical studies in part because it was too risky for Goshen College to have a Bible professor who had studied theology at a German university.[42]

While Mennonites expended a great deal of energy on theology throughout the twentieth century, much of the discussion took place under terms dictated by the debates of the broader American church. The most prominent examples might be the exposition of "Bible doctrines" in Daniel Kauffman's three volumes,[43] followed a bit later by Bender's use of historical theology to chart a path for the contemporary church. As already noted, it was not until the 1980s that Mennonites began to be comfortable with such rubrics such as systematic theology. The transition did not go smoothly. The controversy surrounding the initial publication of Norman Kraus's *Jesus Christ our Lord* in 1987 can surely be seen as an attempt to retain theological categories of an earlier generation and a last gasp of the fundamentalist-modernist controversy for Mennonites.[44] Although *Jesus Christ our Lord* was in no way a liberal or modernist statement, it appeared that way to its detractors, whose categories were inherited from earlier Mennonite fundamentalism.

Thus it seems that only in the very recent past—perhaps even the last decade—have we reached the point at which we can truly begin to ask about the far-reaching effects of assumptions first developed in sixteenth-century Anabaptism.[45] In light of this new stage of Mennonite theological affairs, it seems unnecessarily limiting to argue that sixteenth-century Anabaptist references to classic creeds ought to define the current search for a theology that will serve the peace church in the twenty-first century—especially when those Anabaptists themselves were more interested in following Jesus than in being called orthodox.

Thus far, the book has examined Mennonite and Anabaptist theologizing from the late twentieth century back to the sixteenth century. The results have shown that while Mennonite theology on classic issues used language identified primarily with formulas inherited from versions of Christendom, Anabaptists appear to have made tentative beginnings toward reformulating classic doctrines.

Our discussion has also shown how the current context of postmodernity enables us to see more clearly than previous generations that theology inherited from Christendom is not a general or universal one, but rather the particular theology of a specific European tradition.

Whether one chooses to stress Anabaptists' agreement with classic imagery or to interpret their theologizing as the embryonic stage of a new paradigm has enormous significance for the contemporary church which traces its roots to sixteenth-century Anabaptism. To maintain itself as a peace church, the contemporary peace church can; in fact, must, move to express a theology that specifically reflects and articulates the nonviolence that is intrinsic to the story of Jesus that we find in the New Testament. The next chapter will sketch one peace church theology in conversation with some previously unrecognized, potential dialogue partners.

That chapter expands on the historic atonement image of Christus Victor. Harold S. Bender's name has appeared several times in these pages as one who asserted the agreement of Anabaptist and Mennonite theology with Protestant orthodoxy. But Bender might very well support the following proposed theology. In the early 1960s, as a young seminary student at Goshen Biblical Seminary, Gene Stoltzfus struggled with the idea of substitutionary atonement, specifically with why and how salvation in the reign of God should depend on the Father's needing the death of his Son. Stoltzfus shared that struggle with Bender, the seminary dean, and asked for his advice. As Stoltzfus recalled more than thirty years later, Bender told him to read Gustav Aulén's *Christus Victor* because "it will give you more help than anything I can say."[46] One of the seeds that has grown into the following theological sketch was my own initial interaction with Aulén's book some twenty-five years ago.

FIVE

CHAPTER 5

THE FUTURE OF MENNONITE THEOLOGY IN FACE OF BLACK AND WOMANIST THEOLOGY[1]

INTRODUCTION

This book has repeatedly called for construction of a theology that specifically reflects and is shaped by Jesus' rejection of violence. The current chapter sketches one such suggestion. It is developed via a conversation that includes black and womanist theologians and the classic theology of Christendom. This conversation will make clear that the questions raised by postmodernity and the issue of how theology reflects a particular perspective are by no means limited to Mennonites.[2] Of course, it is true that the theological sketch presented here is itself a particular theology, just as are the other theologies discussed throughout these pages.

THEOLOGY IN THE MARGINS

Mennonites as a Footnote

As noted earlier, it may seem audacious to assert that Mennonites as a peace church should construct a theological alternative to the time-honored formulas of Christendom. With reference to Christian history, whether of Europe or North America, Mennonites have appeared on the margins. In the story of the sixteenth-century Reformation, their story seems less significant than that of the "great Reformers": Martin Luther and John Calvin. In accounts of religion in North America, Mennonites rarely rate attention beyond footnote references or inclusion in lists of "other" small groups, after the larger and more important groups have been treated. The persecution recounted in the *Martyrs Mirror,* the traditions of speaking German and wearing "plain" clothing, the harassment of Mennonite pacifists during several U.S. wars (as described in volumes of the Mennonites in America series), and many other factors have contributed to this marginalization, which was sometimes forced on Mennonites and sometimes chosen by them.

In theology as well, Mennonites have been on the periphery. With some notable exceptions, Mennonite theologians have had only marginal roles in conversations about supposed mainstream or general theology. What theology Mennonites did produce served primarily the needs of their community on the presumed margins. The peripheral quality of Mennonite theology appears in a more profound way in an assumption held both by many Mennonite theologians and by their counterparts from the supposed mainstream: namely, that when discussing the classic issues (such as Christology and atonement), theology for Mennonites should develop out of the classic creeds and formulas of European Christendom. As a relatively new and small group, it is assumed, Mennonites will have little original to contribute.

As suggested in earlier chapters, relegating Mennonite theology to the margins has served to anoint another tradition as the authority. To understand theology for Mennonites as peripheral or as necessarily linked to a foundation located in some other tradition is to assume that the other entity is more true or authentic. Thus credibility comes through association with the supposed mainstream.

African-Americans and Theology

African-Americans have also occupied a marginal location in North America. In brutal fashion, they were transported here against their will and forced to live in slavery. After the U.S. Civil War, the marginalization of blacks continued in the form of official segregation in the South and unofficial but nonetheless real exclusion from white institutions in the North.

The marginalization of African-Americans was reflected in theology. Many African-American churches appropriated a version of European theology. It seemed difficult for either whites or blacks to believe that African-Americans could or should articulate a theology shaped by their experience as an alternative to the received theology of Christendom.[3]

In *Black Religion*, African-American scholar Joseph Washington made a forthright statement of the idea that black churches took their religious validity from European Christianity. James H. Cone noted Washington's contention that though there was a distinct black culture and distinctive black religion, "black churches are not genuine Christian churches." In Washington's view, Cone said, "black religion exists only because blacks have been excluded from genuine Christianity of white churches." Washington's book was received enthusiastically by the white church but denounced in the black church community, which contended that black religion was genuine Christian faith. The desire to refute Washington's book was one of the impulses that spurred the creation of black theology.[4]

In theological discussion, names often indicate the perceived marginal character of a theological perspective. A specifying name, such as Mennonite or black, appears to mean that the perspective designated applies only to the named group and has little relevance either for other named theologies or for the presumed mainstream.

But appearances can be deceiving. The discussion to follow will not only show that black and womanist theologies are relevant to Mennonite theology, but also that each of these so-called marginal theologies can be read as, in fact, central to all theology that goes by the name Christian. Black and womanist theologies have been shaped by the experiences and historical tradition of African-Americans in North America. From these particular experiences, African-American writers have developed comprehensive theologies that focus concerns for justice and peace. These theologies stand both as challenges to the white-oriented theology of many black churches and as critiques and alternatives to Christendom's theology. Black and womanist theologies may exhibit significant parallels as well as contribute major learnings to peace church theological efforts.

Mennonite theology reflects experiences in Europe and North America. The supposedly marginal Mennonite tradition professes to believe that following Jesus produces a community of disciples in visible contrast to the world. Since rejection of the sword is integral to the teaching and life of Jesus, who forms the community, the community of Jesus' disciples—the church—is inherently a peace church. These assumptions provide a different perspective on the classic formulas than that found in the standard account of the history of doctrine.

CHRISTENDOM THEOLOGY

Christendom's theology encompasses theology of the so-called mainstream, or majority Protestant tradition, as well as elements held in common with Catholic theology. In very broad brush strokes, we can note two characteristics of Christendom theology. First, it is of European origin. Second, it assumes for itself the mantle of givenness or of being universally applicable to all Christians.

The benchmark christological formulas of Christendom come from the councils of Nicaea (325 C.E.) and Chalcedon (451 C.E.). Nicaea proclaimed Jesus as "one substance with the Father," and Chalcedon added that Jesus was both "truly God and truly man." As I have already stated, these formulas are not wrong in and of themselves. If one is asking the christological question in terms of Greek philosophical, ontological categories and wants the answer shaped in a fourth-century worldview, then Nicaea and Chalcedon are clearly valid. It is important to state that Jesus is of God and also of humanity (which was Chalcedon's concern).

However, when examined from the particular perspective identified above—that following Jesus produces a community of disciples in visible contrast to the world—a significant absence becomes evident. A Jesus identified only in the abstract categories of "man" and "God" cannot be followed. When faith in Jesus Christ, or being *Christ*ian, means to shape one's life by his teaching and example, these formulas are insufficient; they have omitted the specifics of the New Testament narrative on which faith can be based.

Most specifically, these formulas describe Jesus apart from his rejection of the sword and teaching about love of enemies. Identifying Jesus in terms of abstract categories of humanity and deity allows one to claim him without acknowledging and being shaped by his life and teaching. The formulas do not give shape to the peaceable community of Jesus' disciples that poses a contrast to the world. In effect, they have marginalized ethics from christological understanding, or have provided the space for ethics to express convictions that do not stem from the particularity of Jesus.

Stated another way, these christological formulas seem more the problem than the answer to Jesus' question, "Why do you call me 'Lord, Lord,' and do not do what I tell you? I will show you what someone is like who comes to me, hears my words, and acts on them. That one is like a man building a house, who dug deeply and laid the foundation on rock. . ." (Luke 6:46-49).

Christendom theology has claimed universality via theological categories of fourth- and fifth-century philosophy that required consistency in ontology. These formulas have had sway for centuries. The argument here, however, is that these philosophical formulas are not as important to Christian discipleship as whether our theology conforms to or ignores the gospel, the good news of Jesus Christ. That the classic formulas are particular is not their problem. Peace church theology is also particular. The important question is the reference point for the particularity of our theology. Is it to the particular story of Jesus Christ as it is revealed in the New Testament? Or is it a to particular theological-philosophical formula from the fourth and fifth-centuries, when the church was coming to identify itself with the Roman social order?

Similar observations and conclusions apply to the several versions of satisfaction atonement, which developed from its first full articulation in Anselm's *Cur Deus Homo?* (1098). Some version of satisfaction has been the prevailing atonement image since the medieval church. This image depicts sinful humanity as being unable to satisfy the debt owed to God. In Anselm's version, Christ as man offered his death to satisfy the debt humankind owed to God, while at the same time Christ as deity satisfied the debt, which only God could do. For Anselm, Christ's death thus explained the necessity of Jesus as God and man. For later Protestantism, Christ's death bore the penalty of sin that a wrathful God required of sinners.[5] In either version, Christ's death satisfies a requirement established by God. The sinner who accepts Jesus' death escapes the debt owed or the deserved penalty and is thus reconciled to God.

In either case, atonement consists of an abstract, legal transaction between God and the sinner, which takes place outside of history and without reference to the particularity of Jesus, except for his sinless death. This transaction results in the sinner's salvation, but does not change the ongoing life of the saved individual. Sanctification is separated from justification.

Like the christological formulas, these atonement formulations allow one to claim salvation in Christ, understood as escape from deserved punishment, while neglecting or rejecting Jesus' teaching and example on the sword. Emperor Constantine, who legalized Christianity in 313 C.E., is a symbol of how the early church accommodated the sword and of the rise of Christianity as the favored religion of the empire. The marginalization of Jesus' particular teachings from the formulas of Christology is reflected, I believe, in the fact that although the origins of the formulas were earlier, they emerged as consensus statements in the church of the fourth and fifth centuries, which was fast becoming the imperial, state church.[6] Anselm's formula for salvation also emerged from that church.

The point here is that these formulations are not helpful to the church that intends to reflect and be shaped by the particularity of Jesus, and which consequently poses a visible contrast and witness to the world, a world not shaped by the particularity of Jesus. The second point is that these several formulations (Nicaea, Chalcedon, Anselm's) are specific to the church for which Emperor Constantine is a symbol; namely, the church that came to identify its course and purpose with that of the existing social order. That specificity is visible in the Greek philosophical categories and fourth-century world picture of the christological formulas, as well as in the Germanic feudal imagery of Anselm's atonement image, which depicts God as the Lord whose honor is offended. Most importantly, the formulations of Christology and atonement reflect the imperial church, for which the story of Jesus does not supply the particularity of Christian ethics.

As postmodernism reminds us, all theologies arise from a specific setting and are culture-related. The particularity of the classic formulas is not itself the problem. But recognizing their particularity opens the door to asking about assumptions behind them and the context these reflect. It becomes evident that the classic christological formulas were written to satisfy a fourth-century philosophical question about ontology (namely, the being of Jesus). While that discussion may produce consistent philosophy, what makes for *Christ*ian theology is a focus on the Gospels, where what Jesus said and did is important.

Again, despite postmodernity's insights, it should be noted that classic theology still appears to set the terms of discussion, by virtue of widespread and time-honored usage that pervades all our theologizing. The advent of postmodernity has not, therefore, made it easy for the supposed marginal theologies to assume an equal voice in the discussion. But it has provided an opening in which they can argue their case.

I object to Christendom's assumption that the characteristics that should shape theology for Mennonites as a peace church are marginal to the gospel. As already indicated, I believe that intrinsic to the gospel is the idea that following Jesus produces a community of disciples in visible contrast to the world. Likewise, rejection of the sword is integral to the teaching and life of Jesus, who forms the community.

Mennonites ought not allow the superior number of adherents of Christendom to decide what is central or marginal. With regard to the issues of the normativity of Jesus and of a visible, witnessing peaceful community, it is really Christendom's theology that is marginal. It has little relationship to the story of Jesus and to the good news about life in Christ. To build a theology for Mennonites as a peace church on the classic creeds and formulas of Christendom is to claim a foundation that has already discounted peace church assumptions.

A PEACE CHURCH THEOLOGY

As an alternative to Christendom's theological foundation in the classic formulas, I suggest that construction of Christology and atonement might begin with an atonement image that appears at both ends of the New Testament. On one end, in the book of Revelation, there is the image that has been called Christus Victor. The classic imagery of Christus Victor depicts a cosmic battle between the forces of God and the forces of evil, who hold captive the souls of humankind. Although the forces of evil kill Jesus, God triumphs through the resurrection. In Christ the Victor, humanity is freed to celebrate salvation in the reign of God.

While Revelation is a multifaceted statement, proper understanding of its symbols locates the confrontation of God and the forces of evil within the historical arena. The book's images refer to the Old Testament, especially to the book of Daniel, and to first-century figures and events. For example, the seven-headed dragon with seven crowns and ten horns seems a transparent reference to Rome, which according to legend was built on seven hills. The seven crowns and ten horns appear to represent the seven crowned emperors and three pretenders (for a total of ten emperors and pretenders) between the time of Jesus' crucifixion and the date of the book's composition. Such antecedents make clear that the clash between the reign of God and the reign of Satan has occurred within history. This conflict involved Jesus Christ and his church (the earthly manifestation of the reign of God) and the Roman empire (the earthly representative of all that is not under the rule of God).[7]

At the beginning of the New Testament, the Gospels depict the same confrontation between the representative of the reign of God, namely Jesus, and everything and everyone that is not under God's rule. The Gospels portray a Jesus who challenged violent, exploitive, or oppressive conditions in a number of ways. A few examples: his deliberate defiance of the prevailing understanding of the law when he healed on the Sabbath (Luke 6:6-11; 13:10-17; 14:1-6); his encounter with the Samaritan woman, which broke conventional standards for dealing both with a woman and a Samaritan (John 4:1-30); his other acts that defended or raised the status of women (Luke 7:36-50; 8:1-3; 10:38-42; John 7:53-8:11; 12.1-8); the cleansing of the temple, which precipitated his arrest (Luke 19:45-48), and the rebuke of Peter, when Peter attempted to defend Jesus with a sword at Jesus' arrest (Matt. 26:51-54; John 18:10-11).

Observing the picture of Jesus in the Gospels makes clear that his confrontation of evil occurs nonviolently and that the reign of God made present in Jesus is nonviolent. By identifying who Jesus was, this construction of what I call a historicized Christus Victor also functions as a narrative Christology. It needs the particularity of Jesus; indeed, it is this particularity that shows how God's rule confronts evil and that reveals the nature of God's reign in history. To be reconciled to God—to be saved—means to become part of that story of the reign of God made visible by Jesus, which stretches from creation to the eschaton.

This story is about God's grace to sinners. On their own, sinners are helpless before the reign of evil, and it is God's grace that calls them and catches them up into God's reign. The story is also about human responsibility, since it is the lives of believing people that make visible and testify to the reality of the reign of God in the world. Our participation in this story clearly fits Paul's words: "But by the grace of God I am what I am, and his grace toward me has not been in vain. On the contrary, I worked harder than any of them—though it was not I, but the grace of God that is with me" (1 Cor. 15:10).

After Constantine, however, this image of Christus Victor gradually died out. When the church became the state church and came to embrace the world rather than witness to it, an atonement image of confrontation between reign of God and reign of Satan no longer made sense. It was replaced by the atonement image developed by Anselm, which reflected the church of Christendom.

BLACK THEOLOGY: JAMES H. CONE

A great deal of literature exists in black and womanist theology. This chapter puts the foregoing sketch of peace church Christology and atonement in conversation with works by James H. Cone and by Karen and Garth Kasimu Baker-Fletcher.

Black theology developed out of the black church in the 1960s with a multifaceted agenda. It was a response to black militants, who rejected Christianity entirely as the oppressive religion of white folks. And it challenged the black church, which too willingly accepted the gospel of white theology that supported continued marginalization of African-Americans.[8] Womanist theology emerged in the 1980s. It was the result of black women's challenge to the racism of the women's movement, as well as a critique of sexism and male dominance in the black church.[9]

But black and womanist theology also speak to white Christians. They are a powerful challenge to people in the white church, including white Mennonites, to reexamine both their attitudes and their theology. Mennonites need to face that challenge if they expect to be a faithful church: one that values ethnic and cultural diversity in a world of increasing racial and ethnic strife.

I had already developed an early form of my ideas about a peace church theology[10] before I encountered black theology in a systematic way a few years ago. Having these ideas in mind made it a startling experience to read *God of the Oppressed*, written by James H. Cone, founder of the black theology movement.[11] In some form, every point made earlier in this chapter regarding a supposedly marginal theology for Mennonites is also identifiable in the development of Cone's theology. The previously noted marginal status of African-Americans provided the potential for a different view of the classic theology of European Christendom. This alternative reading supplied the roots of James Cone's black theology.

If slaves became Christians, they did not accept the proffered Christianity outright. When the white owners read the Bible aloud, they stressed "Slaves obey your masters," and said that a future home in heaven depended on earthly obedience. Behind that warning was a theology that depicted Jesus as a spiritual Savior, who delivered people from sin and guilt but said nothing about conditions in this world. This spiritual salvation could be offered to slaves without challenging the master-slave relationship and offered to supposedly free African-Americans who were still unwelcome in white churches.[12]

But when the Bible was read, the slaves heard a different message. They heard the Exodus as a story which placed God squarely on the side of the oppressed. The story promised that as God had freed the Hebrew slaves, so one day God would also free the African slaves in America. Slaves heard the story of Jesus who lifted up the lowly. They saw Jesus as a liberator, whose salvation included freedom from the physical bondage of slavery and support in the struggle against the continuing evils of segregation and racism in post-slavery America.[13]

In Cone's analysis, the white reading of the Bible rested comfortably on the christological formulations of Nicaea and Chalcedon and Anselm's satisfaction atonement. In themselves the abstract categories of humanity and deity of classic Nicene-Chalcedonian theology lacked an explicit ethical content. This, Cone noted, reflected its location in a church that was growing in favor with the Roman empire. He wrote:

> Few, if any, of the early Church Fathers grounded their christological arguments in the concrete history of Jesus of Nazareth. Consequently, little is said about the significance of his ministry to the poor as a definition of his person. The Nicene Fathers showed little interest in the christological significance of Jesus' deeds for the humiliated, because most of the discussion took place in the social context of the Church's position as the favored religion of the Roman State."[14]

White Christians could claim Jesus as defined by Nicaea and Chalcedon. They could see themselves—correctly—as within the orthodox theological tradition, yet at the same time own slaves or, later, continue racial segregation and discrimination.

Cone emphasized that reconciliation is "primarily an act of God." This act is neither a mere inward state nor a mystical transaction but happens "in history." It produces "a new relationship with *people* [emphasis Cone's] created by God's concrete involvement in the political affairs of the world," whether the suffering of biblical Israel or that of oppressed peoples of the modern world.[15]

The link between liberation and reconciliation provides the basis for Cone's critique of classic atonement concepts. This link, Cone said, has been cut for most of the history of Christian thought. A major reason for this was that the post-Constantinian church "produced a 'gospel' that was politically meaningless for the oppressed." Reconciliation was separated from God's liberating acts in history, and definitions of atonement developed "that favored the powerful and excluded the interests of the poor."[16]

Cone applied the critique specifically to Anselm's satisfaction theory, which depicts salvation in terms of a spiritual transaction that spoke neither to the social conditions of Africans in slavery nor to the oppressive character of racism in contemporary society. Cone called it "a neat rational theory but useless as a leverage against political oppression. It dehistoricizes the work of Christ, separating it from God's liberating act in history."[17]

Cone's reconstruction of an atonement motif anchored in the concrete reality of history builds on Christus Victor. Cone noted that Christus Victor focuses on the "objective reality of reconciliation as defined by God's victory over Satan and his powers."[18] This image offers an opportunity for contemporary theology "to return to the biblical emphasis on God's victory over the powers of evil." Included among the powers confronted and ultimately defeated by the resurrected Christ are not only the powers of evil mythically expressed in the figure of Satan but such earthly realities as "the American system," symbolized by government officials who "oppress the poor, humiliate the weak, and make heroes out of rich capitalists"; "the Pentagon"; and a justice system that treats African-Americans differently from whites.[19]

To be sure, James Cone and I come from quite different backgrounds. The discussion here has demonstrated, however, that our supposedly marginal starting points have produced remarkably similar critiques of the classic, supposedly universal formulas for Christology and atonement. Where I noted that the formulas accommodated the violence of the sword, Cone pointed out their accommodation of the violence of racism and slavery. Both of us constructed alternatives that appealed to the specifics of the narrative of Jesus, and that used a restructured version of the Christus Victor atonement motif.

BLACK AND WOMANIST THEOLOGY:
KAREN AND GARTH KASIMU BAKER-FLETCHER

James Cone represents the first generation of black theology. The themes and emphases he identified continue in a second generation. As one example, I comment briefly on *My Sister, My Brother* by Karen and Garth Kasimu Baker-Fletcher.

Garth Kasimu Baker-Fletcher writes as a second-generation representative of black theology, while Karen Baker-Fletcher writes from the perspective of developing womanist theology. Befitting the emerging nature of these theological movements, the style and agenda of *My Sister, My Brother* differ from Cone's. While the reconstructions by the Baker-Fletchers are less parallel to mine than are Cone's, they and I agree on the need to critique the accommodation of violence (whether war, racism, and slavery) in classic formulations, and the concern to pose an alternative theology specifically shaped by concerns for justice, peace, and liberation.

Methodological Affinities

I resonate with Garth Kasimu Baker-Fletcher's question in the introduction: "Is our future that of complete and utter assimilation into Euro-Americanness, or are we to stand firm as a distinct 'Black culture amid the 'White' United States of America?"[20]

This desire not to be entirely assimilated is written with passion, as one can easily observe in the language of XODUS, Garth's name for the "various liberative responses—in second-generation Black male theology—to the crisis in African-American hope and vision in the early 1990s."[21] XODUS uses capitalized words, boldface, and italics, all "designed with the intent to bring to the *WRITTEN WORD* something of the salty, tangy, pungent urgency and expressiveness which *is* BLACK ENGLISH."[22] That passion to maintain and nurture an identity not homogenized into U.S. society plays like the full band jazz version of the call in chapter 1 to resist "the bulldozer of modernity that would flatten all strange bumps" such as the peace church.

But the passion of this book and its mission both to maintain and develop an African-American identity over against the European-derived culture of white America is much more than merely preserving a cultural and historical identity. This is theology that matters. The book constructs a theology that is to be lived as though the justice of God's reign is present in the world.

Theology articulates what we are committed to. The theology of *My Sister, My Brother* expresses how people who are "followers of Jesus"[23] should live justly in an unjust world. This is theology that makes clear that ethics and theologizing are two different ways to express the same beginning assumptions. As the authors say in the introduction, "This book is a Creative Space where systematic theology dances with ethics, the two intertwining and flowing into each other." The Baker-Fletchers appeal to comments of Katie Cannon in saying that this methodology "makes it possible for African-American religious folk to see the tasks of theology and ethics as both fundamentally united and necessarily inseparable."[24] Given our own commitment to discipleship, Anabaptists and Mennonites ought to find this a congenial approach.

Christology and Atonement

As was the case with James Cone, I agree with Karen and Garth Kasimu Baker-Fletcher on the need to restructure Christology and atonement in ways that do not accommodate injustice.

In her description of the conversation in womanist theology about the meaning of the cross, Karen Baker-Fletcher cites the work of Delores Williams.[25] Williams questions the focus on sacrifice in traditional atonement theology (linked to Anselm), because of the connections it encourages between black women's suffering and Jesus' suffering. For Protestant churches, Williams says, "Jesus represents 'the ultimate surrogate figure.'" In place of a Christology that glorifies the cross, and thus encourages black women to accept their suffering, Williams proposes a new image. Jesus did not come to die, she argues; rather he "came to show humans *life*—to show redemption through a perfect *ministerial* vision of right relations between body (individual and community), and mind (of humans and of tradition), and spirit."[26]

But as Karen Baker-Fletcher points out, while "atonement theory is problematic, we are still left with historical reality of the cross."[27] She suggests that an emphasis on the resurrected Jesus refocuses the interpretation of Jesus' death as well. We need to rethink "*how* we preach Christ crucified," she writes.[28]. Glorifying the cross as though Jesus came to die actually glorifies the "human capacity to oppress others."[29] By contrast, emphasizing the resurrection shifts the focus to God's power to overcome oppression. Then it becomes clear that the persecution and violence experienced by those who resist evil does not constitute salvific suffering, nor is it a form of bearing the cross of Jesus. Rather this suffering is the result of an "ethic of risk," which is part of "actively struggling for social justice."[30] This ethic of risk is an "alternative to the ethic of sacrifice" that has glorified suffering.[31] A crucial implication of this ethic is that it makes clear that Jesus' death is not a divinely willed sacrifice but the product of human evil.

Garth Kasimu Baker-Fletcher also appropriates Williams's critique of sacrifice in traditional atonement doctrine. He notes that "it seems to be a particularly 'male' construction in our community that one must be willing to 'die' for something in order for it to be valuable."[32] But "in XODUS," he says, "we JOURNEY toward the future *following a living Jesus*, not tied to a Cross of death."[33] A part of the author's Christology is "Jesus as Conqueror." Taken from the book of Revelation, this is an image of Jesus as the one who conquers evil.[34]

These reconstructions by the Baker-Fletchers make questions about justice and just peace integral to formulations of Christology and atonement: an emphasis also found in my sketch and in James Cone's theology. I agree with the need to fashion a theology that confronts evil and understands that suffering can and does result from that confrontation, yet does not glorify suffering or making it redemptive in and of itself.[35]

Ecclesiology

Concerning ecclesiology, black theology and the peace church tradition are dealing with a similar issue: how to preserve a visible church in a way that confronts justice issues and is redemptive for the wider world. The best understandings of ecclesiology from peace church theologians would say that, as the church, we are a people rather than a collection of individuals. In other words, the church is a creation of God and is more than a mere voluntary assembly of saved individuals. This understanding differs from much of mainstream Protestantism, for which the real (or true) church is invisible, while what is visible are the ministerial functions of preaching and the sacraments. With the real church invisible, the church that is visible has little theological meaning. By contrast, in the believers church tradition to which Mennonites belong, the church is visible through the relationships among its members and the way it makes justice and peace visible in the world.

Garth Kasimu Baker-Fletcher distinguishes first- and second-generation tasks of the church, or the move from liberation to institution building. He illustrates the difference by pointing out the stress on liberation and the rhetoric of prophetic denunciation in the work of James Cone, followed by the emphasis on church life and family in the writing of J. Deotis Roberts, and Dwight Hopkins's work to develop resources out of the African-American experience for use in sustaining the church.[36] These emphases are all concerns of a visible church that seeks not to be swallowed up in the American social order. The author notes the four traditional "marks" of the church—one, holy, catholic, apostolic— which are inherited from European orthodoxy and says that a church seeking to be the visible outpost of God's justice on earth "needs *more than*" these.[37] In a similar way, contemporary Mennonites are engaged in debate about prophetic critique and the building and sustaining of institutions.

A Mennonite view of the church as a people rather than a collection of individuals is akin to Karen Baker-Fletcher's depiction of church as "event" or her statement that going to church is not the same as having church. We have church, she says, when God's Spirit moves and makes us into the church. We have that church when it encompasses class differences, when it is liberating rather than oppressive for women, when it values all generations, when it is in harmony with God's creation, and when it transcends gender norms.[38]

Eschatology

The Baker-Fletchers' chapters on eschatology are important ones in relation to the historic Mennonite emphasis on discipleship. The authors emphasize that that the future reign of God is already lived now. Garth Kasimu Baker-Fletcher urges readers to "embrace a this-worldly eschatology because to do otherwise is to surrender to a spirituality of political quietism."[39] Karen Baker-Fletcher writes that "eschatology involves the transformation of society and all creation with it from what it is to what it ought to be according to God's vision for the world."[40] She observes that "the reign of God's strength for life is an ever-present reality. The hereafter is in the here and now." Thus "black women and men can transform present existence by actively remembering and practicing the prophetic, generative wisdom of the ancestors, particularly the greatest of our ancestors: Jesus."[41]

SOME IMPLICATIONS

The brief comments on Christology and atonement, ecclesiology, and eschatology indicate where the perspectives of supposedly marginal traditions parallel one another vis-à-vis the presumably general, mainstream theology of Christendom. Let me suggest a few implications for Mennonites.

On Theology-in-General

Observations from black and womanist theology clearly support the arguments for discarding a view of Nicea, Chalcedon, and Anselmian atonement as theological givens. These classic formulations do not represent a standard program that every theology should build on. Rather, the independent but parallel critiques from peace church, black, and womanist perspectives reveal that Christendom's formulas have a particular orientation and social context, just as surely as does black theology or a theology for Mennonites.

God of the Oppressed and *My Sister, My Brother* present theology that is embodied in a history quite different from that of Anabaptists and Mennonites generally, or from my own ethnic background. Black theology as a movement has a stronger empathy with left-wing Protestantism than with the mainstream, while most African-Americans in the U.S. have religious roots in Methodist, Baptist, or Pentecostal traditions. Yet I feel great affinity with these authors in their effort to develop a theology of just peace out of the African-American tradition. In many ways, their endeavor corresponds to that of Mennonite theologians trying to root a theology in their own peace church tradition.

In its critique of Christendom theology, James Cone's work not only parallels mine but anticipates the acceptance of postmodernity's insight regarding particularity. Before this understanding was popular, James Cone was writing that "theology is not a universal language; it is *interested* language and thus is always a reflection of the goals and aspirations of a particular people in a definite social setting."[42]

As demonstrated both by black theology and peace church theology, the classic theology of orthodoxy represents the particular tradition of European Christendom. This is the tradition claimed by the rulers of society in defense of the status quo. It has supported crusades and accommodated extending the church by the sword, has countenanced colonial expansion and domination, and has condoned slavery, apartheid, and more.

Instead of continuing to construct theology for our particular traditions on the basis of classic Euro-orthodoxy,[43] theological reconstructions are necessary. As we have seen, it is black, womanist, and peace church theologies and not classic orthodoxy that make explicit the justice and peace that are inherent in the gospel of Jesus Christ. Like African-Americans, the peace church is free to read the Bible afresh and to develop new images that articulate better than Nicaea-Chalcedon-Anselm the peaceful and just reign of God made visible in the New Testament story of Jesus.

The Character of Violence

While they speak from a specific historical tradition, particular theologies carry a message of *universal intent and significance.*

The conversation with black and womanist theology makes abundantly clear for contemporary Mennonites that the gospel has social dimensions and that the question of violence is not limited to the issues of pacifism and refusal of military violence. It is no coincidence that Cone and I articulated parallel statements about the absence of ethics in the classic formulas. Slavery, racism, and the enjoyment of white privilege are forms of violence just as surely as war and the use of swords and guns are. Poverty, male dominance, and patriarchy are equally forms of violence. The list could continue. Engagement with black theology makes clear that a concern for nonviolence must encompass a wider range of justice issues than has been the case in the Mennonite past.

Nonviolence and Violence

From the Mennonite side of the conversation, the concept of violent resistance presents an important potential point of disagreement with black theology.

Martin Luther King, Jr.'s deep and principled commitment to nonviolence is well known. By contrast, black militants and early black power advocates made a point of saying that blacks rejected white calls for nonviolence.[44] One impetus for the development of black theology was to provide an answer to the militants that was Christian but that also challenged rather than accommodated oppressive white religion. With the challenge of the militants clearly in view, Cone wrote with great passion about the "white theologians and preachers who condemned black violence but said nothing about the structural violence that created it," and who quoted Jesus' sayings about loving enemies and turning the other cheek "but ignored their application to themselves."[45]

From a black perspective, this advocacy of nonviolence was one more instance of white folks trying to define the reality of black folks. And in that context, denying white calls for nonviolence and asserting that blacks should liberate themselves "by any means necessary"[46] was as much a statement that blacks would define their own reality as it was a comment about violence.[47]

In a further point, Cone distinguished nonviolence from self-defense. Cone called self-defense a "human right" and said that white people should not tell black people what means they may use to confront racism. At the same time, he asserted that nonviolence is "resistance" and was "the only creative way that an African-American minority of 10 percent could fight for freedom and at the same time avoid genocide" during the era of the Civil Rights Movement.[48]

Nevertheless, Cone argued that one cannot absolutize the nonviolence of Jesus, even if we could be completely sure of the biblical evidence. To make what Jesus did an infallible guide would mean being "enslaved to the past."[49] These comments seem to place Cone somewhat closer to Malcolm X than to Martin Luther King, Jr.

As a response to Cone, I suggest that there is a disjuncture between claiming that the New Testament narrative says Jesus is liberator of the oppressed yet using form criticism to challenge that same narrative at the point of Jesus' rejection of violence.[50] While there has been great disagreement over the centuries about how to appropriate the narrative, a rather broad consensus exists that Jesus himself rejected the option of the sword. I might also point out that self-defense remains the classic example of justifiable violence. This suggests that some caution is in order when appealing to theories of justifiable violence on the basis of self-defense.

In a related area, further analysis might raise an ecclesiological question: namely, whether Cone's understanding of the relationship of the church to oppressed social groups opens the door to another version of the Constantinian temptation, which his theological analysis challenged so effectively.[51] The temptation is to create a new, potentially oppressive force by identifying the church with a social group, rather than functioning as a faith community that seeks the liberation of all.[52]

Other writers of black theology occupy a number of points on a spectrum between Cone and King on the question of violence. Garth Kasimu Baker-Fletcher has affirmed both the radical challenge to white Americans posed by Malcolm X and the principled nonviolent tactics of Martin Luther King, Jr. Baker-Fletcher contends, however, that nonviolence "worked" as a tactic when it concerned the limited agenda of public access in the late 1950s and early 1960s, but seems ineffective against the systemic problems of U.S. society which require revolutionary social change. He also praises King's latter move to embrace a "pan-African" vision that demanded more for African-Americans than merely becoming part of the U.S. mainstream.

The goal of XODUS, Baker-Fletcher writes, "is to change the mainstream so that it will have enough room for us to be Afrikan without discipline, punishment, or banishment."[53] The stress is on achieving this end, rather than on nonviolent tactics.

Karen Baker-Fletcher describes an ethic of survival, resistance, and liberation. Survival is a "creative quality" that can make "something out of nothing," she writes. "Resistance involves active unwillingness to perpetuate injustice." This refusal can involve "subtle and explicit rebellious and insurrectionary acts against systems of oppression." Such acts may range from kicking and fighting to resist removal from a segregated railroad car to refusing to allow others to write down one's thoughts to "physically resistant and liberating acts . . . such as abolitionist activities." Liberation, she says, "is the act of reclaiming the power of freedom."[54] This threefold ethic clearly incorporates nonviolent tactics but stresses the wholeness of African-American women rather than nonviolence itself.

In spite of potential differences, the conversation with black theology need not fall into debates about absolute nonviolence. If Mennonites are concerned about this issue, it is incumbent on us to examine our lives and the structures of our church. We must seek ways to develop greater resistance to the systemic violence in which we participate, as individuals and as a church. Our pursuit of that task, rather than our absolutist arguments, should be the clear witness to the integrity of our commitment to nonviolence. From this standpoint, a productive and mutually enriching discussion can develop between Mennonite theology and black theology about the forms of violence and oppression that we encounter at all levels in the world around us, and then about appropriate ways to resist the violence and to achieve liberation from it.

Nonviolence and Nonresistance

The recognition that there are systemic forms of violence such as racism (as well as sexism, patriarchy, poverty, and more) makes clear why the principle of nonresistance is no longer an adequate peace stance. The term *nonresistance* identified the Mennonite peace stance for much of this century. We were taught to obey Jesus' words: "Do not resist an evildoer. But if anyone strikes you on the right cheek, turn the other also" (Matt.: 5:39). To resist, even if doing so did not involve lethal violence, was to violate this sacred principle of nonresistance.

In the late 1950s and 1960s, Mennonites discussed whether to support the civil rights movement; after all, Martin Luther King, Jr. was leading *resistance*. For myself, I still recall that I arrived at college believing that marches and sit-ins were resistance, and I was rather disturbed by two professors who defended King's nonviolent activism.

Nonresistance can have a powerful impact when it constitutes a refusal to reply to evil and violence with another evil or violent act. It means little, however, in the face of systemic violence such as racism or poverty. In fact, to refuse to resist in that context is to accept the status quo and its violence. To witness against and to resist systemic violence may require engaging in active nonviolent resistance. The church founded on Jesus Christ, whose life and teaching make visible the reign of God in history, should be the locus of such nonviolent social change. If the church is not confronting injustice, then it is not being the church.

The ethic of resistance that the Baker-Fletchers describe (in differing ways) supports this analysis of nonresistance and nonviolence. Today I am grateful to the professors who first opened my eyes to the reality that nonresistance means acquiescence to systemic violence. We need to hear Karen Baker-Fletcher's statement that resistance "involves active unwillingness to perpetuate injustice."[55]

Such resistance empowers people who have believed that they had no power. It also is important for folks in the white majority. It puts us on record as recognizing that we cannot avoid the question of racism and other kinds of systemic violence. To live as a white person in this white-dominated society without actively resisting is to support injustice.

Continuation as a Peace Church

Black theology clearly has an agenda: confronting racism and advocating liberation from its oppression. Theologians from this stream state explicitly that if theology does not deal with racism and related issues, it is accommodating injustice.

The depth of this commitment should give us pause when we compare it to our corresponding reluctance to make liberation from violence an intrinsic element of our peace-church theology. I am disturbed by the apparent erosion of the Mennonite churches' commitment to nonviolence. I am troubled by the increasing number of occasions when Mennonite ethicists and theologians say that we cannot be quite so sure as in times past about the rejection of violence, or that we need to decide whether to allow nonviolence to be a hindrance to evangelism or to further ecumenical conversation. It seems obvious that we would be uncomfortable telling black theologians to soften their stance on racism for the sake of evangelism. Why then are we increasingly willing to make that request of our own tradition in the area for which we are best known in the wider world?

Some people have argued that white Mennonites' complicity in the systemic violence of North American society shows that we cannot escape violence, and that therefore the peace church should modify its stance. I would argue, on the contrary, that such complicity demonstrates why the would-be peace church needs to become more active in nonviolent resistance to systemic violence.

ECUMENICAL AND INTERCHURCH DIALOGUE

When Mennonites have contemplated ecumenical conversation, they have tended to think in terms of the several theological traditions of mainstream Christendom. I suggest that Mennonites have as much or more to learn from interaction with black and womanist theology, which can discuss with us what it means to be a minority religious tradition. Such conversations would cause us to face more forthrightly the whiteness of our theological tradition and ecclesiastical practice. It would test the seriousness of our commitment to justice and our willingness to engage this cause with the black church. Such interaction would add considerably to our understanding of how to be a prophetic voice in violence-accommodating Christendom.

Both black theology and Mennonite theology are vulnerable to the allure of civil religion and to the temptation to blur the distinction between church and social order. Likewise, both African-Americans and Anabaptist Mennonites are seeking ways to cherish a historical tradition in an open and welcoming manner while also professing ultimate allegiance to Jesus Christ. There is great potential for mutually enriching dialogue.

This chapter began with reference to groups on the margin. The discussion has demonstrated, however, that if the peace church is truly the peace church, what Western Christendom has considered marginal is really integral to our understanding of Jesus Christ. The same is true for black and womanist theology. Postmodernity provides a recognition of the particularity of the Christendom tradition. This offers an opening for supposedly marginal voices to articulate a theology of Jesus Christ that has universal import. It is my hope and prayer that the peace church will have the courage to make central what the world considers peripheral and to engage others who have similar concerns.

CONCLUSION

As noted in the introduction, this book is not about postmodernity. Rather, it deals with the character of theology for the peace church in light of learnings currently labeled postmodern.

Yet the primary concern of this book goes beyond theology. It has to do with the future of Mennonites and whether the Mennonite church of the new millennium will continue to be a peace church.

DECLINE OF SEPARATIST SOCIOLOGY

As we have seen, Mennonites over the years have had little theology that was consistently shaped by assumptions of nonviolence. Nor have they sought very vigorously to develop this. Until John H. Yoder, Mennonite theologizing (at least in the nineteenth and twentieth centuries) had consisted primarily of affirming agreement with some version of a presumed general orthodoxy and then adding peace church emphases to it.

Into the 1960s, Mennonites were still something of a rural and separate people. Distinctive dress or German language, even if employed by only some segments of the Mennonite population, reminded all in the church that Mennonites were set apart from the social order. A number of factors made visible the nonresistant and nonviolent dimension of the church. Older people still had memories of rough treatment experienced by conscientious objectors in World War I, and many men and women told of life-changing experiences in

144 / ANABAPTIST THEOLOGY

and around Civilian Public Service camps during World War II. The military draft, during U.S. wars in Korea and Vietnam, continued to stock the church's voluntary service programs with conscientious objectors. Thus Swiss, German, or Dutch ethnic identities, underscored by an idea of separation from the world and coupled with the fact that pacifism was not always popular in American society, reinforced the conviction that a church which followed a nonviolent Jesus was an alternative or witness to the world.

No doubt the best thinking would have declared that rejection of violence was intrinsic to the gospel of Jesus Christ. Nonetheless, it was the sociological dimensions of being a separate people, rather than a specifically nonviolent theology, that defined Mennonites as a peace church.

Today much of this separatist sociology is gone. In less than a generation, the marker of plain dress has virtually disappeared from the Mennonite Church, aligning its members with the General Conference Mennonite Church, which was never characterized by plain dress.[1] Meanwhile both groups have imbibed deeply of modern technology and modern culture. Few acculturated Mennonites continue to use German. As we envision the future of an integrating the Mennonite Church and General Conference Mennonite Church, few visible signs remain to remind us that the church is not identified with the social order.

THE INCREASED IMPORTANCE OF THEOLOGY

We need not lament cultural change and the loss of ethnic identity. Rather, these shifts indicate what most plain-dressing Mennonites would also state: namely, that salvation is not dependent on a particular style of clothing or a specific cultural identity (although conservative groups do see plain dress as a witness to certain beliefs and commitments). The cultural changes have helped to ease some interactions and involvements for service and mission in the wider society.

Yet the disappearance of traditional external markers also renders the issue of theology more acute for acculturated Mennonites. Theology articulates our commitments, while ethical practices constitute the lived version of those commitments. For Christians that commitment is to Jesus Christ, whose particular story we read in the New

Testament. In its best light, Mennonite ethics has attempted to live Jesus' rejection of violence (although never fully attaining the goal), and our theology ought to embrace and express his rejection of violence as an integral component. Modern Anabaptists ought to have an ethics and a theology which make clear that Jesus' story is intrinsically a story about nonviolent resistance to evil.

If Mennonites profess to share a foundational theology with some version of either evangelical or ecumenical Protestantism that does not embrace Jesus' rejection of violence, then they are left without explicit guidance in the way of peace. In the absence of sociological markers, the would-be peace church is left standing on a theology that has already moved to the periphery what we have believed to be central to our understanding of Jesus Christ. If the foundational theology for Mennonites comes from Protestantism, then it follows that the unique points of Bender's Anabaptist Vision—discipleship, community ecclesiology, love, and nonresistance—are add-ons to a presumed general theology, rather than integral dimensions of the whole gospel.[2]

When rejection of violence is seen as intrinsic to who Jesus is, the church shaped by that gospel will have a different perspective on Christology and atonement than the church which does not link social issues intrinsically to the message of Christ. If we truly believe that Jesus' rejection of the sword is central to his teaching and mission, then that dimension of his story should shape and appear plainly in our words about his person and work. The effort to articulate a specifically peace church view of Christology and atonement reflects the recognition that the peace church can articulate a comprehensive worldview as an alternative to the worldview of the established church and to the classic theology that emerged from it.

TOWARD A RENEWED PEACE CHURCH

The postmodern context provides one of the greatest opportunities in several centuries to envision the church specifically shaped by the story of Jesus. The answer to the demise of ethnic identity is to renew our understanding that the social dimensions of Jesus' work and teachings are essential to the gospel and should be intrinsic dimensions of Mennonite theology.

A theology shaped in this way is meant to be lived. This theology is not a self-contained entity that exists for its own sake or that will renew and sustain the peace church by itself. The faithful church is not defined by mere allegiance to correct theology, even theology that is shaped by Jesus' rejection of violence. Theology is the articulated dimension of our commitment to Jesus Christ. How the church lives—our ethics—is the lived version of that commitment. Gerald Biesecker-Mast is correct when he writes:

> We must find a way to live our theology, not merely affirm it. We must learn to become motivated at our very core of being to follow Christ and not merely assent to his views. To do this we must teach a gospel of action and discipleship, of lived faith, and of moral fruits.

Biesecker-Mast goes on to argue that we need to cultivate "a discipleship of performance" that understands "words as deeds" and "deeds as words."[3]

The renewed peace church, whose words and deeds enflesh Jesus Christ, will remain as a distinct witness over against North American society. That witness will not be located in the church's ethnicity—food, dress, and language patterns. Rather, it will be seen in the church's actions for peace and justice, in its practices of discipleship. These actions are a much more significant witness to U.S. society, and pose a much greater threat to it, than plain dress, a rural lifestyle, or Germanic language.

As we begin the third millennium, will Mennonites and other Anabaptists have the courage and the commitment to Jesus Christ to be the kind of witness that will make them seem a danger to American society? Will Mennonites have the courage to articulate that prophetic gospel? Or will we be content to jettison the social dimensions of the gospel in exchange for increased numbers and membership in larger U.S. religious groupings?

EPILOGUE: MENNONITE THEOLOGY
IN FACE OF ANABAPTIST VISION[1]

In the midst of World War II, Harold S. Bender's Anabaptist Vision sought to establish a credible pacifist Mennonite identity on two fronts: with mainline Protestants who might have questions about Mennonites' non-participation in the war effort, and with Mennonites themselves, who perhaps felt guilty about their non-participation.[2]

Bender's effort to forge a distinct identity for Mennonites has been judged highly successful—so much so that we are still talking about it more than fifty years later. The Anabaptist Vision also contains an ecclesiological and theological tension that is much more apparent in postmodern perspective than it was in Bender's era, a half a century ago. How we understand and respond to that tension poses another version of the question of chapter 2: namely whether the future faithfulness of Mennonites in North America is best found through plugging into North American Christendom or by posing a specific witness to it.

The Anabaptists, as described by Bender, looked in two directions with respect to the Protestant Reformers and established church Protestantism. Writing some eighteen years after Anabaptist Vision in the article "Walking in the Resurrection," Bender stated that the

Anabaptist doctrine of regeneration and discipleship was developed both "in the context of Reformation theology and practice, and in conscious opposition to it."[3]

On the one hand, Bender legitimized and identified Anabaptists in terms of established church or magisterial Protestants. In well known words from Anabaptist Vision, Bender described Anabaptism as "the culmination of the Reformation, the fulfillment of the original vision of Luther and Zwingli." Anabaptism was thus a "consistent evangelical Protestantism seeking to recreate without compromise the original New Testament church, the vision of Christ and the apostles."[4]

This identification with mainline Protestantism included an espousal of the core of Protestantism theology. Following his acknowledgment of the bidirectional stance of Anabaptism, quoted above from his "Walking in the Resurrection," Bender went on to claim the theology of mainline Protestantism for Anabaptists and their Mennonite descendants:

> It is not that the Anabaptists differed basically from the Reformation on such doctrines as the sole authority of the Scriptures, grace, and justification by faith, or in the classic Christian loci of doctrine, for they did not. In fact, they had much in common with the Reformers.[5]

Already prior to Anabaptist Vision, Bender had spelled out the "classic Christian loci" in his description of American Mennonites in an address to the 1936 Amsterdam Mennonite World Conference:

> All the American Mennonite groups, without exception stand upon a platform of conservative evangelicalism in theology, being thoroughly orthodox in the great fundamental doctrines of the Christian faith such as the unity of the Godhead, the true deity of Christ, the atonement by the shedding of blood, the plenary inspiration and divine authority of the Holy Scriptures as the Word of God.[6]

Bender's evangelical Anabaptists clearly stood on a common foundation with mainline Protestantism and shared a good deal of its superstructure.[7]

On the other hand, the Anabaptism of Bender's vision posed a clear alternative to magisterial Protestantism. According to Bender,

Luther and Zwingli had begun their reformations with the goal of establishing "an earnest Christianity": "the true Christian church" composed of "earnest Christians."[8] However, while Luther and Zwingli made the decision "to surrender their original vision," returning to the concept of a mass church established by governments, the Anabaptists "retained the original vision of Luther and Zwingli, enlarged it, gave it body and form, and set out to achieve it in actual experience,"[9] an accomplishment achieved in the face of great persecution at the hands of "Catholic, Lutheran, and Zwinglian authorities."[10] Thus for Bender, the commitment of Anabaptists clearly distinguished them from magisterial Protestantism.

Not only did Anabaptists persist with the vision abandoned by Luther and Zwingli, they extended it further. The three points central to Bender's view of the teachings of Anabaptism: discipleship as the essence of Christianity, a new concept of the church, and nonresistance, were important *precisely because* they posed a contrast to mainline Protestantism. These central teachings were not merely different emphases or teachings missing from the Protestant agenda. In at least one case—the concept of the church—the Anabaptist position was mutually exclusive from that of the magisterial Reformers.

Calling "voluntary church membership based upon true conversion" the "absolutely essential heart" of the new concept of the church, Bender wrote that Anabaptist ecclesiology posed a "sharp contrast" to that of the Reformers, who had "retained the medieval idea of a mass church with membership of the entire population from birth to the grave compulsory by law and force."[11] In short, after stressing Anabaptism's common foundation with magisterial Protestantism, Bender also defined an Anabaptist ecclesiology which seems to place Protestantism and Anabaptism in separate domains.

Bender seemed to want it both ways. Anabaptists were part of the Protestant Reformation, but also different from it: different enough, in fact, that Anabaptism became a distinct movement.

Bender's description of the relationship of Anabaptism to Protestantism contains a rather obvious ambiguity. Which Anabaptism was the more real, the Protestant one or the non-Protestant one?

We have long recognized the extent to which Bender used his interpretation of Anabaptist history to provide Mennonites with a credible tradition and pacifist identity in the midst of the second world war, while also avoiding the Scylla and Charybdis of fundamentalism and liberalism. And after all, there is no sense in defining a distinct Anabaptist Vision if it does not pose some kind of contrast to Protestantism. This leaves the distinct impression that, for Bender, the stress fell on Anabaptism as an *alternative* to Protestantism.

Two Current Examples of Ambiguity

Half a century after Anabaptist Vision, amid the process of bringing together two Mennonite denominations and in face of a rapidly fading ethnic identity, one sees an ambiguity regarding wider Protestantism not unlike that in Bender's vision.

Walter Klaassen, for example, once wrote that "Anabaptism was neither Protestant nor Catholic but in fact a movement of different dimensions, . . . that it represents some of the best of both traditions."[12] In a recent address, Klaassen distanced himself from the earlier "neither-nor" categorization and emphasized that Anabaptism had much in common with both Protestantism and Catholicism. Although Anabaptism was part of "'the reformation of the common people' as opposed to the official reformation of the Reformers,"[13] Klaassen said, Anabaptists "shared much" both "with the old [Catholic] church they left and with the others [Protestants] who also separated from the old church."[14] In describing the contribution that Mennonites might make to the whole church in ecumenical discussion, Klaassen noted that on most issues, differences among the Christian traditions are "almost always a matter of relative emphasis along a continuum between two poles" rather than substantial disagreements or mutually exclusive positions.[15] While still acknowledging both similarities and differences between Anabaptism and Protestantism, Klaassen's emphasis has apparently shifted toward identifying Anabaptism with Protestantism (and Catholicism).

Levi Miller's recent comments on Bender and Anabaptist Vision also reflect ambiguity. On the one hand, Miller says, Anabaptist Vision gave Mennonites a way to work in the world without being swallowed up by it. Miller notes that Bender's vision helped Mennonites who came through World War II to "retain a distinctiveness" and emerge from the war "with greater conviction for biblical nonresistance and pacifism." It inspired a generation to serve around the world in the name of Christ, and it gave "mid-century culturally conservative and humble Mennonites a way to think of themselves as progressive and creative."[16]

The problem, Miller says, is that the environment shifted. The vision, which had begun as a perspective on Christian faith, became "*the* central norm by which to judge all Christian identity" [emphasis Miller's].[17] That is, the ethically-oriented "essence of Anabaptism"; namely, discipleship, community, and pacifism, were allowed to become "the essence of the Christian faith."[18]

Pushing Anabaptism in the direction of shared foundations and identity with Protestantism, Miller quoted Bender's Amsterdam statement (cited above), which positioned Mennonites on "a platform of conservative evangelicalism in theology." Anabaptist Vision had behavior categories, Miller says, but lacked categories necessary for Christians in the postmodern, secular world: categories such as worship, spirituality, forgiveness, and grace. Those absent categories come from the wider Christian tradition and from the classical theology alluded to by Bender, Miller implies.

Thus the modern identity of Mennonites should come, not from the distinctiveness of the tradition as portrayed in Anabaptist Vision, but from seeing it as "part of the larger Christian catholic and evangelical tradition."[19] While in Bender's day, Anabaptist Vision supplied Mennonites with a distinctive identity, Miller concludes, today it "has given us Mennonites a biblical and historical place to stand in the modern world."[20]

These comments from Klaassen and Miller show that the ambiguity present in Bender's Anabaptist Vision about the relationship of Anabaptists and Mennonites to the so-called mainline Christian traditions is still with us. What has changed, I suspect, is what Mennonites want to do with that ambiguity. Whereas Bender's emphasis inclined toward the side of Anabaptist distinctiveness, Mennonites today appear to tilt toward identity with the wider tradition

SOME IMPLICATIONS OF AMBIGUITY

The bidirectional stance of Bender's Anabaptists contains the seeds of two other kinds of ambiguity, whose less obvious character veils a potentially more profound impact. The way in which these ambiguities are resolved will have much to do with the future faithfulness of the Mennonite churches.

The first ambiguity deals with the relationship of classic theology to ecclesiology. As already indicated, Bender assumed that Anabaptists and Mennonites agreed with classic orthodoxy on all crucial matters of doctrine. At first glance, it may not be apparent what this assumption has to do with the discussion about ambiguity. However, it is the majority church of Christendom, whose ecclesiology Bender rejected, that developed the classic doctrines accepted by Bender. Bender thus assumed that the classic doctrines exist independent of—or at least unaffected by or unrelated to—the ecclesiology within which they developed.

Bender was not alone in that assumption. It is shared by most of Western Christendom.

But is that assumption fully valid? Isn't it quite thinkable that different, seemingly contradictory ecclesiologies might have differing impacts on the formulation of Christian doctrine? For the past several years, I have argued that different ecclesiologies have the potential to produce different doctrinal formulations. Pursuing questions first provoked by John H. Yoder's informally published *Preface to Theology*,[21] I maintain that the classic formulations of Christology and atonement reflect their genesis in the established church or Constantinian ecclesiology, and that it is therefore logical to develop alternative formulations that reflect a specifically Anabaptist, believers church ecclesiology.[22]

I mention this argument here as a more subtle dimension of the ambiguity of ecclesiology in Bender's Anabaptist Vision. Later I will return to this point in a different way, indicating why this issue is much more than just a question of theology.

Beyond this argument about perspectives on the classic theological questions, Anabaptist Vision conceals an even more subtle ambiguity of ecclesiology. Bender's description of the voluntary nature of Christian commitment and church membership actually can encompass two versions of the voluntary, believers church. The distinction concerns the location of the church in the calculus that links the gospel and the faith of individual believers.

Is the church intrinsic to the gospel, or is it merely the voluntary assembly of saved individuals? Does God's saving work include transformation of structures and relationships among people, or does it envision primarily individuals who subsequently group themselves into a church? When a person comes to the Christian faith, does she join the people assembled by God around Jesus Christ—namely, the church—or does she join a group formed by men and women after they have accepted Christ as Savior? Stated yet one more way, does the gospel have inherently social connotations, or does it deal primarily with individual guilt and salvation?

In the first half of each pair of questions, the church is identified in some way as the result of God's work; in the second half, it is created by men and women.[23] In either case, the individual joins voluntarily, as a result of, in Bender's words, a "true conversion and . . . a commitment to holy living and discipleship."[24] In the first formulations, stress falls on the Christian *community*; faith is expressed in the context of the community, and an individual's activity takes its meaning from the community. The second formulations focus more on the spiritual life of the individual and the individual's quest for God. The church functions primarily as a support group for these individuals, as they encourage one other both in their pursuit of God and in the expression of Christian ethics in their individual lives.[25]

THE IMPLICATIONS OF TWO FORMS OF VOLUNTARY ECCLESIOLOGY

The question whether or not social ethics or the church is intrinsic to the gospel may seem a loaded one. It is. Nonetheless, our practice sometimes differs from the right theological answer.

There is a significant distinction between the two images of ecclesiology. Some of the tension in recent Mennonite theological dialogue is at least in part a reflection of the interaction of these two ecclesiologies, each of which can find shelter under the roof of the voluntary, "brotherhood" church that Bender attributed to Anabaptism. While Bender did not intentionally pose an ambiguous ecclesiology, the rise of postmodernity in the world external to Mennonites, as well as evolutionary changes within the Mennonite world, bring to light an ambiguity that Bender likely did not perceive. More on that point later.

Whether the church is intrinsic to the gospel or is simply the voluntary assembly of saved individuals is a question with many implications.[26] It is a way to ask whether the gospel has social implications or applies only to individuals. Pacifism and the principled rejection of violence illustrate this distinction. If the social teachings of Jesus, such as his rejection of the sword, are intrinsic to the gospel, one cannot accept Christ without those teachings. While the church as a visible social structure is in no way synonymous with the reign of God, the church's mission is to symbolize and witness to the presence in the world of the social dimension of the gospel. If the social teachings of Jesus are intrinsic to the gospel, the church cannot be the church if it lacks a visible witness to the rejection of violence.

On the other hand, if the gospel envisions primarily the salvation of individuals, then the social dimensions of Christian faith are a step removed from experience with Christ. In this case, an individual can voluntarily choose salvation without yet broaching a social question, such as the rejection of violence. When such saved individuals then band together in the church, the social dimensions of the gospel are secondary considerations. The question of violence is then not definitional for the church. Rejecting violence is an option, but failing to choose this option does not challenge the church's integrity.

Given Bender's insistence on discipleship as the essence of Christianity and nonresistance as a specific application of Christian discipleship, there is no doubt that Bender would opt for the formulation that proclaims the church as intrinsic to the gospel. However, the church as the voluntary assembly of the saved also fits Bender's description of the voluntary church of truly converted individuals committed to holy living.

The distinction between these differing ecclesiologies can take several forms. I recall a comment made by a colleague during a heated disagreement over such central theological issues as atonement and whether nonviolence is intrinsic to the gospel. My colleague said, "But at least we can *worship* together."

That comment has remained with me for a long time. Its meaning depends on the ecclesiology behind it. On the one hand, it may reflect a primarily individual and experiential understanding of the gospel, with social and ethical questions and doctrinal issues relegated to a secondary status. Christian unity then is then located in a worship experience that supersedes the impetus to struggle with social implications. One can experience unity in a worship experience *because* the social issues are not intrinsic to the gospel and to the church. On the other hand, my colleague's comment might suggest that because the gospel has clear social implications, a shared worship experience of the grace by which God creates and assembles the believing people might undergird our commitment to continue to struggle with the issues.

These two interpretations reflect the two models of voluntary church that I have sketched. My point is not that consensus on social issues is required or must always precede communion. It is rather to recognize that the social implications of the gospel imply that the church as a witnessing community is intrinsically linked to the gospel. It is really a question about the nature of the church.[27]

Remarks from Archbishop Desmond Tutu illustrate a concept of the church with specific social concerns that is intrinsic to the gospel. Describing Jesus as "the man for others," Tutu remarked: "We qualify ourselves for heaven by whether we have fed the hungry, clothed the naked, or visited the sick and those imprisoned." Jesus cannot be accused of "using religion as a form of escapism from the harsh realities of life. . . . Jesus was heir to the prophetic tradition. . . [The prophets] all condemned as worthless religiosity a concern with offering God worship when we were unmindful of the sociopolitical implications of our religion."

Yet, Tutu added, this social agenda is "only half the truth" about Jesus. He was also a "man of prayer, a man of God. . . . So we conclude that prayer and spirituality were central in the life of our Lord and that indeed he could have been the man for others only because first and foremost he had been the man of God." Tutu asserted that the followers of Jesus can only do likewise: "This twofold movement and pattern in our Lord's life must be ours as well." He noted that in the Council of Churches of South Africa, "an authentic spirituality is central and crucial. . . Our belief is that a relevant and authentic spirituality cannot but constrain us to be involved, . . . in the sociopolitical realm." In Tutu's words, "It is not our political creed that makes us be involved as we are with the families of political prisoners and those detained without trial . . . . No, it is not our politics. It is our Christian faith that says, 'Thus saith the Lord.'"[28]

Evangelical historian Timothy L. Smith poses the question of the relevance of these two versions of the voluntary church in another way. He describes North American evangelicals by way of a threefold definition, which has characterized them since the eighteenth century: "commitment to scriptural authority, the experience of regeneration or 'new life in Christ,' and the passion for evangelism." Smith attributes these characteristics to four groups of evangelicals. The fourth category consists of "Mennonites, Brethren, and Quakers," the so-called "peace churches."[29] Such a description invites Mennonites and other peace churches to accept an identity within a widely recognized and accepted grouping of North American denominations, namely evangelicals.

That opportunity for a wider identity also poses a significant question to Mennonites and to peace churches generally: how seriously they regard the social implications of the gospel—and the church—to be integral to what it means to be Christian. Smith's definition of *evangelical* lacks a concept of the church. By not mentioning the social dimensions of faith, such as pacifism, Smith's definition relegates the rejection of violence to the periphery. Thus it does not affect the unity between evangelical communions.

It appears that the understanding of the church assumed within this definition is that of a group created by men and women: a group in which social issues—at least the rejection of violence, which should be a central concern of Mennonites—is not intrinsic to the gospel. For Mennonites to accept Smith's definition of them as evangelical would be to accept an identity that discounts the rejection of violence with respect to the gospel of Jesus Christ.

However, Smith's additional comments reveal sensitivity to this problem. His description of competing evangelical groups aims to promote unity among evangelical groups. Behind this push is a recognition that militarism and war, which have been supported by most evangelical groups, have brought humanity to the brink of destruction. In the face of that threat, Smith writes, "I think that history has forced us into a corner where we have no alternative but the ethics of Jesus." Thus he observes: "A prayerful and concerned repentance of our warlikeness, among both ecumenical and evangelical Protestants, may also be the avenue to rapprochement"—not only among evangelicals but also with Roman Catholics, Muslims, "justifiably angry Palestinian refugees," and Jews.[30]

Peace church adherents can only affirm such words. Nonetheless, a fundamental question remains: Is or is not the rejection of violence and war intrinsic to the gospel of Jesus Christ? Smith's definition of what it means to be evangelical does not broach that question. By omitting it, even when he includes a later testimony about the need to reject violence, Smith allows for Christian unity apart from stands taken on that issue.

Mennonites still have to make a decision about whether unity with some wider evangelical grouping is more important than the understanding that nonviolence is intrinsic to the gospel of Jesus Christ. Smith's inclusion of Mennonites in his definition of evangelicals forces us to decide again whether the church as a visible witness to nonviolence is integral to the gospel.

My view is not a rejection of Smith's description, nor a conclusion that Mennonites ought not call themselves evangelicals. However, by describing Mennonites with this term, Smith has not yet said anything distinctive about them. The term *evangelical* as defined by Smith does not get at what I believe is and should be the heart of Christian understanding for Mennonites: namely, that the social teaching of Jesus, especially his rejection of violence, is integral to the good news of Jesus Christ. In our collective haste to apologize for ethnic roots (an unnecessary apology, in my view), I hope that we do not meld into a larger U.S. identity which will erode the truly essential character of Christian faith in Mennonite understanding.

The Inadequacy of "Separation of Church and State"

Closely related to the distinction between two versions of the voluntary church is the issue of the church stance in relation to the social order.

For most of Anabaptist history since the Reformation—at least in North America, where both the U.S. and Canadian constitutions enshrine separation of church and state—it has been assumed that that problem had been solved. After the initial failure to reform the mass church, sixteenth-century Anabaptists came to the position that we now call separation of church and state. For Mennonites (as well as the Church of the Brethren and others), this idea has been a cardinal principle, restated with renewed visibility in Bender's Anabaptist Vision. The formulation of church-state separation, however, has lost much of its cutting edge because North American society as a whole also espouses that principle.

Because it seems almost universally acknowledged, the concept of church-state separation is not the most helpful way to get at the issues that Anabaptists, Mennonites, Brethren, and other peace church adherents historically have tried to address. A more telling question is to ask whether the social concerns of Christian faith are expressed in ways shaped by the church (and frequently through structures of the church), or by the social order (and through the structures of the social order). Does the church expect the state to do the work of the church by instituting laws to promote church positions: promoting prayer in public schools, teaching Judeo-Christian morality, prohibiting abortion, or banning ideas that some Christians find offensive, such as evolution?

When the question is posed in this way, it is axiomatic that if the church is intrinsic to the gospel, and if the social dimensions of faith (such as nonviolence) are intrinsic to the gospel, then Christian social concerns are expressed in structures of the church or in ways shaped by the church.[31] By contrast, the church that is the voluntary assembly of the saved can fit comfortably into the social order, and can coexist with contemporary forms of the state church, since the social dimensions of Christian faith are a step removed from the gospel, which saves individuals. Because the social dimensions of faith (such as nonviolence) are not intrinsic to the gospel, a voluntary assembly of the saved can assume that its members will express their social concerns through the structures of the social order, an assumption also made by the established or state church.

The church whose social concerns are expressed through the church, or in ways shaped by the church, can envision challenging the social order. The church conceived as the assembly of the saved, in which social dimensions of the Christian faith are secondary to the gospel, exists much more comfortably with the social order. Since social questions are secondary to the saving relationship between God and the individual, a person in the assembly of the saved has less impetus to challenge the social order. This voluntary assembly of the saved can coexist with the social order in much the same way as the state church. If saving faith is primarily individual and lacks intrinsically social dimensions, a challenge to the social order is not required. By contrast, if the gospel has intrinsic social dimensions, then some level of confrontation between church and society is inevitable.

Again, while both models assume voluntary faith, they set up potentially different understandings of the way that individuals and the church relate to the social order. If social dimensions of faith are intrinsic to the gospel and thus the church, the church is clearly an alternative to the social order; Jesus represented the reign of God in a fallen world precisely because the world did not recognize God's reign. By contrast, the voluntary church composed of saved individuals has the potential to integrate itself into the social order.[32] If the social dimensions of faith are not intrinsic to the gospel, an individual may claim voluntary faith while allowing the social order to define social ethics. In this case, the voluntary assembly of the saved has a social stance parallel to that of the state church.

A student once stated the view that the difference between the mass or state church and the voluntary, believers church was the personal commitment, sincerity, and intensity of the members' individual faith. In other words, the state church consisted of nominal believers, whereas people in the voluntary church have sincere, personal faith.

If the student was correct, the social order defines Christian social ethics. I dissent. Sincerity is not enough; one still has to state *what* one is personally and sincerely committed to—the ethics of the social order or the ethics of Jesus that are expressed via the church. Not to define it explicitly is to allow the ethics of the social order to prevail. In such a case, the church of voluntary faith can then support and identify with the social order, as does the state church.

An intense personal experience of faith can strengthen one's commitment to the nonviolent church. Or it can undergird one's willingness to carry out a military mission for the nation,[33] whether as a private in a foxhole or the commander in chief in the White House, praying before the war starts.

Both pairs of images conform to Bender's description of the church in the second of Anabaptist Vision's three points: that is, a voluntary church composed of truly converted persons committed to holy living. I suggest that the ethos of Bender's epoch made the potential ambiguity much less apparent than it is now, when Mennonites were a much more rural and separate people.

In less than a generation, as was noted in chapter 5, the marker of plain dress has virtually disappeared from the Mennonite Church. Meanwhile, both it and the General Conference Mennonite Church, presently in the process of integration into one denomination, have imbibed deeply of modern technology and culture. Without the former external boundary markers, numbers of modern Mennonites are left wondering what the church is, where it is, and how to preserve it.

As noted earlier, these cultural changes are not necessarily bad. They do, however, render the question of ecclesiology (as well as theology) much more acute than it used to be.

Again, if Anabaptists and Mennonites share a foundational theology with some version of Protestantism, then the demise of ethnicity leaves them without a peace church foundation. They really are just one more brand of American Protestantism. In such a case the unique points of Anabaptist Vision are of limited importance, perhaps a piece of the gospel but certainly less than the whole of it.[34]

As I indicated earlier, however, I believe that there are links between ecclesiology and the formulations on the classic theological issues. If social issues are intrinsic to the gospel, if the rejection of violence is intrinsic to who Jesus is, then the church shaped by that gospel will have a distinctive perspective on Christology and atonement. When ecclesiology and gospel are linked, then the unique dimensions of Anabaptist Vision are not a truncated gospel. Instead they are the framework that shapes our discussions and formulations of the other issues. And the effort to articulate a specifically peace church or believers church view of Christology and atonement is a part of recognizing the voluntary church as a comprehensive worldview that exists as an alternative to that of the established church and the theology that emerged from it.

To be sure, Harold Bender did not take the step of articulating alternative formulations of Christology and atonement, and in fact he did not ask about unique Anabaptist perspectives on the classic issues. That he did not does not mean that we should not, when the ambiguity of his ecclesiological image compels us to pursue it. In our postmodern context, the desire for an Anabaptist, Mennonite theology which both addresses the world and makes sense of the tradition impels us to pursue the question of a specific voluntary church perspective on Christology and atonement.

FAITHFULNESS

The answer to the question of Mennonite identity is not to restore ethnicity. Nor should we seek a unique identity simply for its own sake. Uniqueness in and of itself says nothing about truth or faithfulness. The real issue concerns the ongoing effort and intent of the church to be faithful to Jesus Christ. The answer to the demise of ethnic identity is to renew our understanding of the social dimensions that are intrinsic to the gospel. This renewed church will remain as a distinct witness to North American society: a witness not located in what others consider quaint, such as food or rural lifestyle, but in actions for peace and justice.

Will Mennonites follow this path of faithfulness, or will we be comfortable as a church built by human beings and concerned only with personal salvation? The way we recognize and respond to the ecclesiological ambiguity of Anabaptist Vision, as well as to the ambiguity of contemporary Mennonite vision statements, will determine the shape of Mennonite identity in the twenty-first century. It will determine whether Mennonites develop a specific peace church theology or adopt a theology that allows them to blend smoothly into the North American world, which makes faith in violence its foundational belief.

NOTES

FOREWORD

1. See, for example, Robert S. Paul, *The Atonement and the Sacraments* (Abingdon Press, 1960), Chapter 1, and pp. 92-96 and 253-7.

2. John H. Yoder, *The Politics of Jesus* (Eerdmans: 1994), chapter 8 and 12.

INTRODUCTION

1. A selection of papers from the conference was published in Gerald Biesecker-Mast and Susan Biesecker-Mast, eds., *Anabaptists and Postmodernity*, The C. Henry Smith Series, vol. 1 (Telford, Pa.: Pandora Press U.S., 2000).

2. John Howard Yoder, "Civil Religion in America," in *The Priestly Kingdom: Social Ethics as Gospel* (Notre Dame, Ind.: University of Notre Dame, 1984), 172-95; John A. Lapp, "Civil Religion is but Old Establishment Writ Large," in *Kingdom, Cross and Community: Essays on Mennonite Themes in Honor of Guy F. Hershberger*, John Richard Burkholder and Calvin Redekop, eds.(Scottdale, Pa.: Herald Press, 1976), 196-207.

3. Susan Biesecker-Mast, "Postmodernism: How We Came to Select Cars and Communion on a Similar Basis," *Christian Living* 45, no. 8 (December 1998): 4-7.

4. Ibid., 5.

5. Ibid.

6. Ibid.

7. Ibid., 6.

8. Although postmodern thinkers are suspicious about the idea of one truth (whether religious or philosophical), they are nonetheless interested in truths, be they philosophical, religious, or historical. As an example, one need only note the turn to religious truths in the recent work of Jacques Derrida.

9. John Howard Yoder, "'But We Do See Jesus?': The Particularity of Incarnation and the Universality of Truth," in *The Priestly Kingdom: Social Ethics as Gospel* (Notre Dame, Ind.: University of Notre Dame, 1984), 62.

10. Ibid., 61.

11. Daniel Kauffman, *Manual of Bible Doctrines, Setting Forth the General Principles of the Plan of Salvation* (Elkhart, Ind.: Mennonite Publishing Co., 1898); Daniel Kauffman, *Bible Doctrine: A Treatise on the Great Doctrines of the Bible* (Scottdale, Pa.: Mennonite Publishing House, 1914); Daniel Kauffman, *Doctrines of the Bible: A Brief Discussion of the Teachings of God's Word* (Scottdale, Pa.: Mennonite Publishing House, 1929).

12. John Christian Wenger, *Introduction to Theology: An Interpretation of the Doctrinal Content of Scripture, Written to Strengthen a Childlike Faith in Christ* (Scottdale, Pa.: Herald Press, 1954).

13. Edmund G. Kaufman, *Basic Christian Convictions* (North Newton, Kan.: Bethel College, 1972).

14. Al Keim, "The Anabaptist Vision: The History of a New Paradigm," *Conrad Grebel Review* 12, no. 3 (Fall 1994), 240-42; Albert N. Keim, *Harold S. Bender 1897-1962* (Scottdale, Pa.: Herald Press, 1998), 165-66, 178-82.

15. James M. Stayer, "The Swiss Brethren: An Exercise in Historical Definition," *Church History* 47.2 (June 1978), 175.

16. Harold S. Bender, "The Anabaptist Vision," *Church History* 13, no. 1 (March 1944): 3-24; Harold S. Bender, "The Anabaptist Vision," *Mennonite Quarterly Review* 18, no. 2 (April 1944): 67-88. Reprinted with slight revisions as Harold S. Bender, *The Anabaptist Vision* (Scottdale, Pa.: Herald Press, 1944). Citations in the following are taken from the reprinted text. As the foregoing indicates, Bender's Anabaptist Vision originally emerged in the form of a pamphlet. Over time, however, the Vision has become part of common Anabaptist parlance. Consistent with this nearly generic ubiquity, except when context inescapably points to the pamphlet itself, the style from this point forward will be to use roman type and not italics in referring to the Vision.

17. The paradigmatic statement of diversity and pluralism is James M. Stayer, Werner O. Packull, and Klaus Deppermann, "From Monogenesis to Polygenesis: The Historical Discussion of Anabaptist Origins," *Mennonite Quarterly Review* 49, no. 2 (April 1975): 83-122 . For a historical survey of Anabaptists written from a "polygenesis" perspective, see J. Denny Weaver, *Becoming Anabaptist: The Origin and Significance of Sixteenth-Century Anabaptism* (Scottdale, Pa.: Herald Press, 1987).

18. The papers from that conference were published in Willard Swartley, ed., *Explorations of Systematic Theology from Mennonite Perspectives*, Occasional Papers no. 7 (Elkhart, Indiana: Institute of Mennonite Studies, 1984).

19. Gordon D. Kaufman, *Systematic Theology: A Historicist Perspective*, reprint 1978 (New York: Scribner's, 1968), 219-22, 493-95, 397n, 449n, 453n.

20. C. Norman Kraus, *Jesus Christ Our Lord: Christology from a Disciple's Perspective*, rev. ed., reprint, 1987 (Scottdale, Pa.: Herald Press, 1990).

21. George R. Brunk II, *A Trumpet Sound: A Crisis Among Mennonites on the Doctrine of Christ* (Harrisonburg, Va: Fellowship of Concerned Mennonites, 1988); Arthur G. Hunsberger, *Christ or Kraus? A Critique of Kraus on Christology* (Harrisonburg, Va.: Fellowship of Concerned Mennonites, 1989); Glenn Lehman, "Brunk and Kraus: Two Paths to Christology," *Gospel Herald*, (7 March 1989), 164-66.

22. Two early efforts that begin to clarify these options are A. James Reimer, "Toward Christian Theology from a Diversity of Mennonite Perspectives," *Conrad Grebel Review* 6, no. 2 (Spring 1988): 147-59; and J. Denny Weaver, "The Search for a Mennonite Theology," in *Mennonite World Handbook*, Diether Götz Lichdi, eds. (Carol Stream, Il.: Mennonite World Conference, 1990), 143-52.

23. Thomas N. Finger, *Christian Theology: An Eschatological Approach, Vol. 1, 2* (Scottdale, Pa.: Herald Press, 1985-89).

24. Daniel Liechty, *Theology in Postliberal Perspective* (London: SCM Press, 1990).

25. Gordon D. Kaufman, *In Face of Mystery: A Constructive Theology* (Cambridge, Mass.: Harvard, 1993).

26. See for example, A. James Reimer, "Trinitarian Orthodoxy, Constantinianism, and Theology from a Radical Protestant Perspective," in *Faith to Creed: Ecumenical Perspectives on the Affirmation of the Apostolic Faith in the Fourth Century*, S. Mark Heim, ed. (Grand Rapids, Mi.: Eerdmans, 1991), 129-61 and A. James Reimer, "Doctrines: What Are They, How Do They Function, and Why Do We Need Them?" *Conrad Grebel Review* 11, no. 1 (Winter 1993): 21-36.

27. J. Denny Weaver, "Christus Victor, Ecclesiology, and Christology," *Mennonite Quarterly Review* 68, no. 3 (July 1994): 277-90; "Some Theological Implications of Christus Victor," *Mennonite Quarterly Review* 68, no. 4 (October 1994): 483-99; and *Keeping Salvation Ethical: Mennonite and Amish Atonement Theology in the Late Nineteenth Century*, foreward C. Norman Kraus (Scottdale, Pa.: Herald Press, 1997), 39-49.

28. See note 16.

CHAPTER ONE

1. This chapter is a revised version of J. Denny Weaver, "The United States Shape of Mennonite Theologizing: Some Preliminary Observations," *Mennonite Quarterly Review* 73, no. 3 (July 1999): pp. 631-44. (Its earliest version was presented at the conference "One People, Many Voices" at Columbia Bible College, Abbotsford, British Columbia, 9 May 1998.)

2. An earlier version of this description of two national characters appeared as Harry Huebner and J. Denny Weaver, "We Dare Not Restructure Along National Boundaries," *Gospel Herald*, 22 (October 1991), pp. 8-10; Harry Huebner and J. Denny Weaver, "Don't Stop at the Border," *The Mennonite* 106, no. 20 (22 October 1991): pp. 468-69.

3. Catherine L. Albanese, *America: Religions and Religion* (Belmont, Calif.: Wadsworth, 1992), ch. 12.

4. Russell E. Richey and Donald G. Jones, eds., *American Civil Religion* (New York: Harper & Row, 1974), 6. An extensive literature is available on civil religion. Although the term first appeared in an essay by Jean-Jacques Rousseau, the current widespread use of the term was stimulated by Robert N. Bellah's "Civil Religion in America," *Daedalus* 96.1 (Winter 1967), 1-21. This watershed article has been reprinted several times, including Richey and Jones, eds., *American Civil Religion*, 21-44. This book remains one of the best introductions to the topic of civil religion. Among a host of additional books are Catherine L. Albanese, *Sons of the Fathers: The Civil Religion of the American Revolution* (Philadelphia: Temple University Press, 1976); Robert N. Bellah, *The Broken Covenant: American Civil Religion in Time of Trial* (New York: Crossroad, 1975); Robert N. Bellah and Phillip E. Hammond, *Varieties of Civil Religion* (San Francisco: Harper & Row, 1980); Conor Cruise O'Brien, *God Land: Reflections on Religion and Nationalism* (Cambridge, Mass.: Harvard University Press, 1988); William G. McLoughlin, *Revivals, Awakenings and Reform: An Essay on Religion and Social Change in America, 1607-1977*, Chicago history of American religion (Chicago: University of Chicago Press, 1978); Sidney E. Mead, *The Nation with the Soul of a Church* (New York: Harper & Row, 1975); Mark A. Noll, Nathan O. Hatch, and George M. Marsden, *The Search for Christian America* (Colorado Springs: Helmers & Howard, 1989); John F. Wilson, *Public Religion in American Culture* (Philadelphia: Temple University Press, 1979).

Among writings which have shaped my critique of civil religion are: Stanley Hauerwas, *After Christendom? How the Church is to Behave If Freedom, Justice, and a Christian Nation Are Bad Ideas* (Nashville: Abingdon, 1991); Donald B. Kraybill, *Our Star-Spangled Faith*, Intro. Martin E. Marty (Scottdale, Pa.: Herald Press, 1976); John A. Lapp, "Civil Religion is but Old Establishment Writ Large," in *Kingdom, Cross and Community: Essays on Mennonite Themes in Honor of Guy F. Hershberger*, John Richard Burkholder and Calvin Redekop (Scottdale, Pa.: Herald Press, 1976), 196-207; John Howard Yoder, ed ,"Civil Religion in America," in *The Priestly Kingdom: Social Ethics as Gospel* (Notre Dame, Ind.: University of Notre Dame, 1984), 172-95.

5. John Howard Yoder, "Civil Religion"; Lapp, "Civil Religion is but Old Establishment Writ Large."

6. Lyman Beecher, "On Disestablishment in Connecticut," John F. Wilson, ed. in *Church and State in American History* (Boston: D.C. Heath, 1965), 92-93.

7. In my congregation of First Mennonite in Bluffton, Ohio, I have heard stories from a pacifist couple who were members of a prominent U.S. denomination at the time of the 1991 Gulf War. They experienced so much hostility from the congregation for their pacifist stance that they were on the point of leaving when the war ended. Two pacifist teachers have told of being harassed in the teachers' lounge during the Gulf War—one for refusing to support the troops by displaying a patriotic symbol in her classroom window. Her refusal meant that the school could not convey one hundred percent support of the war.

8. On the contrasts between the United States and Canada, see William A. Stahl, "The New Christian Right," *The Ecumenist* 25, no. 6 (September-October 1987): 81-87; Mark A. Noll, "The End of Canadian History?" *First Things* 22 (April 1992): 29-36; John Cruickshank, "Canada's Search for Identity," *Christian Science Monitor*, (26 February 1992):19.

9. Roland H. Bainton, "The Left Wing of the Reformation," in *Studies on the Reformation*, Roland H. Bainton, Collected Papers in Church History, Series 2 (Boston: Beacon Press, 1963), 119-29.

10. John S. Coffman, "Spirit of Progress," *Christian Monitor* 5, no. 6 (June 1913): 179.

11. C. H. Wedel, *Die Geschichte der Täufer und Mennoniten in der Schweiz, in Mähren, in Süddeutschland, Am Niederrhein und in Nordamerika*, Abriß der Geschichte der Mennoniten, vol. 4 (Newton, Kan.: Bethel College, 1904), 204.

12. C. Henry Smith, *Mennonite Country Boy: The Early Years of C. Henry Smith*, Mennonite Historical Series (Newton, Kan.: Faith and Life Press, 1962), 199.

13. Harold S. Bender, *The Anabaptist Vision* (Scottdale, Pa.: Herald Press, 1944), 4.

14. See James C. Juhnke, "Mennonite Benevolence and Revitalization in the Wake of World War I," *Mennonite Quarterly Review* 60, no. 1 (January 1986): 26; James C. Juhnke, *Vision, Doctrine, War: Mennonite Identity and Organization in America 1890-1930*, Mennonite Experience in America, vol. 3 (Scottdale, Pa.: Herald Press, 1989), 254.

15. When it appeared, the Anabaptist Vision underscored a distinct identity for Mennonites, even while stating that they shared a theological core with mainstream Protestantism. In recent years, it would appear that Mennonite observers bent on moving Mennonites closer to the mainstream have emphasized Bender's agreements with mainstream Protestantism. For discussion of the two faces of Anabaptist Vision, see my Epilogue on the ambiguity of ecclesiology in the Anabaptist Vision.

16. For development of these two sets of lists, see chapter 3 to follow.

17. Thomas N. Finger, *Christian Theology: An Eschatological Approach, Vol. 1, 2* (Scottdale, Pa.: Herald Press, 1985-89).

18. A more thorough analysis and description of Finger's methodology and synthesis appears in chapter 2.

19. John H. Yoder, *Preface to Theology: Christology and Theological Method* (Elkhart, Ind.: Goshen Biblical Seminary; distributed by Co-op Bookstore, 1981), 121-58.

20. In October 1980, Bluffton College hosted a Believers Church Conference that examined the question, "Is there a Believers Church christology?" In remarks added to his conference keynote address at a later date, John H. Yoder noted that one element that made relevant the question of the conference was the "narrative and relativizing approach" he had "taken to the development of early Christian

dogma, with special reference to the development of the christological creedal statements," in his *Preface to Theology*. John H. Yoder, "That Household We Are," unpublished paper (1980), 9.

21. See J. Denny Weaver, "Christology in Historical Perspective," in *Jesus Christ and the Mission of the Church: Contemporary Anabaptist Perspectives*, Erland Waltner, ed. (Newton, Kan.: Faith and Life Press, 1990), 83-105; J. Denny Weaver, "Atonement for the NonConstantinian Church," *Modern Theology* 6, no. 4 (July 1990): 307-23; J. Denny Weaver, "Christus Victor, Ecclesiology, and Christology," *Mennonite Quarterly Review* 68, no. 3 (July 1994): 277-90.

22. I make a distinction between saying the creeds are not required and saying they are wrong. If one assumes their worldview and frame of reference, and if one is asking the specific question that they address, then their answer is probably the best response in that context. However, being right in those particular circumstances does not make them a general, required touchstone of all future christological thought.

23. I am borrowing the image of the "bulldozer of modernity" from Vincent Harding who used it in this very context at a conference in 1994.

24. Whereas civil religion in the United States poses a direct challenge to Mennonites as a peace church, the cultural mosaic of Canada poses an indirect challenge. As noted earlier, the absence of a direct challenge makes it possible for Mennonites to lose sight of the distinction between the church and the surrounding societal environment. When this happens, it becomes more difficult for the church to see the need for prophetic critique.

25. (That was the import of a presentation by Rachel Reesor, which comprised the other half of the session at the Abbotsford conference at which this paper was first presented [see note 1]). For published version, see Rachel Reesor, "A Mennonite Theological Response to a Canadian Context: A. James Reimer," *Mennonite Quarterly Review* 73, no. 3 (July 1999): 644-54.

26. Recent actions by the Mennonite Church and General Conference Mennonite Church to create separate national bodies (Mennonite Church Canada, Mennonite Church USA) within a new, integrated Mennonite denomination appear to be following the path of emphasizing national identity. In a time of postmodern uncertainty about Mennonite identity, it is perhaps not surprising that nationalism—one of the primary institutions of modernity—may play a determinative role in structuring the newly integrated church.

27. For references, see chapter 5.

CHAPTER TWO

1. This chapter is a revised version of J. Denny Weaver, "The General Versus the Particular: Exploring Assumptions in 20th-Century Mennonite Theologizing," *The Conrad Grebel Review* 17, no. 2 (1999 Spring 1999): 28-51. (An earlier form was presented at the conference "Mennonites, Brethren and Twentieth-Century Theologies" at the Young Center, Elizabethtown College,

Elizabethtown, Pa., 19-21 June 1997.)

2. John Horsch, *The Mennonite Church and Modernism* (Scottdale, Pa.: Mennonite Publishing. House, 1924), 7-8.

3. John Horsch, *Mennonites in Europe* (Scottdale, Pa.: Mennonite Publishing House, 1942), 325, 370-72, 378-80.

4. Ibid., 373, 359-69.

5. Ibid., 354.

6. J. E. Hartzler, "Essential Fundamentals of Christian Faith," in *Report of Third All-Mennonite Convention Held in First Mennonite Church, Bluffton, Ohio, September 2-3, 1919*, A. S. Bechtel, ed. (Bluffton, Ohio, 1919), 84.

7. Horsch, *Mennonite Church and Modernism*, 74.

8. Ibid., 68.

9. Daniel Kauffman, "Upon What Fundamentals Should All Christian People Agree?" *Gospel Herald* 3, no. 19 (11 August 1910), 292, 302; Daniel Kauffman, "Upon What Fundamentals Should All Christian People Agree? II," *Gospel Herald* 3, no. 20 (18 August 1910), 307, 317; Daniel Kauffman, "Upon What Fundamentals Should All Christian People Agree? III," *Gospel Herald* 3, no. 21 (25 August 1910), 325.

10. Daniel Kauffman, "The Mennonite Church and Current Issues," *Gospel Herald* 9, no. 37 (14 December 1916), 682.

11. Ibid.

12. Daniel Kauffman, "Two Kinds of Fundamentalists," *Gospel Herald* 12, no. 51 (18 March 1920), 961.

13. Daniel Kauffman, *The Mennonite Church and Current Issues* (Scottdale, Pa.: Mennonite Publishing House, 1923), 18-26.

14. Kauffman, *Current Issues*, 26. Emphasis Kauffman's.

15. Daniel Kauffman, "Unfundamental Fundamentalists," *Gospel Herald* 24, no. 48 (25 February 1932), 1025-26.

16. Daniel Kauffman, "Real Fundamentalism," *Gospel Herald* 34, no. 4 (24 April 1941), 81.

17. Daniel Kauffman's three volumes of Bible doctrines (see below) do not use the language of two lists. Yet their outlines of doctrines follow the pattern of listing what would be the general Christian doctrines followed by the particular doctrines and emphases of Mennonites. Despite this, the titles of these volumes clearly indicate that whatever the internal subdivisions, all contents are necessary as biblical.

These three volumes also retained the category of "restrictions." Restrictions were negative commands of scripture and contained specifically Mennonite distinctives that when obeyed would keep the Christian saved. The restrictions were one element in completing the general gospel borrowed from revivalism or fundamentalism. Restrictions included nonresistance, nonconformity to the world, nonswearing of oaths, not suing at law, not belonging to secret societies, and not buying life insurance. For more, see Daniel Kauffman, "Restrictions," *The Gospel Witness* 1, no. 23 (6 September 1905): 178, 184; Daniel Kauffman,

Bible Doctrines Briefly Stated, Second ed. (Scottdale, Pa.: Mennonite Publishing House, 1922), 27; Daniel Kauffman, *Manual of Bible Doctrines, Setting Forth the General Principles of the Plan of Salvation* (Elkhart, Ind.: Mennonite Publishing Co., 1898), 12-14; Daniel Kauffman, *Bible Doctrine: A Treatise on the Great Doctrines of the Bible* (Scottdale, Pa.: Mennonite Publishing House, 1914), 458, 510-87; Daniel Kauffman, *Doctrines of the Bible: A Brief Discussion of the Teachings of God's Word* (Scottdale, Pa.: Mennonite Publishing House, 1929), 490-544. For John Horsch's discussion of restrictions, see Horsch, *Mennonite Church and Modernism*, 92-100.

18. Harold S. Bender, *The Anabaptist Vision* (Scottdale, Pa.: Herald Press, 1944), 13.

19. Harold S. Bender, "The Mennonites of the United States," *Mennonite Quarterly Review* 11, no. 1 (January 1937): 79.

20. Harold S. Bender, "'Walking in the Resurrection': The Anabaptist Doctrine of Regeneration and Discipleship," *Mennonite Quarterly Review* 35, no. 2 (April 1961): 102.

21. Al Keim's biography of Bender makes clear that Bender's own theology was orthodox and that he developed significant components of it from seminary studies at Princeton and graduate study in Europe. See Albert N. Keim, *Harold S. Bender 1897-1962* (Scottdale, Pa.: Herald Press, 1998), 152-56, and comments throughout.

22. Bender, *Anabaptist Vision*, 20, 13.

23. John C. Wenger, *Glimpses of Mennonite History and Doctrine*, 2nd ed., rev. and enlarged (Scottdale, Pa.: Herald Press, 1947), 137, 147.

24. Ibid., 137-47.

25. Ibid., 147-79. On restrictions, see note 17 above.

26. The sense that the distinct Mennonite practices are indeed part of a full-orbed biblical faith is clear in Wenger's *Introduction to Theology*. This book claims the Bible as its foundational reference point, and does not distinguish general Christian from Mennonite doctrines and practices. The particular practices of nonresistance, nonconformity, and so on are no longer called restrictions. They appear in a section on "The Nature and Function of the Church," which is found in Part III on "God as Redeemer." See John Christian Wenger, *Introduction to Theology: A Brief Introduction to the Doctrinal Content of the Scripture Written in the Anabaptist-Mennonite Tradition*, reprint, 1954 (Scottdale, Pa.: Herald Press, 1966), 225-27.

27. Ronald J. Sider, "Evangelicalism and the Mennonite Tradition," in *Evangelicalism and Anabaptism*, C. Norman Kraus, ed. (Scottdale, Pa.: Herald Press, 1979), 159-68.

28. Ibid., 149-50.

29. Ibid., 150.

30. Ibid., 155.

31. Ronald J. Sider, *Genuine Christianity* (Grand Rapids, Mich.: Zondervan,

1996), 104-08.

32. Ibid., 104.

33. Sider, *Genuine Christianity*, 106-07. Quote, 107

34. Rodney J. Sawatsky, "Defining 'Mennonite' Diversity and Unity," *Mennonite Quarterly Review* 57, no. 3 (July 1983): 285-87; Rodney Sawatsky, *Authority and Identity: The Dynamics of the General Conference Mennonite Church*, Cornelius H. Wedel Historical Series, vol. 1 (North Newton, Kan.: Bethel College, 1987), 63-66.

35. For the rise of state church Christendom and then the Waldensian alternative which merged into Anabaptism of the 16th century, see C. H. Wedel, *Die Geschichte Ihrer Vorfahren Bis Zum Beginn Des Täufertums Im 16. Jahrhundert*, Abriß der Geschichte der Mennoniten, vol. 1 (Newton, Kans: Bethel College, 1900). For Wedel's description of the characteristics of *Gemeindechristentum*, see C. H. Wedel, *Randzeichnungen zu Den Geschichten Des Neuen Testaments* (Newton, Kans.: Bethel College, 1900), 60-63, 89-90; Wedel, *Abriß I*, 4-6, 14-16, 28-30; C. H. Wedel, *Die Geschichte Des Täufertums Im 16. Jahrhundert*, Abriß der Geschichte der Mennoniten, vol. 2 (Newton, Kan.: Bethel College, 1902), 149-58, 171-76.

36. C. H. Wedel, *Glaubenslehre*, in 4 Hefte (North Newton, Kans.). For an in-depth analysis of Wedel's theology, see the Wedel sections of J. Denny Weaver, *Keeping Salvation Ethical: Mennonite and Amish Atonement Theology in the Late Nineteenth Century*, foreward C. Norman Kraus (Scottdale, Pa.: Herald Press, 1996).

37. Weaver, *Keeping Salvation Ethical*, 86-91.

38. Hartzler, "Essential Fundamentals," 88.

39. Ibid., 88-91.

40. J. E. Hartzler, "Christian Fundamentals," *The Mennonite* 35, no. 45 (11 November 1920): 4-5; J. E. Hartzler, "Christian Fundamentals," *The Mennonite* 35, no. 46 (18 November 1920): 5; J. E. Hartzler, "Christian Fundamentals," *The Christian Evangel* 10, no. 12 (December 1920): 267-69.

41. J. E. Hartzler, "The Faith of Our Fathers," *Christian Exponent* 1, no. 3 (1 February 1924): 38-39.

42. Ibid., 38.

43. J. E. Hartzler, "Philosophy in the Mennonite Tradition," *Mennonite Life* 3, no. 2 (April 1948): 44. For a third listing of these principles of Anabaptist faith that are added to the Protestant core see J. E. Hartzler, "Witmarsum Theological Seminary," in *Report of Fourth All-Mennonite Convention Held in Eighth Street Mennonite Church, Goshen, Indiana* (n.p.: n.p., 1922), 44.

44. J. E. Hartzler's theology was not as liberal as many of his contemporaries believed or feared. While he was a cultural liberal and accommodator, his specific views on the classic issues were orthodox, if not as sharply defined as fundamentalists wanted. See Janeen Bertsche Johnson, "J. E. Hartzler: The Change in His Approach to Doctrine," unpublished paper (1986).

45. Hartzler, "Faith of Our Fathers," 38.

46. Hartzler, "Essential Fundamentals," 89-90.

47. Edmund G. Kaufman, *Basic Christian Convictions* (North Newton, Kan.: Bethel College, 1972).

48. My reading of Kaufman agrees with the analysis of James C. Juhnke, *Creative Crusader: Edmund G. Kaufman and Mennonite Community*, ed. John D. Thiesen, Cornelius H. Wedel Historical Series (North Newton, Kan.: Bethel College, 1994), 270-73. Quote, 271.

49. Edmund G. Kaufman, *Basic Christian Convictions*, 201-02.

50. The materials for *Basic Christian Convictions* came from the course that Kaufman taught for many years at Bethel College. James Juhnke notes that "Kaufman both added to, and subtracted from, the materials from his course in ways that made the book more ecumenical and less sectarian. One major subtraction was the unit on 'the Mennonite Church,'" which was reduced to an extended footnote. Juhnke, *Creative Crusader*, 270-71.

51. Juhnke, *Creative Crusader*, 108.

52. See Chapter 1, note 20.

53. A. James Reimer, "Trinitarian Orthodoxy, Constantinianism, and Theology from a Radical Protestant Perspective," in *Faith to Creed: Ecumenical Perspectives on the Affirmation of the Apostolic Faith in the Fourth Century*, S. Mark Heim, ed. (Grand Rapids, Mich.: Eerdmans, 1991), 131-40.

54. Ibid., 148, 150-52.

55. Reimer, "Trinitarian Orthodoxy," 142, 150, 152, 156. Quote, 150.

56. Reimer, "Trinitarian Orthodoxy," 150.

57. Ibid., 156-59.

58. Ibid., 161.

59. Ibid., 160.

60. For Reimer's conclusions, see Reimer, "Trinitarian Orthodoxy," 160-61. What I perceive as a different form of the problem between a general core and a specific peace church addition appears in commentary on an analysis of John H. Yoder's thought by Gayle Gerber Koontz. Reimer identifies general revelation, ongoing revelation, final revelation, and special revelation. General revelation "is that which is common to all of us" without regard to "nationality, religion, denomination, sex or class"; ongoing revelation is an acknowledgment that our truth is "always relative and on the way"; final revelation is an eschatological matter, which means that we cannot know the end with clarity, while special revelation refers to Jesus Christ. While Reimer acknowledges with Koontz that "Jesus Christ is Lord" is a confessional claim, he adds that "we need to make this confessional claim in the context of general, ongoing, and final revelation. To do this is to make a general philosophical-theological truth claim." However, this assertion is also problematic for Reimer. It is at this point, he says, that "our peace theology can become idolatrous. How? By absolutizing the finite understanding of the meaning of Christ of one particular minority group within the Christian and religious

world." A. James Reimer, "Response to Gayle Gerber Koontz," *The Conrad Grebel Review* 14, no. 1 (Winter 1996): 88. I suggest that the flaw in Reimer's argument is the unacknowledged contradiction of claiming that general revelation, common to us all, is also identified with the particular, special revelation that is Jesus Christ, which is revelation precisely because it is different from that which is common to all.

61. R. P. C. Hanson, *The Search for the Christian Doctrine of God: The Arian Controversy 318-381* (Edinburgh: T. & T. Clark, 1988), 854.

62. Thomas N. Finger's synthesis contains a great deal of helpful historical and analytical data. Thomas N. Finger, *Christian Theology: An Eschatological Approach*, Vol. 1, 2 (Scottdale, Pa.: Herald Press, 1985-89). For a recent statement of his methodology, see Thomas Finger, "Appropriating Other Traditions While Remaining Anabaptist," *The Conrad Grebel Review* 17, no. 2 (1999 Spring 1999): 52-68. Other examples include Thomas Finger, "The Place to Begin Mennonite Theology," *Gospel Herald*, (30 July 1996), 1-3; Thomas Finger, "From Biblical Intentions to Theological Conceptions: Some Strengths and Some Tensions in Norman Kraus's Christology," *Conrad Grebel Review* 8, no. 1 (Winter 1990): 53-76; Thomas Finger, "Still Something Essential in the Creeds," in *Jesus Christ and the Mission of the Church: Contemporary Anabaptist Perspectives*, Erland Waltner, ed (Newton, Kan.: Faith and Life Press, 1990), 106-14.

63. Quotes from Scott Holland, "Anabaptism as Public Theology," *Conrad Grebel Review* 11, no. 3 (Fall 1993): 269-74. See also Scott Holland, "Theology is a Kind of Writing: The Emergence of Theopoetics," *The Mennonite Quarterly Review* 71, no. 2 (April 1997): 227-41; Scott Holland, "Intellectual and Aesthetic Freedom in the Anabaptist Academy," for conference on Church-Related Institutions (Elizabethtown College, 1996).

64. One might compare, for example, Mennonite and non-Mennonite reviews of Thomas Finger's synthesis. Mennonite reviewers have pointed out its Anabaptist, believers church dimensions along with the imported components. Helmut Harder, "*Christian Theology: An Eschatological Approach*, Volume II, by Thomas N. Finger," review, *Conrad Grebel Review* 8, no. 2 (Spring 1990): 229-31; Dan Liechty, "*Christian Theology: An Eschatological Approach* by Thomas N. Finger," review, *The Mennonite*, (25 September 1990), 426-27; Donald B. Stoesz, "*Christian Theology: An Eschatological Approach*, 2 Vol., by Thomas N. Finger," review, *Mennonite Quarterly Review* 67, no. 1 (January 1990): 104-07. In contrast, a reviewer who is not a Mennonite identified Finger's theological orientation as "generally conservative, favoring a historical premillennial position eschatologically," noted his defense of "inerrancy," and cited his weakening of the atonement section by refusing to emphasize "penal substitutionary" atonement—all positions which identify Finger in terms of a grid from evangelical orthodoxy. Yet the review made no mention at all of Finger's believers church ecclesiology and the insertion of nonviolence into his synthesis. Robert L. Saucy, "Two Innovative Theologies," *Journal of Psychology and Theology* 17, no. 2 (Summer 1989): 187-89.

65. Chapters 3 and 4 include additional discussion of the theological tension of holding together peace church ecclesiology with established church theology.

66. For example, it is quite obvious that since the fourth century, the theology of Western Christianity has accommodated war. The formulas of Christology and atonement, which most often supply the heart of the supposed theology-in-general, are the formulations of the church that began to accommodate violence. Since the basis of Christian faith is Jesus and not formulas which emerge in and after the fourth century, it is quite logical to ask why peace church adherents should base their theology on those violence-accommodating formulas rather than on other options that are based on and shaped more explicitly by the biblical narratives of Jesus.

67. Current efforts to reconstruct theology shaped at least in part by the assumption of nonviolence include John H. Yoder's analysis of classic creeds and creedal statements in John H. Yoder, *Preface to Theology: Christology and Theological Method* (Elkhart, Ind.: Goshen Biblical Seminary; distributed by Co-op Bookstore, 1981), 120-58; C. Norman Kraus, *Jesus Christ Our Lord: Christology from a Disciple's Perspective*, rev. ed., reprint, 1987 (Scottdale, Pa.: Herald Press, 1990); Daniel Liechty, *Theology in Postliberal Perspective* (London: SCM Press, 1990); C. Norman Kraus, *God Our Savior: Theology in a Christological Mode* (Scottdale, Pa.: Herald Press, 1991); J. Denny Weaver, "Christus Victor, Ecclesiology, and Christology," *Mennonite Quarterly Review* 68, no. 3 (July 1994): 277-90; Weaver, *Keeping Salvation Ethical*; James Wm. McClendon, Jr., *Systematic Theology: Ethics*, Systematic Theology, vol. 1 (Nashville: Abingdon, 1986); James Wm. McClendon, Jr., *Systematic Theology: Doctrine*, Systematic Theology, vol. 2 (Nashville: Abingdon, 1994); John Dear, *The God of Peace: Toward a Theology of Nonviolence* (Maryknoll, N.Y.: Orbis, 1994).

Gordon Kaufman's reconstruction of theology is clearly shaped by the assumption of nonviolence, as well as by concerns for social justice and ecology. Gordon D. Kaufman, *In Face of Mystery: A Constructive Theology* (Cambridge, Mass.: Harvard, 1993). However, Kaufman's retention of the world as a whole as the venue of restored humanity and restored community (thus retaining something of Christendom's understanding of the church's relationship to the social order), and his near privileging of Western, technological ways of knowing make it arguable that Kaufman has not entirely surrendered the idea that there is (or ought to be) a theology-in-general.

CHAPTER THREE

1. This chapter is a greatly revised version of J. Denny Weaver, "Amish and Mennonite Soteriology: Revivalism and Free Church Theologizing in the Nineteenth-Century," *Fides et Historia* 27, no. 1 (Winter/Spring 1995): 30-52. Both that essay and the current chapter draw on research developed for J. Denny Weaver, *Keeping Salvation Ethical: Mennonite and Amish Atonement Theology in the Late Nineteenth Century*, (Scottdale, Pa.: Herald Press, 1997).

2. For example, Donald G. Bloesch, *The Evangelical Renaissance* (Grand Rapids, Mich.: William B. Eerdmans Publishing Company, 1973), 60-62; Walter A. Elwell, ed., *Evangelical Dictionary of Theology* (Grand Rapids, Mich.: Baker, 1984), s.v. "Evangelicalism," by Richard V. Pierard.

3. For references, see Weaver, *Keeping Salvation Ethical: Mennonite and Amish Atonement Theology in the Late Nineteenth Century*, 189-216.

4. Anselm, "Why God Became Man," in *A Scholastic Miscellany: Anselm to Ockham*, edited and trans. Eugene R. Fairweather, The Library of Christian Classics (Philadelphia: Westminster, 1956), 100-83.

5. John Holdeman, *A Treatise on Redemption, Baptism, and the Passover and the Lord's Supper* (Carthage, Mo.: self-published, 1890), 7-8.

6. The primary source for Jacob Stauffer's thought is his *Eine Chronik oder Geschicht-Büchlein von der Sogenannten Mennonisten Gemeinde*, (Lancaster, Pa.: Johann Bär, 1855). A facsimile of the 1855 edition was printed in 1972 by Wilson Martin, New Holland, Pa. The facsimile carries no modern date.

7. Stauffer, *Eine Chronik*, 164.

8. Ibid., 22,29,50,64, quote 402.

9. Based on Jesus' words in Matt. 5: 38-48, the historic Mennonite doctrine of nonresistance not only rejected participation in war but also precluded the use of any kind of force or coercive power, such as boycotts, strikes, or lawsuits. Thus nonresistance included pacifism, but pacifism as a distinct position was looked upon with suspicion by the most traditional Mennonites, who saw it as having a political rather than a biblical and theological basis and as not going far enough in its rejection of force and violence.

10. *Eine Chronik*, 78, 80. Stauffer gave the following summary to the chapter from which this quote comes: "How the weaponless and defenseless church of God, the truly reborn disciples of Jesus, are called through the gospel to walk without violence, revenge or self-vindication." *Eine Chronik*, 78.

11. The three major primary sources to David Beiler are John Umble, ed. and trans., David Beiler, "Memoirs of an Amish Bishop,", *Mennonite Quarterly Review* 22, no. 2 (April 1948): 94-115; David Beiler, *Das Wahre Christenthum. Eine Christliche Betrachtung Nach Den Lahren der Heiligen Schrift* (Lancaster, Pa.: Johann Bär's Söhnen, 1888); and David Beiler, *Eine Betrachtung Über Den Berg Predig Christi und Über Den Ebräer, das 11 Cap.*, with an introduction by Amos B. Hoover, reprint, 1861 (Alymer, Ont.: available from Pathway Bookstore, LaGrange, Ind., 1994).

12. "The Amish believed that the sacrifice of the Lamb of God on the cross atoned—more correctly, potentially atoned—for the sin of Adam and Eve and the sins of the whole world." Paton Yoder, *Tradition & Transition: Amish Mennonites and Old Order Amish 1800-1900*, Studies in Anabaptist and Mennonite History, no. 31 (Scottdale, Pa.: Herald Press, 1991), 88.

13. Theron Schlabach writes of Beiler, "The earnest religion he called for was

to be inner and subjective as well as outer, objective, and governed by *Ordnung.*" *Peace, Faith, Nation: Mennonites and Amish in Nineteenth-Century America,* The Mennonite Experience in America, vol. 2 (Scottdale, Pa.: Herald, 1988), 212. Beiler's meditation on John 3 (*Wahre Christenthum,* 215-73) perhaps best illustrates his frequently expressed understanding of the relationship of inner and outer.

14. For example, Beiler, *Wahre Christenthum,* 227-28.

15. *Wahre Christenthum,* 226. Numerous similar references could be cited.

16. Such points supply the main themes of chapters in *Wahre Christenthum,* while the ideas such as humility and nonresistance, and the admonition to be obedient, occur repeatedly throughout the book.

17. Gerhard Wiebe left one written source, penned shortly before his death in 1900 and then copied and published by his son Diedrich. This small work is Gerhard Wiebe, *Ursachen und Geschichte der Auswanderung der Mennoniten Aus Rußland Nach Amerika* (Winnipeg, Manitoba: Druckerei des Nordwesten, 1900). The English edition is Gerhard Wiebe, *Causes and History of the Emigration of the Mennonites from Russia to America,* trans. Helen Janzen, Documents in Manitoba Mennonite History, no. 1 (Winnipeg, Manitoba: Manitoba Historical Society, 1981). Except when noted, the following discussion uses Janzen's translation and supplies both German and English references.

18. Accepting a date for the resignation late in 1881 or early in 1882 are Dennis E. Stoesz, "*A History of the Chortitzer Mennonite Church of Manitoba 1874-1914,*" (M.A. thesis, Department of History, University of Manitoba, Winnipeg, 1987), 192-93; William Schroeder, *The Bergthal Colony,* rev. ed., Bergthal historical series, vol. 1 (Winnipeg, Manitoba: CMBC Publications, 1986), 130; *Dictionary of Canadian Biography,* s.v. "Wiebe, Gerhard," by Adolf Ens. Older literature assumes he resigned in 1887, probably because ministers and bishops continued to consult with Wiebe after he left office. Stoesz, "History," 193-94.

The precise nature of Wiebe's offense remains unclear, as well as whether it was his own scrupulousness or pressure from the church that forced the resignation. It is also unclear whether his church continued to hold Wiebe in high regard after the resignation, or if the later publication of the *Ursache* served to restore his image with the church. Lack of detailed information on these questions, however, does not materially affect the interpretation of Wiebe's theology for the purposes of this essay.

19. For particular claims of such divine protection, see incidents described in *Ursachen,* 31-33; *Causes,* 40-41.

20. Wiebe, *Ursachen,* 1-8, 46-49; Wiebe, *Causes,* 1-7,59-63.

21. See esp. *Ursachen,* 49-58; references to end of world, 54, 58; *Causes,* 68, 72-73; references to end of world, 68, 72-73.

22. Wiebe, *Ursachen,* 9; Wiebe, *Causes,* 9.

23. Wiebe, *Ursachen,* 8; Wiebe, *Causes,* 8-9.

24. Wiebe, *Ursachen,* 1; Wiebe, *Causes,* 1.

25. Wiebe, *Ursachen*, 10; Wiebe, *Causes*, 10.

26. Wiebe, *Ursachen*, 10; see also 48-49; *Causes*, 10; see also 61-62.

27. Wiebe, *Ursachen*, 11; Wiebe, *Causes*, 12.

28. Wiebe, *Ursachen*, 13; Wiebe, *Causes*, 13-14.

29. Wiebe, *Ursachen*, 12; Wiebe, *Causes*, 13.

30. For additional passages linking the Constantinian shift and advanced education, see Wiebe, *Ursachen*, 48-49; Wiebe, *Causes*, 61-62.

31. Mennonites in southern Manitoba faced three revivalist-oriented options: John Holdeman's revival preaching among the Kleine Gemeinde in the winter of 1881-82; the travelling preachers of the Mennonite Brethren who began coming after 1883; and the General Conference Mennonites, particularly after 1890. None of these had a significant impact on Gerhard Wiebe's people in the East Reserve. Frank H. Epp, *Mennonites in Canada, 1786-1920: The History of a Separate People*, Mennonites in Canada, vol. 1 (Toronto: Macmillan, 1974), 290, 294-97; Henry J. Gerbrandt, *Adventure in Faith: The Background in Europe and the Development in Canada of the Bergthaler Mennonite Church of Manitoba* (Altona, Manitoba: Bergthaler Mennonite Church of Manitoba, 1970), 85-88, 103-07.

32. Wiebe, *Ursachen*, 7; Wiebe, *Causes*, 7.

33. Wiebe, *Ursachen*, 9, 13; Wiebe, *Causes*, 9, 14. In order to assure and ensure that the preacher was not displaying his own arrogance or pushing new ideas, the conservative worship tradition of Gerhard Wiebe read sermons collected from earlier generations of ministers.

34. Wiebe, *Ursachen*, 19-20, 51-52; Wiebe, *Causes*, 23, 64-66.

35. Among Wedel's published writings, his most explicit theological statement is the C. H. Wedel, *Meditationen zu Den Fragen und Antworten Unseres Katechismus* (Newton, Kans.: Wedel, 1910). Wedel's unpublished *Glaubenslehre* is a comprehensive systematic theology. It exists handwritten in German script, in four Hefte [copy books] totaling approximately 475 pages, which belong to the C. C. Wedel collection of the Mennonite Library and Archives at Bethel College, North Newton, Kansas. The notebooks contain C. C. Wedel's copies of notes made by student William Unrau from C. H. Wedel's class in Christian doctrine at Bethel College. Unrau's originals have been lost. C. C. Wedel's copies survive, along with an English translation of the first 353 pages made by David C. Wedel, son of C. C. Wedel, and a transliteration in modern type prepared by Hilda Voth of the untranslated portion of *Glaubenslehre*.

Inside of the front cover of Heft I is written in German script: "*Glaubenslehre bearbeitet von Prof. C. H. Wedel.* Permission of copyright secured." Since the material reads coherently, much better than one would expect from student notes made in the midst of a lecture, and is divided into short, numbered sections in the format of Wedel's six-volume history of the church (See note 50 below), these materials are treated as a primary source equal to that of C. H. Wedel's published writings. References to *Glaubenslehre* will list the page number of the appropriate

German note book as well as David C. Wedel's English translation when available. The translations in the current essay are my own.

36. C. H. Wedel, *Glaubenslehre* (North Newton, Kan.), 189-93,

37. Ibid., 197-98.

38. Wedel, *Glaubenslehre*, 197, 198, Heft IV:32-33. Similar comments on the moral influence theory appear in the *Meditionen*. There Wedel called it the perspective of a "positive-thinking theologian." He characterized this theory as a statement that the life and death of Jesus are a rich and unfathomable testimony of Christ's love. He replied that there is certainly much of value in this treasuring of the death of Christ, but that "it is nonetheless one-sided and cannot be reconciled with the words of scripture." Wedel, *Meditationen zu Den Fragen und Antworten Unseres Katechismus*, 147.

39. Wedel, *Glaubenslehre*, 193, Heft IV:27.

40. Wedel, *Meditationen zu Den Fragen und Antworten Unseres Katechismus*, 247-55. While Wedel does not have the absolutist positions of his more conservative Amish and Mennonite brothers on governmental service and nonswearing of oaths, the point in the current context is that he accepted the traditional Anabaptist categories as the appropriate external expression of the inner, spiritual faith.

41. Wedel, *Meditationen zu Den Fragen und Antworten Unseres Katechismus*, 11.

42. Wedel, *Glaubenslehre*, IV:83.

43. Ibid., IV:85.

44. Wedel, *Meditationen zu Den Fragen und Antworten Unseres Katechismus*, 12.

45. Wedel, *Glaubenslehre*, IV:54.

46. Ibid., IV:59.

47. Ibid.

48. See James C. Juhnke, *Vision, Doctrine, War: Mennonite Identity and Organization in America 1890-1930*, Mennonite Experience in America, vol. 3 (Scottdale, Pa.: Herald Press, 1989), 82-83.

49. Wedel, *Glaubenslehre*, IV:62-69, quote 66.

50. Six volumes developed the syntheses from the beginning of the Old Testament through history to Wedel's own time. These six are: C. H. Wedel, *Randzeichnungen zu Den Geschichten Des Alten Testaments* (Newton, Kan.: Bethel College, 1899); C. H. Wedel, *Randzeichnungen zu Den Geschichten Des Neuen Testaments* (Newton, Kan.: Bethel College, 1900), 96 pp.; C. H. Wedel, *Die Geschichte Ihrer Vorfahren Bis Zum Beginn Des Täufertums Im 16. Jahrhundert*, Abriß der Geschichte der Mennoniten, vol. 1 (Newton, Kan: Bethel College, 1900); C. H. Wedel, *Die Geschichte Des Täufertums Im 16. Jahrhundert*, Abriß der Geschichte der Mennoniten, vol. 2 (Newton, Kan.: Bethel College, 1902); C. H. Wedel, *Die Geschichte der Niederländischen, Preußischen und Russischen Mennoniten*, Abriß der Geschichte der Mennoniten, vol. 3 (Newton, Kan.: Bethel

College, 1901); C. H. Wedel, *Die Geschichte der Täufer und Mennoniten in der Schweiz, in Mähren, in Süddeutschland, Am Niederrhein und in Nordamerika, Abriß der Geschichte der Mennoniten,* vol. 4 (Newton, Kan.: Bethel College, 1904).

In the following discussion of Wedel's world view, I am indebted to James C. Juhnke, *Dialogue with a Heritage: Cornelius H. Wedel and the Beginnings of Bethel College* (North Newton, Kan.: Bethel College, 1987). Juhnke situated C. H. Wedel in his historical context in James C. Juhnke, "Gemeindechristentum and Bible Doctrine: Two Mennonite Visions of the Early Twentieth Century," *Mennonite Quarterly Review* 57, no. 3 (July 1983): 206-21.

51. Wedel's *Apriß 1* deals with the rise of state church Christendom and then the Waldensian alternative that supposedly merged into the Anabaptism of the 16th century. For Wedel's description of the characteristics of *Gemeindechristentum,* see Wedel, *Neuen Testaments,* 60-63, 89-90; Wedel, *Abriß 1,* 4-6, 14-16, 28-30; Wedel, *Abriß 2,* 149-58, 171-76.

52. Wedel borrowed the idea of a historical link between Anabaptists, Waldensians and the medieval sectarians from Ludwig Keller. The fact that such a historical link has come to be almost universally rejected ought not discredit in our eyes his effort to understand a *theological* alternative to the established church throughout Christian history.

53. See in particular, Wedel, *Abriß 4,* 193-208.

54. Primary sources for the theology of Johannes Moser are the 64 articles he wrote for the Mennonite periodicals *Herold der Wahrheit* and *Christlicher Bundes-Bote.*

55. Nonresistance headed a list of thirteen topics discussed at a conference of the Swiss Mennonite congregations on 15 October 1878 and reported in *Herold der Wahrheit* 15 (December 1878): 209. In his introductory comments in "Ueber die Wehrlosigkeit," *Herold der Wahrheit* 16, no. 1, 2 (January, February 1879): 1-4, 21-25, Moser stated that the article constituted further thoughts on the conclusions reached by the Swiss Mennonite conference.

56. Moser, "Ueber," 1-2.

57. Ibid., 2.

58. Ibid.

59. Johannes Moser, "Der Menschen Sterblichkeit," *Herold der Wahrheit* 15, no. 9 (September 1878): 147; Johannes Moser, "Siehe, Ich Komme Bald," *Herold der Wahrheit* 21, no. 22 (15 November 1884): 341.

60. Moser, "Menschen"; Johannes Moser, "Die Erziehung der Jugend," *Herold der Wahrheit* 16, no. 3 (March 1879): 41-44; Johannes Moser, "Das Völligerwerden," *Herold der Wahrheit* 21, no. 19 (1 October 1884): 292-93; Moser, "Siehe"; Johannes Moser, "Ein Vortrag Über Nachbarschaft," pt. 1, *Herold der Wahrheit* 22, no. 4 (14 February 1885): 49-51; Johannes Moser, "Ein Vortrag Über Nachbarschaft," pt. 2, *Herold der Wahrheit* 22, no. 5 (1 March 1885): 65-68; Johannes Moser, "Die Veranlassung und Beeinflussung Zur

Sünde," *Christlicher Bundes-Bote* 7, no. 30 (2 August 1888): 2-3; Johannes Moser, "Das Reizen Zur Liebe und zu Guten Werken," *Christlicher Bundes-Bote* 7, no. 32 (16 August 1888): 2; Johannes Moser, "Hindernisse der Mission," *Christlicher Bundes-Bote* 11, no. 19 (12 May 1892): 1; Johannes Moser, "Festigkeit in Prüfungen," *Christlicher Bundes-Bote* 11, no. 27 (14 July 1892): 2-3; Johannes Moser, "Keiner Wiederholung der Taufe," pt. 1, *Christlicher Bundes-Bote* 12, no. 40 (12 October 1893): 2; Johannes Moser, "Keiner Wiederholung der Taufe," pt. 2, *Christlicher Bundes-Bote* 12, no. 41 (19 October 1893): 2-3; Johannes Moser, "Gedanken Über Spaltungen," pt. 1, *Herold der Wahrheit* 21, no. 7 (1 April 1884): 102-03; Moser, "Gedanken 1"; Moser, "Gedanken 1"; Moser, "Gedanken 1"; Moser, "Gedanken 1"; Moser, "Gedanken 1"; Moser, "Gedanken 1"; Johannes Moser, "Göttlicher Natur Teilhaftig Werden," *Christlicher Bundes-Bote* 24, no. 23 (8 June 1905): 1-2.

61. Moser, "Vortrag 2," 65, 67.

62. Ibid., 68.

63. For one major treatment, see Moser, "Vortrag 1"; Moser, "Vortrag 2".

64. Primary sources include several small books and numerous articles in *Herold der Wahrheit* and *Herald of Truth*.

65. Men such as Jacob Stauffer and David Beiler represented the early manifestations of opposition to these changes—hence their designation as belonging to the Old Order.

66. Theron F. Schlabach, *Gospel Versus Gospel: Mission and the Mennonite Church, 1863-1944*, Studies in Anabaptist and Mennonite History, no. 21 (Scottdale, Pa.: Herald Press, 1980), 31.

67. Joseph C. Liechty, "Humility: The Foundation of Mennonite Religious Outlook in the 1860s," *Mennonite Quarterly Review* 54, no. 1 (January 1980): 5-31; J. Denny Weaver, "The Quickening of Soteriology: Atonement from Christian Burkholder to Daniel Kauffman," *Mennonite Quarterly Review* 61, no. 1 (January 1987): 5-45.

68. Schlabach, *Gospel Versus Gospel*, 31.

69. See "Repentance," in John M. Brenneman, *Plain Teachings, or Simple Illustrations and Exhortations from the Word of God* (Elkhart, Ind.: Mennonite Publishing Co., 1876); original version in *Herald of Truth* 1.7 (July 1864): 37-39.

70. Brenneman, *Plain Teachings, or Simple Illustrations and Exhortations from the Word of God*, 35-37.

71. First reprinted by John Funk's press in 1867; references to *Pride and Humility* in what follows come from John M. Brenneman, *Pride and Humility: A Discourse Setting Forth the Characteristics of the Proud and the Humble. Also an Alarm to the Proud*, 3rd ed. (Elkhart, Ind.: J. F. Funk & Bro., 1873).

72. Point made by Liechty, "Humility," 23.

73. Brenneman, *Pride and Humility*, 10.

74. Ibid., 14.

75. Ibid., 31-45.

76. John M. Brenneman, *Christianity and War: A Sermon Setting Forth the Sufferings of Christians* (Elkhart, Ind.: John F. Funk, 1868).

77. This chapter uses three of John Holdeman's books, the first two of which he produced himself in both German and English. 1) John Holdeman, *Der Alte Grund und Fundament Aus Gottes Wort Gefaßt und Geschrieben* (Lancaster, Pa.: Johann Bär's Söhnen, 1862) and John Holdeman, *The Old Ground and Foundation* (Lancaster, PA.: Holdeman, 1863). 2) John Holdeman, *Eine Geschichte der Gemeinde Gottes* (Lancaster, Pa.: Johannes Bär's Söhnen, 1875) and John Holdeman, *A History of the Church of God*, 4th printing, 1978 (Moundridge, Ks.: Gospel Publishers, 1978). The English version has been reprinted several times. Citations in what follows refer to the most recent printing by Gospel Publishers of Moundridge, Kansas, 1978. Since Holdeman considered these two English editions as more complete versions as well as translations (*Old Ground*, ii; *History*, 10.), they are quoted in this study. 3) Holdeman, *Spiegel der Wahrheit* (Lancaster, Pa.: Johann Bär's Sohnen, 1880). The English translation, John Holdeman, *A Mirror of Truth*, 5th printing, 1987 (Moundridge, KS: Gospel Publishers, 1956) should be checked against the German.

78. For example, Holdeman, *Old Ground*, 11, 22-23, 89-90.

79. Holdeman, *History*, 13-20.

80. It seems obvious that Holdeman was learning new material. Although noting only a few of the titles, Clarence Hiebert stated that Holdeman had accumulated a personal library of fifty to one hundred books. Clarence Hiebert, *The Holdeman People: The Church of God in Christ, Mennonite, 1859-1969* (South Pasadena, Calif.: William Carey Library, 1973), 379.

81. "Von der Erkenntniß des Dreieinigen Gottes, des Vaters, des Sohnes, und des Heiligen Geistes; und was sie uns lehrt," Holdeman, *Spiegel*, 9. Holdeman's focus is changed a bit by *Mirror*'s rendering of the title, "The Divine Trinity and What It Teaches Us," (17).

82. Holdeman, *Spiegel*, 11.

83. Holdeman, *Mirror*, 20-37.

84. Ibid., 23-31.

85. A change similar to that in Holdeman's outlines appears in Daniel Kauffman's three volumes of Bible doctrines. See Weaver, "Quickening," 34-42.

86. See Holdeman, *Mirror*, 11-16, 270-75, 326-27. On Common Sense philosophy in a form Holdeman could have absorbed, see George M. Marsden, *Fundamentalism and American Culture: The Shaping of Twentieth-Century Evangelicalism: 1870-1925* (New York: Oxford University Press, 1980), 14-16.

87. Menno Simons, *The Complete Writings of Menno Simons c.1496-1561*, ed. John Christian Wenger, trans. Leonard Verduin, with biography by Harold S. Bender (Scottdale, Pa.: Herald Press, 1956), 489-98.

88. At another point, Holdeman's theology certainly followed Menno Simons. After the sixteenth century, Holdeman and his followers were among the few Mennonites and Amish who accepted Menno's celestial flesh Christology. See

Holdeman, *Mirror*, 37.

89. Holdeman, *History*, 98-108; Holdeman, *Mirror*, 356-99.

90. Holdeman, *History*, 18; Holdeman, *Mirror*, 356-57.

91. Holdeman's consideration of the relationship between old and new covenants, including this treatment of the exercise of government and the sword, sounds somewhat like dispensationalism's different kinds of government and distinction between Jews and Gentiles. In contrast to dispensationalism, however, Holdeman considers the church to be the continuation of the people of Israel who have a spiritual but not a secular government. See Holdeman, *Mirror*, 356-58.

92. Holdeman, *Mirror*, 356-99.

93. Holdeman, *History*, 119-21. One mile from the Mennonite congregation in Wayne County, Ohio, in which John Holdeman grew up and was baptized was a congregation of ex-Mennonites. This group formed under the influence of revivalist preaching and had been organized into a congregation of the Church of God by John Winebrenner. In all likelihood, Holdeman had access to revivalist teaching and experience through the ongoing interaction of members of these two congregations, and the name he chose for his new church (Church of God in Christ, Mennonite) seems influenced by Winebrenner's Church of God. Schlabach, *Peace, Faith, Nation*, 108-09.

94. Hiebert, *Holdeman People*, 278-79, 414-15, 618-20.

95. Primary sources for the theology of Heinrich Egly include an "Autobiography" of 25 single-spaced pages, which he wrote in April 1887, and a series of articles. At present we have access to Egly's "Autobiography" only through an English translation, done by Emma Steury of the Evangelical Mennonite Church, Berne, Indiana. Copies of that translation are in the Mennonite Historical Library, Bluffton College; Mennonite Church Archives, Goshen College; archives of the Evangelical Mennonite Church, Administrative Headquarters in Fort Wayne, Indiana; Egly Memorial Library of the EMC of Berne, Indiana. Sometime before Steury's death in 1980, Egly's original manuscript as well as a transcription were lost.

Egly published sixteen articles in *Herold der Wahrheit* and *Christlicher Bundesbote*. Five of these were reprinted posthumously, along with three new ones, in Heinrich Egly, *Das Friedensreich Christi oder Auslegung der Offenbarung St. Johannes und Noch Etliche Andere Artikel*, ed. Jacob Schenbock (Geneva, In.: [John F. Funk], 1895). Jacob Schenbeck was a son-in-law of Heinrich Egly. An undated tract by Egly also exists.

96. Insisting on an experiential, crisis conversion was what distinguished Egly from other Amish bishops and led to some congregational schisms. This, in turn, caused the annual ministers conference to become involved. Yoder, *Tradition & Transition*, 184-85.

97. " Essen und Trinken das Fleisch und Blut Christi," *Herold der Wahrheit* 14, no. 11 (November 1877): 167-68; "Das Osterlamm," *Herold der Wahrheit* 16, no. 6 (June 1879): 102-03, and in *Friedensreich Christi*, 17-20. Other motifs

included eating the entire passover lamb, reaping what one sows, the meek inheriting the earth, a linking of Israelite festivals, and the return of the one healed leper.

98. Virtually all of Egly's articles make this point in some way.

99. J. Y. Schultz, "Besuchsreise nach Indiana und Ohio," *CBB* 6.16 (15 Aug. 1887): 6.

100. "Autobiography," transl. Emma Steury (Adams Co, Indiana, 1887), 11. For Moser, see notes above.

Egly also used revivalism as the criterion for his judgments about John Oberholtzer and William Gehman, principals in a Mennonite schism in Pennsylvania. "Autobiography," 14-15. For details on that schism, see Schlabach, *Peace, Faith, Nation*, 117-27. In addition, absence of a felt conversion was one reason that Egly rejected the so-called "Sleeping Preachers," Amish preachers who gained fame in the 1870s and 1880s for preaching while in a trance. For Egly's response, see his "Lasset Euch Niemand Verfühlen in Keinerlei Weise," *Christlicher Bundes-Bote* 1, no. 16 (15 August 1882): 125-26. On "sleeping preachers," see Schlabach, *Peace, Faith, Nation*, 220 and articles "Kauffman, John D." and "Sleeping Preacher Churches" in *Mennonite Encyclopedia*.

101. Egly was in contact with John Holdeman, who also called for an intense conversion experience. He even contemplated a merger with Holdeman's group. That hope broke down, Egly wrote, because we "could not agree again about water baptism." Egly, "Autobiography," 4.

102. Heinrich Egly, "Unser Bestreben Nach Oben," *Herold der Wahrheit* 10, no. 12 (December 1873): 195-96; Egly, "Essen und Trinken."

103. "Unser Bestreben," 195. See also "Essen und Trinken"; "Ein Neu Gebot," *Herold der Wahrheit* 15, no. 2 (December 1878): 19-20 and *Friedensreich Christi*, 11-16; "Säen und Ernten," *Herold der Wahrheit* 15, no. 12 (December 1878): 201-02; "Die Sanftmüthigen," *Herold der Wahrheit* 16, no. 12 (May 1879): 85; "Suchet und Forschet," *Herold der Wahrheit* 206, no. 14 (15 July 1883): 211-12.

104. Jacob Schenbeck's reprinting of the eight Egly sermons perhaps also reflects this shift. While nonresistance is present in this collection (*Friedensreich Christi*, 1, 4, 11, 15, 31-32), it is not as prominent in the items selected by Schenbeck as in others of Egly's articles.

105. Schlabach points out that during Egly's lifetime his group appeared to learn revivalism without departing radically from Amish faith and practice. Schlabach, *Peace, Faith, Nation*, 116. While Schlabach is correct as far as he goes, and while Egly himself did not reject or abandon nonresistance, the analysis here shows clearly that Egly's espousal of revivalist theology opened wide the door to the major changes which occurred in the era immediately following his death.

106. Marsden, *Fundamentalism and American Culture: The Shaping of Twentieth-Century Evangelicalism: 1870-1925*, 282n 29. Marsden's source was a prepublication version of Stan Nussbaum, *You Must Be Born Again, A History of the Evangelical Mennonite Church* (Fort Wayne: Evangelical Mennonite Church,

1980).

CHAPTER FOUR

1. Harold S. Bender, *The Anabaptist Vision* (Scottdale, Pa.: Herald Press, 1944), 13.

2. Harold S. Bender, "'Walking in the Resurrection': The Anabaptist Doctrine of Regeneration and Discipleship," *Mennonite Quarterly Review* 35, no. 2 (April 1961): 102.

3. Harold S. Bender, "The Mennonites of the United States," *Mennonite Quarterly Review* 11, no. 1 (January 1937): 79.

4. John Horsch, *Mennonites in Europe* (Scottdale, Pa.: Mennonite Publishing House, 1942), 370-80.

5. John C. Wenger, *Glimpses of Mennonite History and Doctrine*, 4th printing, rev., reprint, 1947 (Scottdale, Pa.: Herald Press, 1959), 145-46.

6. Cornelius Krahn, "Prolegomena to an Anabaptist Theology," *Mennonite Quarterly Review* 24, no. 1 (January 1950): 6.

7. Walter Klaassen, "Sixteenth-Century Anabaptism: A Vision Valid for the Twentieth Century?" *Conrad Grebel Review* 7, no. 3 (Fall 1989): 245-46.

8. C. Arnold Snyder, *Anabaptist History and Theology: An Introduction* (Kitchener, Ont.: Pandora Press, 1995), 84. Popular presentations of the idea of a core of doctrines shared with wider Christianity and distinct Anabaptist doctrines include C. Arnold Snyder, "Anabaptist Seed, Worldwide Growth: The Historical Core of Anabaptist-Mennonite Identity, Part I," *Courier* 13, no. 1 (First Quarter 1998): 5-8; "Anabaptist Seed, Worldwide Growth: The Historical Core of Anabaptist-Mennonite Identity, Part II," *Courier* 13, no. 2 (Second Quarter 1998): 9-12; "Anabaptist Seed, Worldwide Growth: The Historical Core of Anabaptist-Mennonite Identity, Part III," *Courier* 13, no. 3 (third Quarter 1998): 9-11, and reprinted as "From Anabaptist Seed (I)," *Canadian Mennonite* 3, no. 3 (1 February 1998): 6-8; "From Anabaptist Seed (II)," *Canadian Mennonite* 3, no. 4 (15 February 1998): 6-8; C. Arnold Snyder, "From Anabaptist Seed (III)," *Canadian Mennonite* 3, no. 5 (1 March 1998): 6-8. This series of popular articles was reprinted as C. Arnold Snyder, *From Anabaptist Seed: The Historical Core of Anabaptist-Related Identity* (Kitchener, Ont.: Pandora Press, 1999).

9. C. Arnold Snyder, "Beyond Polygenesis: Recovering the Unity and Diversity of Anabaptist Theology," in *Essays in Anabaptist Theology*, H. Wayne Pipkin, ed., Text Reader Series (Elkhart, Ind.: Institute of Mennonite Studies, 1994), 11.

10. Klaassen, "Sixteenth-Century Anabaptism," 246.

11. J. Denny Weaver, "The Work of Christ: On the Difficulty of Identifying an Anabaptist Perspective," *Mennonite Quarterly Review* 59, no. 2 (April 1985): 107-29. The following summary depends on this article, which should be consulted for particular references to sixteenth-century sources.

12. Manfred Krebs and Hans Georg Rott, eds., *Elaß, I. Teil: Stadt Staßburg 1522-1532*, Quellen zur Geschichte der Täufer, vol. 7 (Gerd Mohn: Gütersloher, 1959),

110, and Martin Bucer, *Deutsche Schriften, II: Schriften der Jahre 1524-1528*, ed. Robert Supperich, Martini Buceri Opera Omni, Series I (Gütersloh: Gerd Mohn, 1962), 254. Additional writings of Bucer on which this summary is based appear in Martin Bucer, *Deutsche Schriften, I: Frühschriften 1520-1524*, ed. Robert Supperich, Martini Buceri Opera Omni, Series I (Gütersloh: Gerd Mohn, 1960). For sources of Michael Sattler, see materials in *Elsaß I* and John Howard Yoder, trans. and ed., *The Legacy of Michael Sattler*, Classics of the radical Reformation, vol. 1 (Scottdale, Pa.: Herald Press, 1973). For sources of Hans Denck, see Hans Denck, *Schriften, 2. Teil: Religiöse Schriften; Part 3: Exegetische Schriften, Gedichte und Briefe*, ed. Walter Fellmann, Quellen zur Geschichte der Täufer, vol. 6 (1956), in particular his tracts "Was geredt sei, daß die schrift sagt," and "Von der wahren Liebe." An English translation of "Was geredt sei" appears as Hans Denck, "Whether God is the Cause of Evil," in *The Spiritual Legacy of Hans Denck: Interpretations and Translation of Key Texts*, Clarence Bauman, trans. and interp., Studies in Medieval and Reformation Thought, vol. 47 (Leiden: E. J. Brill, 1991), 72-117.

13. J. Denny Weaver, "Hubmaier Versus Hut on the Work of Christ: The Fifth Nicolsburg Article," *Archiv Für Reformationsgeschichte* 82 (1991): 171-92. The following discussion summarizes parts of this article, which should be consulted for particular references to sixteenth-century sources. For the writings of Balthasar Hubmaier, see Balthasar Hubmaier, *Schriften*, Gunnar Westin and Torsten Bergsten, eds., Quellen zur Geschichte der Täufer, Bd. 29 Quellen und Forschungen zur Reformationsgeschichte (Gütersloh: Gerd Mohn, 1962), in particular writings number 7, 8, 9, 10, 15, 16, 22, 25. The English translation of the Hubmaier corpus is H. Wayne Pipkin and John H. Yoder, *Balthasar Hubmaier: Theologian of Anabaptism*, Classics of the Reformation, vol. 5 (Scottdale, Pa.: Herald Press, 1989). For the two tracts of Hans Hut, see Hans Hut, "Von dem Geheimnus der Tauf," in *Glaubenszeugnisse Oberdeutschen Taufgesinnten, I*, ed. Lydia Müller, Quellen und Forschungen zur Reformationsgeschichte, vol. 20 (Leipzig: M. Heinsius Nachfolger, 1938), 12-28 and Hans Hut, "Ein Christlicher Underricht," in *Glaubenszeugnisse, I*, 28-37. The English translation of "Von dem Geheimnus der Tauf" is Hans Hut, "On the Mystery of Baptism," in *Early Anabaptist Spirituality: Selected Writings*, edited and trans. Daniel Liechty, with a preface by Hans J. Hillerbrand, Classics of Western Spirituality (Mahwah, N.J.: Paulist Press, 1994), 64-81.

14. Hut, "Von dem Geheimnus der Tauf," 16, Hut, "On the Mystery of Baptism," 67-68.

15. C. Norman Kraus supports these conclusions. He identifies three areas in which Anabaptist reconceptualizations had a bearing on their understanding of atonement: (1) the human-divine linkage, with greater stress on our participation in the character of Christ; (2) the relationship of God's love to justice, so that the suffering of Jesus for humanity is more representative than penal and forensic; (3) the relationship of law and grace, with the old law replaced by a new law that it is

possible to keep. In addition, Kraus points out, sixteenth-century Anabaptists "rejected the concepts of predestination and of imputation, with its corollary of limited atonement." C. Norman Kraus, "Interpreting the Atonement in the Anabaptist-Mennonite Tradition," *Mennonite Quarterly Review* 66, no. 3 (July 1992): 294-302, quote, 302.

16. The following discussion appeared in a different version in J. Denny Weaver, "Christology in Historical Perspective," in *Jesus Christ and the Mission of the Church: Contemporary Anabaptist Perspectives*, Erland Waltner, ed. (Newton, Kan.: Faith and Life Press, 1990), 99-103.

17. See "Was geredt sei," in Denck, *Schriften*, 2, 27-47 and Denck, "Whether".

18. Comments on aspects of Christology are scattered throughout Marpeck's writings. For representative statements, one might see William Klassen and Walter Klaassen, eds. and trans., *The Writings of Pilgram Marpeck*, Classics of the Reformation (Scottdale, Pa.: Herald Press, 1978), 75-76, 78-85, 98-100, 212, 233, 274, 314-15, 332, 378-79, 412-14, 434-36, 440, 447, 467, 507-15.

19. For Menno's writing on Christology, see Menno Simons, *The Complete Writings of Menno Simons c.1496-1561*, John Christian Wenger, ed., Leonard Verduin, trans., with biography by Harold S. Bender (Scottdale, Pa.: Herald Press, 1956), 422-40, 487-98, 763-72, 792-834. For an analysis of Menno's Christology, see William Keeney, "The Incarnation, a Central Theological Concept," *A Legacy of Faith: The Heritage of Menno Simons: Sixtieth Anniversary Tribute to Cornelius Krahn*, Cornelius J. Dyck, ed., Mennonite Historical Series (Newton, Kan..: Faith and Life Press, 1962), 55-68.

20. Traditional Catholic thought solved this problem in a different way. To give Jesus a sinless mother from whom he could then inherit sinless flesh, Catholic thought posited the "immaculate conception" of Mary—in which the Holy Spirit miraculously interceded to prevent the transmission of original sin when Anne and Joachim, Mary's parents according to tradition, conceived her through sexual intercourse. The resultant sinless Mary could then give birth to a sinless son of her flesh.

21. The Schleitheim *Brotherly Union* may illustrate this point. This statement of points on which the brethren agreed does not mention orthodox creedal statements, nor does any supposed common ground with magisterial Reformers on the basis of these creeds prevent the brethren's departure from Christendom.

22. Abraham Friesen, *Erasmus, the Anabaptists, and the Great Commission* (Grand Rapids, Mich.: William B. Eerdmans Publishing Company, 1998).

23. Ibid., 7-8.

24. The heart of Friesen's analysis of Erasmus's interpretation, and how Anabaptists from the radical followers of Zwingli to Menno had access to it, is found in chapter 3 of Friesen, *Erasmus*.

25. Friesen, *Erasmus*, 27-29.

26. Ibid., 37-42.

27. See Friesen, *Erasmus*, ch. 5.

28. Friesen, *Erasmus*, 100.

29. Snyder, *Anabaptist History and Theology*, 83-98; Snyder, "Beyond Polygenesis," 11-16.

30. For a good, popular introduction to postmodernity, see Susan Biesecker-Mast, "Postmodernism: How We Came to Select Cars and Communion on a Similar Basis," *Christian Living* 45, no. 8 (December 1998), 4-7.

31. Snyder, *Anabaptist History and Theology*, 8; Snyder, "Anabaptist Seed, I"; "Anabaptist Seed, II"; "Anabaptist Seed, III"; "From Anabaptist Seed 1"; "From Anabaptist Seed 2"; "From Anabaptist Seed 3"; and Snyder, *From Anabaptist Seed*.

32. On the difference between seeing the debated issues (such as the sword) as belonging to the heart of Anabaptism because they were central enough to argue about, or as issues not belonging to the real essence because there was no consensus, see Gerald Biesecker-Mast, "Anabaptist Separation and Arguments Against the Sword in the Schleitheim *Brotherly Union*," *Mennonite Quarterly Review*, 74, no. 3 (July 2000); 381-402.

33. For a somewhat related and longer version of these arguments, see J. Denny Weaver, "Some Theological Implications of Christus Victor," *Mennonite Quarterly Review* 68, no. 4 (October 1994): 492-98. These discussions are in reply to A. James Reimer, "Trinitarian Orthodoxy, Constantinianism, and Theology from a Radical Protestant Perspective," in *Faith to Creed: Ecumenical Perspectives on the Affirmation of the Apostolic Faith in the Fourth Century*, S. Mark Heim, ed. (Grand Rapids, Mich.: Eerdmans, 1991), 129-61.

34. So states Snyder, "Beyond Polygenesis," 11, citing article from *Westminster Dictionary of Christian Spirituality*.

35. Snyder, "Beyond Polygenesis," 12-13.

36. See the comments on ethics and the Nicene formula by Roberta C. Bondi, Rosemary Jermann, Paulo D. Siepierski, and A. James Reimer in S. Mark Heim, ed., *Faith to Creed: Ecumenical Perspectives on the Affirmation of the Apostolic Faith in the Fourth Century* (Grand Rapids, Mich.: Eerdmans, 1991). Whereas Reimer argued that Nicaea contains ethics, as the basis of salvaging the creed for the peace church, Bondi, Jermann, and Siepierski all note that Nicaea itself does not contain ethics. In order to salvage it, they contend, one must find ethics elsewhere in the historical context or in the lives of the men who developed the formula.

37. McClendon's chosen term for believers church or free church. James Wm. McClendon, Jr., *Systematic Theology: Ethics*, Systematic Theology, vol. 1 (Nashville: Abingdon, 1986),19.

38. Stanley Hauerwas, *The Peaceable Kingdom: A Primer in Christian Ethics* (Notre Dame, Ind.: University of Notre Dame, 1983), 55.

39. Snyder, "Beyond Polygenesis," 12-16.

40. Abraham Friesen attempted to defend Menno's acceptance of this spurious Christology by showing that Menno probably accepted it under duress, when it

was introduced to him by Obbe and Dirk Philips after his baptism. Friesen, *Erasmus*, 63-64. While I do not disagree with Friesen's suggestion, the possibility that Menno was contemplating a Christology that would work better with his new understanding of discipleship and a visible church might explain his willingness to consider a view that he knew to be questionable. In any case, we need to recognize Menno's struggle and his choice to accept the doctrine. We must account for it in terms of his own theology, rather than easily discount it as unoriginal by tracing the origins elsewhere.

41. Theron F. Schlabach, *Gospel Versus Gospel: Mission and the Mennonite Church, 1863-1944*, Studies in Anabaptist and Mennonite History, no. 21 (Scottdale, Pa.: Herald Press, 1980),116-17, quote 117.

42. Al Keim, "The Anabaptist Vision: The History of a New Paradigm," *Conrad Grebel Review* 12, no. 3 (Fall 1994): 241-42; Albert N. Keim, *Harold S. Bender 1897-1962* (Scottdale, Pa.: Herald Press, 1998), 165-66.

43. Daniel Kauffman, *Manual of Bible Doctrines, Setting Forth the General Principles of the Plan of Salvation* (Elkhart, Ind.: Mennonite Publishing Co., 1898); Daniel Kauffman, *Bible Doctrine: A Treatise on the Great Doctrines of the Bible* (Scottdale, Pa.: Mennonite Publishing House, 1914); Daniel Kauffman, *Doctrines of the Bible: A Brief Discussion of the Teachings of God's Word* (Scottdale, Pa.: Mennonite Publishing House, 1929).

44. See George R. Brunk II, *A Trumpet Sound: A Crisis Among Mennonites on the Doctrine of Christ* (Harrisonburg, Va: Fellowship of Concerned Mennonites, 1988); Arthur G. Hunsberger, *Christ or Kraus? A Critique of Kraus on Christology* (Harrisonburg, Va.: Fellowship of Concerned Mennonites, 1989); Glenn Lehman, "Brunk and Kraus: Two Paths to Christology," *Gospel Herald*, (7 March 1989), 164-66.

45. Chapter 2 identified the beginning of that quest with the work of John Howard Yoder.

46. Anecdote related in private conversation with Gene Stoltzfus. Stoltzfus eventually left seminary because of dissatisfaction with the prevailing answers and went to Vietnam to pursue activist, nonviolent peacemaking. Eventually he came to understand the work of Christ as enabling believers to confront and overcome evil, rather than as payment of a required penalty. Stoltzfus is now the director of Christian Peacemaker Teams.

CHAPTER FIVE

1. The following analysis of James Cone's work is based on J. Denny Weaver, "Confessing Jesus Christ from the 'Margins'," *Direction* 27, no. 1 (Spring 1998): 28-40. (The discussion of Karen Baker-Fletcher and Garth Kasimu Baker-Fletcher, *My Sister, My Brother,* is based on a presentation made to the Black Theology Group of American Academy of Religion/Society of Biblical Literature, meeting in Orlando, Florida, 22 November 1998.)

2. The initial footnotes of some of this book's chapters show that the content

was discussed in particular settings with individuals interested in that particular context. In such discussions, a part of my argument was that we were seeing only a piece of a larger picture. That larger picture, however, seemed rather elusive. For example, in one discussion about the interpretation of sixteenth-century Anabaptist theology, I suggested that an understanding of black theology's response to the inherited theology of Christendom would inform our understanding of early Anabaptist interpretation of that same theology. When one first hears such a comment, it seems like a great leap, and perhaps not surprisingly my interlocutor responded rather incredulously, "But what does black theology have to do with us?" It is when the arguments of the several chapters of this book have been brought together that one can begin to see the parallels and connections between the various discussions, and thus discover that there is a connection even from sixteenth-century Anbaptist theology to recent black theology. The argument of this book is cumulative, and the whole is greater than the sum of the separate parts in their individual settings.

3. A noted exception was Bishop Henry McNeal Turner (d. 1915) of the African Methodist Episcopal Church, who wrote in 1898 that "God is a Negro." Cited in James H. Cone, *For My People: Black Theology and the Black Church* (Maryknoll, N.Y.: Orbis Books, 1984), 60.

4. Cone, *For My People*, 8-9.

5. This formulation of classic atonement concepts follows John Bossy, *Christianity in the West: 1400-1700* (Oxford: Oxford University Press, 1985), 5-6, 93-94.

6. Some writers have defended the classic formulas by arguing that they were not substantially shaped by a historical coincidence—namely by their development within the church of the so-called Constantinian shift described by John Yoder. It has been claimed that finding the formula in a pre-Nicene writer invalidates the argument for the link between the creeds and ecclesiology. However, these arguments neglect to consider that the Constantinian shift happened in evolutionary fashion; its beginnings are apparent already in the second century and its culmination is indeed later than Constantine. Finding an early version of the classic formula simply shows the gradual nature of the shift, and arguing that the Nicene-Chalcedonian formulas became widely accepted only later than the time of their proclamation further underscores that they reflect the church identified with the empire, rather than the New Testament narrative of Jesus. I also suggest that denying a substantial link between the classic formulas and the church in which they developed runs counter to the assumptions of social history and of much recent historical work, which would place great stress on understanding any given formulation in terms of its context.

7. For detailed development of this interpretation of Revelation, see J. Denny Weaver, *Keeping Salvation Ethical: Mennonite and Amish Atonement Theology in the Late Nineteenth Century* (Scottdale, Pa.: Herald Press, 1997), 40-43.

8. James H. Cone, *For My People*, 10-18, 32-39, 54-62, 79-84, 101-05.

9. For the beginnings of these theological movements see James H. Cone and Gayraud S. Wilmore, eds., *Black Theology: A Documentary History: Vol. 1: 1966-1979* (Maryknoll, N.Y.: Orbis Books, 1993); James H. Cone and Gayraud S. Wilmore, eds., *Black Theology: A Documentary History: Vol 2: 1980-1992* (Maryknoll, N.Y.: Orbis Books, 1993); Katie G. Cannon, *Black Womanist Ethics* (Atlanta: Scholars Press, 1988); Jacquelyn Grant, *White Women's Christ and Black Women's Jesus: Feminist Christology and Womanist Response*, American Academy of Religion academy series, no. 64 (Atlanta: Scholars Press, 1989); Kelly Brown Douglas, *The Black Christ*, The Bishop Henry McNeal Turner studies in North American Black religion, no. 9 (Maryknoll, N.Y.: Orbis, 1994).

10. For glimpses of this evolving reconstruction of non-Constantinian theology, see J. Denny Weaver, "Christology in Historical Perspective," in *Jesus Christ and the Mission of the Church: Contemporary Anabaptist Perspectives*, Erland Waltner, ed. (Newton, Kan.: Faith and Life Press, 1990), 83-105; J. Denny Weaver, "Atonement for the Non-Constantinian Church," *Modern Theology* 6, no. 4 (July 1990): 307-23; J. Denny Weaver, "Christus Victor, Ecclesiology, and Christology," *Mennonite Quarterly Review* 68, no. 3 (July 1994): 277-90; J. Denny Weaver, "Narrative Theology in an Anabaptist-Mennonite Context," *Conrad Grebel Review* 12, no. 2 (Spring 1994): 171-88; Weaver, *Keeping Salvation Ethical*, ch. 2.

11. James H. Cone, *God of the Oppressed*, rev. ed. (Maryknoll, N.Y.: Orbis, 1997).

12. Ibid., 42-52.

13. Ibid., 57-76.

14. Ibid., 107.

15. Ibid., 209.

16. Ibid., 211.

17. Ibid., 211-12, quote 212.

18. Ibid., 212.

19. Ibid., 212-13.

20. Karen Baker-Fletcher and Garth Kasimu Baker-Fletcher, *My Sister, My Brother: Womanist and XODUS God-Talk*, Bishop Henry McNeal Turner/Sojourner Truth series in Black religion, vol. 12 (Maryknoll, N.Y.: Orbis Books, 1997), 9.

21. Ibid., 7.

22. Ibid., 15.

23. A part of Garth Baker-Fletcher's self-designation is "follower of Jesus." Baker-Fletcher and Baker-Fletcher, *My Sister, My Brother*, 203.

24. Baker-Fletcher and Baker-Fletcher, *My Sister, My Brother*, 2,3.

25. Delores S. Williams, *Sisters in the Wilderness: The Challenge of Womanist God-Talk* (Maryknoll, N.Y.: Orbis Books, 1993).

26. Delores Williams quoted in Baker-Fletcher and Baker-Fletcher, *My Sister, My Brother*, 76.

27. Baker-Fletcher and Baker-Fletcher, *My Sister, My Brother*, 77.

28. Ibid., 79.

29. Ibid.

30. Ibid.

31. Ibid., 80.

32. Ibid., 103.

33. Ibid., 104.

34. Ibid., 106. It should be noted that Garth Kasimu Baker-Fletcher contrasts this image with the "nonviolent Jesus of orthodoxy." For more on this potential point of difference between black theology and peace church theology, see the section on "Nonviolence and Violence."

35. (See J. Denny Weaver, "Atonement after 'divine child abuse," paper presented at AAR/SBL Annual Meeting, Orlando, Fla., 21-24 November 1998.)

36. Baker-Fletcher and Baker-Fletcher, *My Sister, My Brother*, 232-36.

37. Ibid., 236-42, quote 241.

38. Ibid., 244-57.

39. Ibid., 272.

40. Ibid., 285.

41. Ibid., 286.

42. Cone, *God of the Oppressed*, 36.

43. For the problems of building black theology on a base of Euro-orthodoxy, refer to scattered comments in *My Sister, My Brother* and in the writings of James H. Cone. For Mennonite assertions of the correctness of building peace church theology on classic European orthodoxy, see A. James Reimer, "Trinitarian Orthodoxy, Constantinianism, and Theology from a Radical Protestant Perspective," in *Faith to Creed: Ecumenical Perspectives on the Affirmation of the Apostolic Faith in the Fourth Century*, S. Mark Heim, ed. (Grand Rapids, Mich.: Eerdmans, 1991), 129-61; A. James Reimer, "Towards a Theocentric Christology: Christ for the World," in *The Limits of Perfection: Conversations with J. Lawrence Burkholder*, Rodney J. Sawatsky and Scott Holland, eds.(Waterloo, Ont.: Institute of Anabaptist-Mennonite Studies, Conrad Grebel College, 1993), 95-109; Jim Reimer, "Passing on the Faith: Peter Provides a Model," *Canadian Mennonite* 2, no. 16 (17 August 1998): 8-9.

44. See note 8. Cone, *For My People*, 54-59.

45. James H. Cone, *My Soul Looks Back* (Maryknoll, N.Y.: Orbis Books, 1986), 44.

46. Cone, *For My People*, 45, 58; James H. Cone, *Martin and Malcolm and America: A Dream or a Nightmare* (Maryknoll, N.Y.: Orbis Books, 1991), 303.

47. Cone, *Martin and Malcolm*, 303.

48. Ibid.

49. Cone, *God of the Oppressed*, 204.

50. Ibid., 204-05.

51. For John Yoder's discussion of such questions, see his "The Racial Revolu-

tion in Theological Perspective," *For the Nations: Essays Public and Evangelical* (Grand Rapids, Mich. and Cambridge, U.K.: Eerdmans, 1997), 97-124.

52. " Liberation of all" does not mean that all people and groups are in need of the same kind of liberation. African-Americans need liberation from the oppression of white racism, while white Americans need to be liberated from the power of white privilege that perpetuates racism.

53. Garth Kasimu Baker-Fletcher, *XODUS: An African American Male Journey* (Minneapolis: Fortress Press, 1996), 94-109, quotes 103, 105.

54. Baker-Fletcher and Baker-Fletcher, *My Sister, My Brother*, 157-58.

55. Ibid., 157.

CONCLUSION

1. Plain dress continues alive and well among the more conservative Mennonite and Amish conferences and denominations, which comprise more than a third of the 315,000 members of Mennonite-related groups in the United States. For statistics, see "1999 U.S. Anabaptist/Mennonite Statistics," *Mennonite Weekly Review*, (12 August 1999): 7; Steven Nolt, "The Mennonite Eclipse," *Festival Quarterly* 19, no. 2 (Summer 1992): 8-12.

2. See Stephen F. Dintaman, "The Spiritual Poverty of the Anabaptist Vision," *Conrad Grebel Review* 10, no. 2 (Spring 1992): 205-08; and Levi Miller, "'The Anabaptist Vision' and How It Has Changed the Mennonite Church," *Gospel Herald*, (26 April 1994), 1-4.

3. Gerald Biesecker-Mast, "Recovering the Anabaptist Body (to Separate It for the World)," in *Anabaptists and Postmodernity*, Gerald Biesecker-Mast and Susan Biesecker-Mast eds., C. Henry Smith Series, no. 1 (Telford, Pa.: Pandora Press U.S., 2000), 198, 207, 208, 209.

EPILOGUE

1. This essay is a revised version of J. Denny Weaver, "The Ambiguity of Ecclesiology in 'The Anabaptist Vision': Implications for a Peace-Church Theology," *Faith and Freedom* 6, no. 2 (August 1998): 3-11. (Its first form was a paper presented at the conference "Anabaptist Vision(s) in the 20th Century: Ideas & Outcomes," Goshen College, Goshen, Ind., 15 October 1994.)

2. Albert N. Keim, "History of the Anabaptist Vision," *Mennonite Historical Bulletin* 54, no. 4 (October 1993): 7.

3. Harold S. Bender, "'Walking in the Resurrection': The Anabaptist Doctrine of Regeneration and Discipleship," *Mennonite Quarterly Review* 35, no. 2 (April 1961): 102.

4. Harold S. Bender, *The Anabaptist Vision* (Scottdale, Pa.: Herald Press, 1944), 13.

5. Bender, "Walking," 102.

6. Harold S. Bender, "The Mennonites of the United States," *Mennonite*

Quarterly Review 11, no. 1 (January 1937): 79.

7. As was noted in Chapter 2, Al Keim's biography of Bender makes clear that Bender's own theology was orthodox and contained significant elements developed while a seminary student at Princeton and in graduate study in Europe. See Albert N. Keim, *Harold S. Bender 1897-1962* (Scottdale, Pa.: Herald Press, 1998), 152-56, as well as comments throughout.

8. Bender, *The Anabaptist Vision*, 17.

9. Ibid., 18.

10. Ibid., 7.

11. Ibid., 26.

12. Walter Klaassen, *Anabaptism: Neither Catholic or Protestant* (Waterloo, Ontario: Conrad Press, 1973), 77.

13. (Walter Klaassen, "Reassessing the Radical Reformation and Its Significance for Contemporary Christianity," address [Toronto Mennonite Theological Center, 1993],2. Address was distributed by Toronto Mennonite Theological Centre, 47 Queen's Park Crescent East, Toronto, Ontario, Canada M5S 2C3.)

14. Klaassen, "Reassessing," 4.

15. Ibid., 8.

16. Levi Miller, "'The Anabaptist Vision' and How It Has Changed the Mennonite Church," *Gospel Herald* (26 April 1994), 2.

17. Ibid., 3.

18. Ibid.

19. Ibid., 4.

20. Ibid., 5.

21. John H. Yoder, *Preface to Theology: Christology and Theological Method* (Elkhart, Ind.: Goshen Biblical Seminary, distributed by Co-op Bookstore, 1981).

22. J. Denny Weaver, "Perspectives on a Mennonite Theology," *Explorations of Systematic Theology from Mennonite Perspectives*, Willard Swartley, ed., Occasional Papers (Elkhart, Ind.: Institute of Mennonite Studies, 1984), 17-36; J. Denny Weaver, "Christology in Historical Perspective," *Jesus Christ and the Mission of the Church: Contemporary Anabaptist Perspectives*, Erland Waltner, ed. (Newton, Kan.: Faith and Life Press, 1990), 83-105; J. Denny Weaver, "Atonement for the NonConstantinian Church," *Modern Theology* 6, no. 4 (July 1990): 307-23; J. Denny Weaver, "Christus Victor, Ecclesiology, and Christology," *Mennonite Quarterly Review* 68, no. 3 (July 1994): 277-90; J. Denny Weaver, *Keeping Salvation Ethical: Mennonite and Amish Atonement Theology in the Late Nineteenth Century*, foreward C. Norman Kraus (Scottdale, Pa.: Herald Press, 1997), ch 2.

23. In light of centuries old male dominance of Western Christianity, it is tempting to say that in the second case, the church is "man's work."

24. Bender, *The Anabaptist Vision*, 26.

25. The creation of the voluntary church of the saved mirrors the formation of government "through voluntary common consent" of the governed in John

Locke's "social contract." Thomas N. Finger, *Christian Theology: An Eschatological Approach*, vol. 2 (Scottdale, Pa.: Herald Press, 1989), 228. In critique of Mennonite adoption of the "social contract" approach to ecclesiology, C. Norman Kraus has written: ". . . we have tended to consider the church under the model of a democratic institution rather than as the 'body of Christ.' Put crassly, but with more than a grain of truth, we have viewed it as a nonprofit corporation formed by freely contracting individuals (its actual legal status under the United States Constitution) for their mutual purposes of nurture, inspiration (worship), and evangelism. From this perspective the church, however solemnly we speak of it, belongs to the *bene esse* and not the *esse* of salvation" [emphasis Kraus's]. C. Norman Kraus, "Toward a Theology for the Discipleship Community," *Kingdom, Cross, and Community: Essays on Mennonite Themes in Honor of Guy F. Hershberger*, John Richard Burkholder and Calvin Redekop, eds. (Scottdale, Pa.: Herald, 1976), 111-12. For a recent theological discussion of the ecclesiological issues, see C. Norman Kraus, *God Our Savior: Theology in a Christological Mode* (Scottdale, Pa.: Herald Press, 1991), 161-86.

26. Only a few of these implications can be treated in this paper. For a longer list, see J. Denny Weaver, "The Socially Active Community: An Alternative Ecclesiology," *The Limits of Perfection: Conversations with J. Lawrence Burkholder*, second ed., Rodney J. Sawatsky and Scott Holland, eds. (Waterloo, Ont. and Kitchener, Ont.: Institute of Anabaptist-Mennonite Studies, Conrad Grebel College; and Pandora Press, 1993), 76-78.

27. It is of course true that practical, pastoral difficulties accompany the claim that the church is intrinsic to the gospel. In some ways, it is not so much a matter of whether the gospel has social implications as it is a question of which social issues belong to the gospel. In this paper, I have used nonviolence as the illustrative issue. More controversial and divisive at this time might be the issue of homosexuality. However, if the church is truly a witness to the reign of God, then we ought not allow the pastoral difficulties of dealing with social issues to undercut the idea that the gospel has intrinsically social implications and that the church is intrinsic to the gospel.

28. Desmond Tutu, *The Rainbow People of God: The Making of a Peaceful Revolution*, John Allen, ed., with a foreword by Nelson Mandela (New York: Doubleday, 1994), 29-31. See also pp. 116-118.

29. Timothy L. Smith, "Evangelical Christianity and American Culture," A. James Rudin and Marvin R. Wilson, eds., *A Time to Speak: The Evangelical-Jewish Encounter* (Grand Rapids, Mich.: and Austin, Tex.: Eerdmans and Center for Judaic-Christian Studies, 1987), 59-60. For similar descriptions of historical groups and threefold definition of evangelicalism, see Timothy L. Smith, "An Historical Perspective on Evangelicalism and Ecumenism," *Mid-Stream* 22, no. 3-4 (1983): 310; and Timothy L. Smith, "The Evangelical Kaleidoscope and the Call to Christian Unity," *Christian Scholar's Review* 15, no. 2 (1986): 127.

30. Smith, "Evangelical Kaleidoscope," 139-40.

31. This is not a statement that all Christians should receive their paychecks from an agency of the church. Rather, it means that when people work within the structures of their host society, they work in ways shaped by the church rather than in ways that merely conform to the conventions of society. That might mean, for example, that a teacher refuses to participate in patriotic displays during wartime and risks being fired. It might mean that a teenager refuses to march in her high school band's Memorial Day parade, and risks expulsion from band because of her absence. It might mean that lawyers accept lower salaries as the result of developing a practice related to questions of poverty and social justice, rather than accepting high-paying positions in corporate law. The list of examples, both small and large, is endless.

32. Of course, the extent to which the church is an alternative, and the intensity of the confrontation between church and world, depends upon the character of the social order. The intensity of confrontation varies greatly from one cultural or national setting to another. However, Anabaptists in socially tolerant North America ought not allow the lack of overt hostility to blur the fact that the church is still an alternative to, rather than a supporter of, the social order. At this juncture, recall chapter 1's warning about the subtle temptation in Canada and the direct invitation in the United States to forget or abandon the distinction between church and social order.

33. One form of the church of the saved that supports the social order is that of the later generations of Pietism. Although early Pietism had a strong social concern, as Dale Brown has argued, it later developed a highly individualistic character and lost its social challenge. See comments throughout Dale W. Brown, *Understanding Pietism*, rev. ed., reprint, 1978 (Nappanee, Ind.: Evangel Publishing House, 1996), as well as his *Anabaptism and Pietism: I. Points of Convergence and Divergence, II. Living the Anabaptist and Pietist Dialectic* (Elizabethtown, Pa.: Young Center for the Study of Anabaptist and Pietist Groups, Elizabethtown College, 1990).

34. For example, Stephen F. Dintaman, "The Spiritual Poverty of the Anabaptist Vision," *Conrad Grebel Review* 10.2 (Spring 1992), 205-208; Levi Miller, "The Anabaptist Vision' and how it changed the church," *Gospel Herald*, (26 April 1994), pp. 1-4.

BIBLIOGRAPHY

"1999 U.S. Anabaptist/Mennonite Statistics." *Mennonite Weekly Review*. 2 August 1999, 7.

Albanese, Catherine L. *America: Religions and Religion*. Belmont, Calif.: Wadsworth, 1992.

Anselm. "Why God Became Man." In *A Scholastic Miscellany: Anselm to Ockham*, ed. and trans. Eugene R. Fairweather. The Library of Christian Classics, 100-83. Philadelphia: Westminster, 1956.

Bainton, Roland H. "The Left Wing of the Reformation." In *Studies on the Reformation*, Roland H. Bainton. Collected Papers in Church History, Series 2, 119-29. Boston: Beacon Press, 1963.

Baker-Fletcher, Garth Kasimu. *Xodus: An African American Male Journey*. Minneapolis: Fortress Press, 1996.

Baker-Fletcher, Karen, and Garth KASIMU Baker-Fletcher. *My Sister, My Brother: Womanist and XODUS God-Talk*. Bishop Henry McNeal Turner/Sojourner Truth Series in Black Religion, vol. 12. Maryknoll, N.Y.: Orbis Books, 1997.

Beecher, Lyman. "On Disestablishment in Connecticut." John F. Wilson, ed. In *Church and State in American History*, 92-93. Boston: D.C. Heath, 1965.

Beiler, David. *Das Wahre Christenthum. Eine Christliche Betrachtung Nach Den Lahren der Heiligen Schrift*. Lancaster, Pa.: Johann Bär's Söhnen, 1888.

———. *Eine Betrachtung Über Den Berg Predig Christi und Über Den Ebräer, das 11 Cap*. With an introduction by Amos B. Hoover. 1861. [Alymer, Ont.]: [Available from Pathway Bookstore, LaGrange, Ind.], 1994.

Bellah, Robert N. *The Broken Covenant: American Civil Religion in Time of Trial.* New York: Crossroad, 1975.

Bender, Harold S. *The Anabaptist Vision.* Scottdale, Pa.: Herald Press, 1944.

——. "The Anabaptist Vision." *Mennonite Quarterly Review.* 18, no. 2 (April 1944): 67-88.

——. "The Anabaptist Vision." *Church History.* 13, no. 1 (March 1944): 3-24.

——. "The Mennonites of the United States." *Mennonite Quarterly Review.* 11, no. 1 (January 1937): 68-82.

——. "'Walking in the Resurrection': The Anabaptist Doctrine of Regeneration and Discipleship." *Mennonite Quarterly Review.* 35, no. 2 (April 1961): 96-110.

Biesecker-Mast, Gerald. "Anabaptist Separation and Arguments Against the Sword in Schleitheim *Brotherly Union. Mennonite Quarterly Review.* 74, no. 3 (July 2000): 381-402.

——. "Recovering the Anabaptist Body (to Separate It for the World)." In *Anabaptists and Postmodernity*, Gerald Biesecker-Mast and Susan Biesecker-Mast, eds. C. Henry Smith Series, no. 1. Telford, Pa.: Pandora Press U..S., 2000.

Biesecker-Mast, Susan. "Postmodernism: How We Came to Select Cars and Communion on a Similar Basis." *Christian Living.* 45, no. 8 (December 1998): 4-7.

Bloesch, Donald G. *The Evangelical Renaissance.* Grand Rapids, Mich.: William B. Eerdmans Publishing Company, 1973.

Bossy, John. *Christianity in the West: 1400-1700.* Oxford: Oxford University Press, 1985.

Brenneman, John M. *Christianity and War: A Sermon Setting Forth the Sufferings of Christians.* Elkhart, Ind.: John F. Funk, 1868.

——. *Plain Teachings, or Simple Illustrations and Exhortations from the Word of God.* Elkhart, Ind.: Mennonite Publishing Co., 1876.

——. *Pride and Humility: A Discourse Setting Forth the Characteristics of the Proud and the Humble. Also an Alarm to the Proud.* 3rd ed. Elkhart, Ind.: J. F. Funk & Bro., 1873.

Brown, Dale W. *Anabaptism and Pietism: I. Points of Convergence and Divergence, II. Living the Anabaptist and Pietist Dialectic.* Young Center for the Study of Anabaptist and Pietist Groups, Elizabethtown College, Elizabethtown, Pennsylvania, 1990.

——. *Understanding Pietism.* Rev. ed. 1978. Nappanee, Ind.: Evangel Publishing House, 1996.

Brunk, George R. II. *A Trumpet Sound: A Crisis Among Mennonites on the Doctrine of Christ*. Harrisonburg, Va: Fellowship of Concerned Mennonites, 1988.

Bucer, Martin. *Deutsche Schriften, I: Frühschriften 1520-1524*. Robert Supperich, ed. Martini Buceri Opera Omni, Series I. Gütersloh: Gerd Mohn, 1960.

———. *Deutsche Schriften, II: Schriften der Jahre 1524-1528*. Robert Supperich, ed. Martini Buceri Opera Omni, Series I. Gütersloh: Gerd Mohn, 1962.

Cannon, Katie G. *Black Womanist Ethics*. Atlanta, Ga.: Scholars Press, 1988.

Coffman, John S. "Spirit of Progress." *Christian Monitor* 5, no. 6 (June 1913): 176-80.

Cone, James H. *For My People: Black Theology and the Black Church*. Maryknoll, N. Y.: Orbis Books, 1984.

———. *God of the Oppressed*. Rev. ed. Maryknoll, N.Y.: Orbis, 1997.

Cone, James H., and Gayraud S. Wilmore, eds. *Black Theology: A Documentary History: Vol. 1: 1966-1979*. Maryknoll, N.Y.: Orbis Books, 1993.

Cone, James H., and Gayraud S. Wilmore, eds. *Black Theology: A Documentary History: Vol. 2: 1980-1992*. Maryknoll, N.Y.: Orbis Books, 1993.

———. *Martin and Malcolm and America: A Dream or a Nightmare*. Maryknoll, N. Y.: Orbis Books, 1991.

———. *My Soul Looks Back*. Maryknoll, N.Y.: Orbis Books, 1986.

Cruickshank, John. "Canada's Search for Identity." *Christian Science Monitor*. 26 February 1992, 19.

Dear, John. *The God of Peace: Toward a Theology of Nonviolence*. Maryknoll, N.Y.: Orbis, 1994.

Denck, Hans. *Schriften, 2. Teil: Religiöse Schriften; Part 3: Exegetische Schriften, Gedichte und Briefe*. Walter Fellmann, ed. Quellen Zur Geschichte der Täufer, vol. 6, 1956.

———. "Whether God is the Cause of Evil." In *The Spiritual Legacy of Hans Denck: Interpretations and Translation of Key Texts*, Clarence Bauman, trans. and interp. Studies in Medieval and Reformation Thought, vol. 47, 72-117. Leiden: E. J. Brill, 1991.

Dintaman, Stephen F. "The Spiritual Poverty of the Anabaptist Vision." *Conrad Grebel Review*. 10, no. 2 (Spring 1992): 205-08.

Douglas, Kelly Brown. *The Black Christ*. The Bishop Henry McNeal Turner Studies in North American Black Religion, no. 9. Maryknoll, N.Y.: Orbis, 1994.

Egly, Heinrich. "Autobiography." Emma Steury, trans. Adams Co, Indiana, 1887.

———. *Das Friedensreich Christi oder Auslegung der Offenbarung St. Johannes und Noch Etliche Andere Artikel*. Jacob Schenbock, ed. Geneva, In.: [John F. Funk], 1895.

————. "Das Osterlamm." *Herold der Wahrheit*. 16, no. 6 (June 1879): 102-03.

————. "Die Sanftmüthigen." *Herold der Wahrheit*. 16, no. 12 (May 1879): 85.

————. "Ein Neu Gebot." *Herold der Wahrheit*. 15, no. 2 (December 1878): 19-20.

————. "Essen und Trinken das Fleisch und Blut Christi." *Herold der Wahrheit*. 14, no. 11 (November 1877): 167-68.

————. "Lasset Euch Niemand Verfühlen in Keinerlei Weise." *Christlicher Bundes-Bote*. 1, no. 16 (15 August 1882): 125-26.

————. "Säen und Ernten." *Herold der Wahrheit*. 15, no. 12 (December 1878): 201-02.

————. "Suchet und Forschet." *Herold der Wahrheit*. 206, no. 14 (15 July 1883): 211-12.

————. "Unser Bestreben Nach Oben." *Herold der Wahrheit*. 10, no. 12 (December 1873): 195-96.

Elwell, Walter A., ed. *Evangelical Dictionary of Theology*. Grand Rapids, Mich.: Baker, 1984.

Epp, Frank H. *Mennonites in Canada, 1786-1920: The History of a Separate People*. Mennonites in Canada, vol. 1. Toronto: Macmillan, 1974.

Finger, Thomas N. "Appropriating Other Traditions While Remaining Anabaptist." *The Conrad Grebel Review*. 17, no. 2 (1999 Spring 1999): 52-68.

————. "From Biblical Intentions to Theological Conceptions: Some Strengths and Some Tensions in Norman Kraus's Christology." *Conrad Grebel Review*. 8, no. 1 (Winter 1990): 53-76.

————. "Still Something Essential in the Creeds." In *Jesus Christ and the Mission of the Church: Contemporary Anabaptist Perspectives*, Erland Waltner, ed., 106-14. Newton, Kan.: Faith and Life Press, 1990.

————. "The Place to Begin Mennonite Theology." *Gospel Herald*. 30 July 1996, 1-3.

————. *Christian Theology: An Eschatological Approach, Vol. 1, 2*. Scottdale, Pa.: Herald Press, 1985-89.

Friesen, Abraham. *Erasmus, the Anabaptists, and the Great Commission*. Grand Rapids, Michigan: William B. Eerdmans Publishing Company, 1998.

Gerbrandt, Henry J. *Adventure in Faith: The Background in Europe and the Development in Canada of the Bergthaler Mennonite Church of Manitoba*. Altona, Manitoba: Bergthaler Mennonite Church of Manitoba, 1970.

Grant, Jacquelyn. *White Women's Christ and Black Women's Jesus: Feminist Christology and Womanist Response*. American Academy of Religion Academy Series, no. 64. Atlanta: Scholars Press, 1989.

Hanson, R. P. C. *The Search for the Christian Doctrine of God: The Arian Controversy 318-381.* Edinburgh: T. & T. Clark, 1988.

Harder, Helmut. "*Christian Theology: An Eschatological Approach,* Volume II, Thomas N. Finger." Review. *Conrad Grebel Review.* 8, no. 2 (Spring 1990): 229-31.

Hartzler, J. E. "Christian Fundamentals." *The Mennonite.* 35, no. 45 (11 November 1920): 4-5.

———. "Christian Fundamentals." *The Mennonite.* 35, no. 46 (18 November 1920): 5.

———. "Christian Fundamentals." *The Christian Evangel.* 10, no. 12 (December 1920): 267-70.

———. "Essential Fundamentals of Christian Faith." In *Report of Third All-Mennonite Convention Held in First Mennonite Church, Bluffton, Ohio, September 2-3, 1919,* A. S. Bechtel, ed., 81-93. Bluffton, Oh., 1919.

———. "Philosophy in the Mennonite Tradition." *Mennonite Life.* 3, no. 2 (April 1948): 43-45.

———. "The Faith of Our Fathers." *Christian Exponent* 1, no. 3 (1 February 1924): 38-39.

———. "Witmarsum Theological Seminary." In *Report of Fourth All-Mennonite Convention Held in Eighth Street Mennonite Church, Goshen, Indiana,* 44-48. N.p.: N.p., 1922.

Hauerwas, Stanley. *After Christendom? How the Church is to Behave If Freedom, Justice, and a Christian Nation Are Bad Ideas.* Nashville: Abingdon, 1991.

———. *The Peaceable Kingdom: A Primer in Christian Ethics.* Notre Dame, Ind.: University of Notre Dame, 1983.

Hiebert, Clarence. *The Holdeman People: The Church of God in Christ, Mennonite, 1859-1969.* South Pasadena, Ca.: William Carey Library, 1973.

Holdeman, John. *A History of the Church of God.* 4th printing, 1978. Moundridge, Ks.: Gospel Publishers, 1978.

———. *A Mirror of Truth.* 5th printing, 1987. Moundridge, Kan.: Gospel Publishers, 1956.

———. *A Treatise on Redemption, Baptism, and the Passover and the Lord's Supper.* Carthage, Mo.: The Author, 1890.

———. *Der Alte Grund und Fundament Aus Gottes Wort Gefaßt und Geschrieben.* Lancaster, Pa.: Johann Bär's Söhnen, 1862.

———. *Eine Geschichte der Gemeinde Gottes.* Lancaster, Pa.: Johannes Bär's Söhnen, 1875.

———. *The Old Ground and Foundation.* Lancaster, Pa.: The author, 1863.

Holdeman. *Spiegel der Wahrheit*. Lancaster, Pa.: Johann Bär's Sohnen, 1880.

Holland, Scott. "Anabaptism as Public Theology." *Conrad Grebel Review*. 11, no. 3 (Fall 1993): 269-74.

———. "Intellectual and Aesthetic Freedom in the Anabaptist Academy." For Conference on Church-Related Institutions. Elizabethtown College, 1996.

———. "Theology is a Kind of Writing: The Emergence of Theopoetics." *The Mennonite Quarterly Review*. 71, no. 2 (April 1997): 227-41.

Horsch, John. *Mennonites in Europe*. Scottdale, Pa.: Mennonite Publishing House, 1942.

———. *The Mennonite Church and Modernism*. Scottdale, Pa.: Mennonite Publishing House, 1924.

Hubmaier, Balthasar. *Balthasar Hubmaier: Theologian of Anabaptism*. H. Wayne Pipkin, trans. and ed. , and John H. Yoder. Classics of the Reformation, vol. 5. Scottdale, Pa.: Herald Press, 1989.

———. *Schriften*. Gunnar Westin and Torsten Bergsten eds. Quellen Zur Geschichte der Täufer. Bd. 29 Quellen und Forschungen zur Reformationsgeschichte. Gütersloh: Gerd Mohn, 1962.

Huebner, Harry, and J. Denny Weaver. "Don't Stop at the Border." *The Mennonite*. 106, no. 20 (22 October 1991): 468-69.

———. "We Dare not Restructure Along National Boundaries." *Gospel Herald*. 22 October 1991, 8-10.

Hunsberger, Arthur G. *Christ or Kraus? A Critique of Kraus on Christology*. Harrisonburg, Va.: Fellowship of Concerned Mennonites, 1989.

Hut, Hans. "Ein Christlicher Underricht." In *Glaubenszeugnisse Oberdeutschen Taufgesinnten, I*, Lydia Müller, ed. Quellen und Forschungen Zur Reformationsgeschichte, vol. 20, 28-37. Leipzig: M. Heinsius Nachfolger, 1938.

———. "On the Mystery of Baptism." In *Early Anabaptist Spirituality: Selected Writings*, Daniel Liechty, trans. and ed., with a preface by Hans J. Hillerbrand. Classics of Western Spirituality, 64-81. Mahwah, N.J.: Paulist Press, 1994.

———. "Von dem Geheimnus der Tauf." In *Glaubenszeugnisse Oberdeutschen Taufgesinnten, I*, Lydia Müller, ed. Quellen und Forschungen Zur Reformationsgeschichte, vol. 20, 12-28. Leipzig: M. Heinsius Nachfolger, 1938.

Johnson, Janeen Bertsche. "J. E. Hartzler: The Change in His Approach to Doctrine." Unpublished paper, 1986.

Juhnke, James C. *Creative Crusader: Edmund G. Kaufman and Mennonite Community*. John D. Thiesen, ed. Cornelius H. Wedel Historical Series. North Newton, Kan.: Bethel College, 1994.

———. *Dialogue with a Heritage: Cornelius H. Wedel and the Beginnings of Bethel College.* North Newton, Kan.: Bethel College, 1987.

———. "Gemeindechristentum and Bible Doctrine: Two Mennonite Visions of the Early Twentieth Century." *Mennonite Quarterly Review.* 57, no. 3 (July 1983): 206-21.

———. "Mennonite Benevolence and Revitalization in the Wake of World War I." *Mennonite Quarterly Review.* 60, no. 1 (January 1986): 15-30.

———. *Vision, Doctrine, War: Mennonite Identity and Organization in America 1890-1930.* Mennonite Experience in America, vol. 3. Scottdale, Pa.: Herald Press, 1989.

Kauffman, Daniel. *Bible Doctrine: A Treatise on the Great Doctrines of the Bible.* Scottdale, Pa.: Mennonite Publishing House, 1914.

———. *Bible Doctrines Briefly Stated.* 2nd. ed. Scottdale, Pa.: Mennonite Publishing House, 1922.

———. *Doctrines of the Bible: A Brief Discussion of the Teachings of God's Word.* Scottdale, Pa.: Mennonite Publishing House, 1929.

———. *Manual of Bible Doctrines, Setting Forth the General Principles of the Plan of Salvation.* Elkhart, Ind.: Mennonite Publishing Co., 1898.

———. "Real Fundamentalism." *Gospel Herald.* 34, no. 4 (24 April 1941): 81.

———. "Restrictions." *The Gospel Witness.* 1, no. 23 (6 September 1905): 178, 184.

———. "The Mennonite Church and Current Issues." *Gospel Herald.* 9, no. 37 (14 December 1916): 682-83.

———. *The Mennonite Church and Current Issues.* Scottdale, Pa.: Mennonite Publishing House, 1923.

———. "Two Kinds of Fundamentalists." *Gospel Herald.* 12, no. 51 (18 March 1920): 961.

———. "Unfundamental Fundamentalists." *Gospel Herald.* 24, no. 48 (25 February 1932): 1025-26.

———. "Upon What Fundamentals Should All Christian People Agree?" *Gospel Herald.* 3, no. 19 (11 August 1910): 292, 302-03.

———. "Upon What Fundamentals Should All Christian People Agree? II." *Gospel Herald.* 3, no. 20 (18 August 1910): 307, 317.

———. "Upon What Fundamentals Should All Christian People Agree? III." *Gospel Herald.* 3, no. 21 (25 August 1910): 323.

Kaufman, Edmund G. *Basic Christian Convictions.* North Newton, Kan.: Bethel College, 1972.

Kaufman, Gordon D. *In Face of Mystery: A Constructive Theology.* Cambridge, Mass.: Harvard, 1993.

————. *Systematic Theology: A Historicist Perspective.* New York: Scribner's, 1968. Reprint 1978.

Keeney, William. "The Incarnation, a Central Theological Concept." In *A Legacy of Faith: The Heritage of Menno Simons: Sixtieth Anniversary Tribute to Cornelius Krahn,* Cornelius J. Dyck, ed. Mennonite Historical Series, 55-68. Newton, Kan.: Faith and Life Press, 1962.

Keim, Albert N. *Harold S. Bender 1897-1962.* Scottdale, Pa.: Herald Press, 1998.

————. "History of the Anabaptist Vision." *Mennonite Historical Bulletin.* 54, no. 4 (October 1993): 1-7.

Keim, Al. "The Anabaptist Vision: The History of a New Paradigm." *Conrad Grebel Review.* 12, no. 3 (Fall 1994): 239-58.

Klaassen, Walter. *Anabaptism: Neither Catholic or Protestant.* Waterloo, Ontario: Conrad Press, 1973.

————. "Reassessing the Radical Reformation and Its Significance for Contemporary Christianity." Address. Toronto Mennonite Theological Center, 1993.

————. "Sixteenth-Century Anabaptism: A Vision Valid for the Twentieth Century?" *Conrad Grebel Review.* 7, no. 3 (Fall 1989): 241-51.

Krahn, Cornelius. "Prolegomena to an Anabaptist Theology." *Mennonite Quarterly Review.* 24, no. 1 (January 1950): 5-11.

Kraus, C. Norman. *God Our Savior: Theology in a Christological Mode.* Scottdale, Pa.: Herald Press, 1991.

————. "Interpreting the Atonement in the Anabaptist-Mennonite Tradition." *Mennonite Quarterly Review.* 66, no. 3 (July 1992): 291-311.

————. *Jesus Christ Our Lord: Christology from a Disciple's Perspective.* Rev. ed. 1987. Scottdale, Pa.: Herald Press, 1990.

————. "Toward a Theology for the Discipleship Community." In *Kingdom, Cross, and Community: Essays on Mennonite Themes in Honor of Guy F. Hershberger,* John Richard Burkholder and Calvin Redekop, eds., 103-17. Scottdale, Pa.: Herald, 1976.

Kraybill, Donald B. *Our Star-Spangled Faith.* Intro Martin E. Marty. Scottdale, Pa.: Herald Press, 1976.

Krebs, Manfred, and Hans Georg Rott, eds. *Elaß, I. Teil: Stadt Staßburg 1522-1532.* Quellen Zur Geschichte der Täufer, vol. 7. Gerd Mohn: Gütersloher, 1959.

Lapp, John A. "Civil Religion is but Old Establishment Writ Large." In *Kingdom, Cross and Community: Essays on Mennonite Themes in Honor of Guy F. Hershberger,* John Richard Burkholder and Calvin Redekop, eds., 196-207. Scottdale, Pa.: Herald Press, 1976.

Lehman, Glenn. "Brunk and Kraus: Two Paths to Christology." *Gospel Herald.* 7 March 1989, 164-66.

Liechty, Daniel. *Theology in Postliberal Perspective.* London: SCM Press, 1990.

———. "*Christian Theology: An Eschatological Approach* by Thomas N. Finger." Review. *The Mennonite.* 25 September 1990, 426-27.

Liechty, Joseph C. "Humility: The Foundation of Mennonite Religious Outlook in the 1860s." *Mennonite Quarterly Review.* 54, no. 1 (January 1980): 5-31.

Marpeck, Pilgram. *The Writings of Pilgram Marpeck..* William Klassen and Walter Klaassen, trans. and eds. Classics of the Reformation. Scottdale, Pa.: Herald Press, 1978.

Marsden, George M. *Fundamentalism and American Culture: The Shaping of Twentieth-Century Evangelicalism: 1870-1925.* New York: Oxford University Press, 1980.

McClendon, James Wm., Jr. *Systematic Theology: Doctrine.* Systematic Theology, vol. 2. Nashville: Abingdon, 1994.

———. *Systematic Theology: Ethics.* Systematic Theology, vol. 1. Nashville: Abingdon, 1986.

McLoughlin, William G. *Revivals, Awakenings and Reform: An Essay on Religion and Social Change in America, 1607-1977.* Chicago History of American Religion. Chicago: University of Chicago Press, 1978.

Mead, Sidney E. *The Nation with the Soul of a Church.* New York: Harper & Row, 1975.

Menno Simons. *The Complete Writings of Menno Simons c. 1496-1561.* John Christian Wenger, ed.. Leonard Verduin, trans., with biography by Harold S. Bender. Scottdale, Pa.: Herald Press, 1956.

Miller, Levi. "'The Anabaptist Vision' and How It Has Changed the Mennonite Church." *Gospel Herald.* 26 April 1994, 1-4.

———. "Das Reizen Zur Liebe und zu Guten Werken." *Christlicher Bundes-Bote.* 7, no. 32 (16 August 1888): 2.

———. "Das Völligerwerden." *Herold der Wahrheit.* 21, no. 19 (1 October 1884): 292-93.

———. "Der Menschen Sterblichkeit." *Herold der Wahrheit.* 15, no. 9 (September 1878): 146-47.

———. "Die Erziehung der Jugend." *Herold der Wahrheit.* 16, no. 3 (March 1879): 41-44.

———. "Die Veranlassung und Beeinflussung Zur Sünde." *Christlicher Bundes-Bote.* 7, no. 30 (2 August 1888): 2-3.

———. "Ein Vortrag Über Nachbarschaft." Pt. 1. *Herold der Wahrheit.* 22, no. 4 (14 February 1885): 49-51.

———. "Festigkeit in Prüfungen." *Christlicher Bundes-Bote* 11, no. 27 (14 July 1892): 2-3.

———. "Gedanken Über Spaltungen." Pt. 1. *Herold der Wahrheit* 21, no. 7 (1 April 1884): 102-03.

———. "Göttlicher Natur Teilhaftig Werden." *Christlicher Bundes-Bote.* 24, no. 23 (8 June 1905): 1-2.

———. "Hindernisse der Mission." *Christlicher Bundes-Bot.* 11, no. 19 (12 May 1892): 1.

———. "Keiner Wiederholung der Taufe." Pt. 1. *Christlicher Bundes-Bote.* 12, no. 40 (12 October 1893): 2.

———. "Keiner Wiederholung der Taufe." Pt. 2. *Christlicher BundesBote.* 12, no. 41 (19 October 1893): 2-3.

———. "Siehe, Ich Komme Bald." *Herold der Wahrheit.* 21, no. 22 (15 November 1884): 338-41.

———. "Ueber die Wehrlosigkeit." *Herold der Wahrheit.* 16, no. 1-2 (February 1879): 1-4, 21-25.

Noll, Mark A., Nathan O. Hatch, and George M. Marsden. *The Search for Christian America.* Colorado Springs: Helmers & Howard, 1989.

———. "The End of Canadian History?" *First Things.* 22 (April 1992): 29-36.

Nolt, Steven. "The Mennonite Eclipse." *Festival Quarterly.* 19, no. 2 (Summer 1992): 8-12.

Nussbaum, Stan. *You Must Be Born Again, A History of the Evangelical Mennonite Church.* Fort Wayne: Evangelical Mennonite Church, 1980.

Reesor, Rachel. "A Mennonite Theological Response to a Canadian Context: A. James Reimer." *Mennonite Quarterly Review.* 73, no. 3 (July 1999): 644-54.

Reimer, A. James. "Doctrines: What Are They, How Do They Function, and Why Do We Need Them?" *Conrad Grebel Review.* 11, no. 1 (Winter 1993): 21-36.

———. "Toward Christian Theology from a Diversity of Mennonite Perspectives." *Conrad Grebel Review.* 6, no. 2 (Spring 1988): 147-59.

———. "Response to Gayle Gerber Koontz." *The Conrad Grebel Review.* 14, no. 1 (Winter 1996): 86-89.

———. "Towards a Theocentric Christology: Christ for the World." In *The Limits of Perfection: Conversations with J. Lawrence Burkholder,* Rodney J. Sawatsky and Scott Holland, eds., 95-109. Waterloo, Ont.: Institute of Anabaptist-Mennonite Studies, Conrad Grebel College, 1993.

———. "Trinitarian Orthodoxy, Constantinianism, and Theology from a Radical Protestant Perspective." In *Faith to Creed: Ecumenical Perspectives on the Affirmation of the Apostolic Faith in the Fourth Century*, S. Mark Heim, ed, 129-61. Grand Rapids, Mich.: Eerdmans, 1991.

Reimer, Jim. "Passing on the Faith: Peter Provides a Model." *Canadian Mennonite.* 2, no. 16 (17 August 1998): 8-9.

Richey, Russell E., and Donald G. Jones, eds. *American Civil Religion.* New York: Harper & Row, 1974.

Saucy, Robert L. "Two Innovative Theologies." *Journal of Psychology and Theology.* 17, no. 2 (Summer 1989): 187-89.

Sawatsky, Rodney. *Authority and Identity: The Dynamics of the General Conference Mennonite Church.* Cornelius H. Wedel Historical Series, vol. 1. North Newton, Kan.: Bethel College, 1987.

———. "Defining 'Mennonite' Diversity and Unity." *Mennonite Quarterly Review.* 57, no. 3 (July 1983): 282-92.

Schlabach, Theron F. *Gospel Versus Gospel: Mission and the Mennonite Church, 1863-1944.* Studies in Anabaptist and Mennonite History, no. 21. Scottdale, Pa.: Herald Press, 1980.

———. *Peace, Faith, Nation: Mennonites and Amish in Nineteenth-Century America.* The Mennonite Experience in America, vol. 2. Scottdale, Pa.: Herald, 1988.

Schroeder, William. *The Bergthal Colony.* Rev. ed. Bergthal Historical Series, vol. 1. Winnipeg: CMBC Publications, 1986.

Sider, Ronald J. "Evangelicalism and the Mennonite Tradition." In *Evangelicalism and Anabaptism*, C. Norman Kraus, ed, 159-68. Scottdale, Pa.: Herald Press, 1979.

———. *Genuine Christianity*, 183. Grand Rapids, Mich.: Zondervan, 1996.

Smith, C. Henry. *Mennonite Country Boy: The Early Years of C. Henry Smith.* Mennonite Historical Series. Newton, Kan.: Faith and Life Press, 1962.

Smith, Timothy L. "An Historical Perspective on Evangelicalism and Ecumenism." *Mid-Stream.* 22, no. 3-4 (1983): 308-25.

———. "Evangelical Christianity and American Culture.". A. James Rudin, ed., and Marvin R. Wilson. In *A Time to Speak: The Evangelical-Jewish Encounter*, 58-75. Grand Rapids, Mich. and Austin, Texas: Eerdmans and Center for Judaic-Christian Studies, 1987.

———. "The Evangelical Kaleidoscope and the Call to Christian Unity." *Christian Scholar's Review.* 15, no. 2 (1986): 125-40.

Snyder, C. Arnold. *Anabaptist History and Theology: An Introduction.* Kitchener, Ontario: Pandora Press, 1995.

————. "Anabaptist Seed, Worldwide Growth: The Historical Core of Anabaptist-Mennonite Identity, Part I." *Courier.* 13, no. 1 (First Quarter 1998): 5-8.

————. "Anabaptist Seed, Worldwide Growth: The Historical Core of Anabaptist-Mennonite Identity, Part II." *Courier.* 13, no. 2 (Second Quarter 1998): 9-12.

————. "Anabaptist Seed, Worldwide Growth: The Historical Core of Anabaptist-Mennonite Identity, Part III." *Courier.* 13, no. 3 (Third Quarter 1998): 9-11.

————. "Beyond Polygenesis: Recovering the Unity and Diversity of Anabaptist Theology." In *Essays in Anabaptist Theology,* H. Wayne Pipkin, ed.. Text Reader Series, 1-34. Elkhart, In.: Institute of Mennonite Studies, 1994.

————. *From Anabaptist Seed: The Historical Core of Anabaptist-Related Identity.* Kitchener, Ont.: Pandora Press, 1999.

————. "From Anabaptist Seed (I)." *Canadian Mennonite.* 3, no. 3 (1 February 1998): 6-8.

————. "From Anabaptist Seed (II)." *Canadian Mennonite.* 3, no. 4 (15 February 1998): 6-8.

————. "From Anabaptist Seed (III)." *Canadian Mennonite.* 3, no. 5 (1 March 1998): 6-8.

Stahl, William A. "The New Christian Right." *The Ecumenist.* 25, no. 6 (September-October 1987): 81-87.

Stauffer, Jacob. *Eine Chronik oder Geschicht-Büchlein von der Sogenannten Mennonisten Gemeinde.* 1855. Lancaster: Johann Bär, 1972.

Stayer, James M., Werner O. Packull. "From Monogenesis to Polygenesis: The Historical Discussion of Anabaptist Origins." *Mennonite Quarterly Review.* 49, no. 2 (April 1975). 83-122.

Stayer, James M. "The Swiss Brethren: An Exercise in Historical Definition." *Church History.* No. 2 (June 1978): 174-95.

Stoesz, Donald B. "*Christian Theology: An Eschatological Approach,* 2 Vol., by Thomas N. Finger." Review. *Mennonite Quarterly Review.* 67, no. 1 (January 1990): 104-07.

Swartley, Willard, ed. *Explorations of Systematic Theology from Mennonite Perspectives.* Occasional Papers. Elkhart, Indiana: Institute of Mennonite Studies, 1984.

Tutu, Desmond. *The Rainbow People of God: The Making of a Peaceful Revolution.* John Allen, ed., with a foreword by Nelson Mandela. New York: Doubleday, 1994.

Umble, John, ed. and trans. "Memoirs of an Amish Bishop." By David Beiler. *Mennonite Quarterly Review.* 22, no. 2 (April 1948): 94-115.

Weaver, J. Denny. "Amish and Mennonite Soteriology: Revivalism and Free Church Theologizing in the Nineteenth-Century." *Fides et Historia*. 27, no. 1 (Winter/Spring 1995): 30-52.

———. "Atonement for the NonConstantinian Church." *Modern Theology*. 6, no. 4 (July 1990): 307-23.

———. *Becoming Anabaptist: The Origin and Significance of Sixteenth-Century Anabaptism*. Scottdale, Pa.: Herald Press, 1987.

———. "Christology in Historical Perspective." In *Jesus Christ and the Mission of the Church: Contemporary Anabaptist Perspectives*, Erland Waltner, ed, 83-105. Newton, Kansas: Faith and Life Press, 1990.

———. "Christus Victor, Ecclesiology, and Christology." *Mennonite Quarterly Review*. 68, no. 3 (July 1994): 277-90.

———. "Confessing Jesus Christ from the 'Margins'." *Direction* 27, no. 1 (Spring 1998): 28-40.

———. "Hubmaier Versus Hut on the Work of Christ: The Fifth Nicolsburg Article." *Archiv Für Reformationsgeschichte*. 82 (1991): 171-92.

———. "The Search for a Mennonite Theology." In *Mennonite World Handbook*, Diether Götz Lichdi, ed., 143-52. Carol Stream, Il.: Mennonite World Conference, 1990.

———. *Keeping Salvation Ethical: Mennonite and Amish Atonement Theology in the Late Nineteenth Century*. Foreword C. Norman Kraus. Scottdale, Pa.: Herald Press, 1997.

———. "Narrative Theology in an Anabaptist-Mennonite Context." *Conrad Grebel Review*. 12, no. 2 (Spring 1994): 171-88.

———. "Perspectives on a Mennonite Theology." In *Explorations of Systematic Theology from Mennonite Perspectives*, Willard Swartley, ed., Occasional Papers, 17-36. Elkhart, Indiana: Institute of Mennonite Studies, 1984.

———. "Some Theological Implications of Christus Victor." *Mennonite Quarterly Review*. 68, no. 4 (October 1994): 483-99.

———. "The Ambiguity of Ecclesiology in 'the Anabaptist Vision': Implications for a Peace-Church Theology." *Faith and Freedom*. 6, no. 2 (August 1998): 3-11.

———. "The General Versus the Particular: Exploring Assumptions in 20th-Century Mennonite Theologizing." *The Conrad Grebel Review*. 17, no. 2 (1999 Spring 1999): 28-51.

———. "The Quickening of Soteriology: Atonement from Christian Burkholder to Daniel Kauffman." *Mennonite Quarterly Review*. 61, no. 1 (January 1987): 5-45.

————. "The Socially Active Community: An Alternative Ecclesiology." In *The Limits of Perfection: Conversations with J. Lawrence Burkholder*. Second ed., Rodney J. Sawatsky and Scott Holland, eds., 71-94. Waterloo, Ont. and Kitchener, Ont.: Institute of Anabaptist-Mennonite Studies, Conrad Grebel College; and Pandora Press, 1993.

————. "The United States Shape of Mennonite Theologizing: Some Preliminary Observations." *Mennonite Quarterly Review*. 73, no. 3 (July 1999): 631-44.

————. "The Work of Christ: On the Difficulty of Identifying an Anabaptist Perspective." *Mennonite Quarterly Review*. 59, no. 2 (April 1985): 107-29.

Wedel, C. H. *Die Geschichte Ihrer Vorfahren Bis Zum Beginn Des Täufertums Im 16. Jahrhundert*. Abriß der Geschichte der Mennoniten, vol. 1. Newton, Kans: Bethel College, 1900.

————. *Die Geschichte Des Täufertums Im 16. Jahrhundert*. Abriß der Geschichte der Mennoniten, vol. 2. Newton, Kan.: Bethel College, 1902.

————. *Die Geschichte der Niederländischen, Preußischen und Russischen Mennoniten*. Abriß der Geschichte der Mennoniten, vol. 3. Newton, Kan.: Bethel College, 1901.

————. *Die Geschichte der Täufer und Mennoniten in der Schweiz, in Mähren, in Süddeutschland, Am Niederrhein und in Nordamerika*. Abriß der Geschichte der Mennoniten, vol. 4. Newton, Kan.: Bethel College, 1904.

————. *Glaubenslehre*. North Newton, Kan., n.d.

————. *Meditationen zu Den Fragen und Antworten Unseres Katechismus*. Newton, Kans.: The author, 1910.

————. *Randzeichnungen zu Den Geschichten Des Alten Testaments*. Newton, Kan.: Bethel College, 1899.

————. *Randzeichnungen zu Den Geschichten Des Neuen Testaments*, 96 pp. Newton, Kan.: Bethel College, 1900.

————. *Ursachen und Geschichte der Auswanderung der Mennoniten Aus Rußland Nach Amerika*. Winnipeg, Mb.: Druckerei des Nordwesten, 1900.

Wenger, John Christian. *Glimpses of Mennonite History and Doctrine*. 4th printing, rev. 1947, 258 pp. Scottdale, Pa.: Herald Press, 1959.

————. *Introduction to Theology: An Interpretation of the Doctrinal Content of Scripture, Written to Strengthen a Childlike Faith in Christ*. Scottdale, Pa.: Herald Press, 1954.

Wiebe, Gerhard. *Causes and History of the Emigration of the Mennonites from Russia to America*. Helen Janzen, trans. Documents in Manitoba Mennonite History, no. 1. Winnipeg, Mb.: Manitoba Historical Society, 1981.

Williams, Delores S. *Sisters in the Wilderness: The Challenge of Womanist God-Talk.* Maryknoll, N.Y.: Orbis Books, 1993.

Yoder, John Howard. *The Priestly Kingdom: Social Ethics as Gospel.* Notre Dame, Ind.: University of Notre Dame, 1984.

———. *Preface to Theology: Christology and Theological Method.* Elkhart, Ind.: Goshen Biblical Seminary; distributed by Co-op Bookstore, 1981.

———. "That Household We Are." Unpublished paper, 1980.

———. *For the Nations: Essays Public and Evangelical,* 97-124. Grand Rapids, Mich. and Cambridge, U.K.: William B. Eerdmans Publishing Company, 1997.

Yoder, John Howard, trans. and ed. *The Legacy of Michael Sattler.* Classics of the Radical Reformation, vol. 1. Scottdale, Pa.: Herald Press, 1973.

Yoder, Paton. *Tradition & Transition: Amish Mennonites and Old Order Amish 1800-1900.* With a foreword by Donald B. Kraybill. Studies in Anabaptist and Mennonite History, no. 31. Scottdale, Pa.: Herald Press, 1991.

INDEX

General Conference Mennonite
Church, 40, 48, 144, 159,
168, 177
General theology. *See* theology-in-
general
Geneva, Indiana, 90
Goshen Biblical Seminary, 120
Goshen College, 23, 118
Gospel Herald, 53-54
Graham, Billy, 35
Gulf War, 166

H
Hanson, R. P. C., 63
Harding, Vincent, 168
Hartzler, J. E., 43, 52, 60-61, 67, 171
Hauerwas, Stanley, 115
Holdeman, John, 73-74, 87-89,
92, 177, 181-183
and atonement, 87-89
Holdeman Mennonites, 73
Holland, Scott, 65, 67
Homosexuality, 36, 194
Hopkins, Dwight, 135
Horsch, John, 43, 51-52, 54, 58,
61, 67, 95-96
Hubmaier, Balthasar, 100-102,
105, 115-116
Atonement, 100-102
Humility, 77-79, 85-87, 176
Hut, Hans, 100-102, 105
and atonement, 100-102

I
Individualism, 20

J
Jesus Christ. *See* Christology;
Nonviolence of Jesus.

Juhnke, James C., 41, 62, 172,
179
Just war, 57
Justice, 29

K
Kansas, 59, 72
Kauffman, Daniel, 23, 43, 52-58,
63, 67, 118, 169
Kaufman, Edmund G., 23, 43,
61-62, 67, 172
and atonement, 61
Kaufman, Gordon, 24-25, 174
Keim, Albert, 118, 170, 193
Keller, Ludwig, 82
King, Martin Luther, Jr., 138-140
Klaassen, Walter, 95-96, 112,
150-151
Kleine Gemeinde, 177
Koontz, Gayle Gerber, 172
Korean War, 144
Krahn, Cornelius, 95-96
Kraus, C. Norman, 24, 118-19,
185-186, 194

L
Lapp, John A., 37
Liberalism, 61, 66, 118, 150, 171
Liechty, Daniel, 25
Locke, John, 194
Lord's Supper, 90, 109
Luther, Martin, 30, 51, 103, 122,
148-149

M
Malcolm X, 138-139
Manitoba, 72, 77, 79, 177
Marpeck, Pilgram, 103-105, 186
Christology of, 103-104

Unrau, William, 177

V
Vietnam War, 144

W
Waldensians, 18, 83, 179
Washington, George, 35
Washington, Joseph, 123
Wedel, Cornelius H., 41, 43, 59-
    60, 67, 72-74, 80-85, 90-91,
    93, 177-179
  and atonement, 74, 80, 82
  Gemeindechristentum, 59, 82-83
Wedel, Cornelius P., 81
Wedel, David C., 177
Wenger, John C., 23-24, 43, 55-
    58, 63, 67, 95-96, 170
Wesleyans, 57
Wiebe, Gerhard, 72, 76-80, 176-
    177
  atonement, 76, 80
Williams, Delores, 133-134
Winebrenner, John, 182
Womanist theology, 29, 121, 123,
    129, 132-142
World War I, 52, 143
World War II, 62, 144, 147, 149-
    150

X
Xodus, 132-134, 139

Y
Yoder, John Howard, 18, 22, 37,
    42-44, 46, 62, 65, 143, 152,
    167-168, 172

Z
Zurich, 109
Zwingli, Ulrich, 51, 109, 112,
    148-149

THE AUTHOR

J. Denny Weaver is Professor of Religion and chair of the Department of History and Religion at Bluffton (Oh.) College. He teaches courses in Christian theology and ethics and a variety of historical studies. His research interests deal with the conversation between Anabaptist and Mennonite theology and the contextual theologies such as black, womanist, and feminist.

Weaver was born in 1941 to Alvin and Velma Weaver, of Kansas City, Kansas. With his family he attended and was a member of the local Argentine Mennonite Church. He attended Hesston College and graduated from Goshen College in 1963 with a major in mathematics. Following graduation, he spent two years at Associated Mennonite Biblical Seminary (Elkhart, Ind.), with a particular focus on Old Testament studies.

While the Vietnam War was widening, Weaver volunteered with Mennonite Central Committee for a term of alternative service as a conscientious objector. He and his wife spent a year in French language study and then served during 1966-1968 in Algeria under the MCC Teachers Abroad Program (TAP). Weaver taught English in an Algerian public school, using French as the language of instruction.

Weaver was keenly interested in events and attitudes in the newly liberated Algeria as well as in France, its former colonial ruler. Efforts to understand made him much more aware of the need to know history in order to interpret contemporary events. This insight reoriented his academic interests toward historical studies. After the MCC asignmet, Weaver focused on church history for a year at Kirchliche Hochschule Bethel, in Germany, and continued that emphasis in his final year at AMBS. At Duke University, his doctoral studies were in church history, with a speciality in sixteenth-century Anabaptism.

After teaching at Goshen College for a year, Weaver joined the Bluffton faculty. For twenty years he has been refining historical perspectives that shape his work in theology. His goal is to develop theology for the peace church that incorporates the belief that rejection of violence is an intrinsic and indispensable aspect of the good news about Jesus Christ.

Weaver is a frequent participant in conferences on Mennonite and believers church theology, and has written widely on aspects of Mennonite history and thought. *His Becoming Anabaptist* (Herald Press, 1987) was the first book to synthesize the account of Anabaptist origins from the perspective of polygenesis historiography. His *Keeping Salvation Ethical* (Herald Press, 1997) shed new light on previously uncharted nineteenth-century Mennonite and Amish theologizing and developed its relevance for contemporary understandings of peace-church atonement theology.

His many articles and essays have appeared in books and dictionaries such as *Evangelical Dictionary of Theology* and *The Oxford Encyclopedia of the Reformation*, and in academic and church periodicals, such as *Mennonite Quarterly Review, Conrad Grebel Review, Modern Theology, Archiv fur Reformationsgeschichte, Fides et Historia, Journal of Mennonite Studies, Christian Scholar's Review, Mennonite Life, Pennsylvania Mennonite Heritage, Gospel Herald,* and *The Mennonite.* Subjects include Anabaptist and Mennonite theology from the sixteenth-century to the present, use of a peace church perspective to analyze the classic statements of Christology and atonement from the early and medieval church, and the development of statements of Christology and atonement for the contemporary peace churches.

Weaver is a member of the executive committee of the Mennonite Historical Society. He also belongs to the American Academy of Religion, the American Society of Church History, and the Conference on Faith and History.

He is a member of First Mennonite Church of Bluffton, where he has served as deacon, chair of the pastoral search committee, and frequent teacher of adult Sunday School classes. He served on the Peace, Service, and Justice Committee of the Central District Conference of the General Conference Mennonite Church, and on three Christian Peacemaker Team delegations to Haiti. In 1990-1991, Weaver was visiting professor of theology at Canadian Mennonite Bible College (Winnipeg).

In 1965, Weaver married Mary Lois Wenger. They have three adult daughters, Sonia Katharina, Lisa Denise, and Michelle Therese, and four grandchildren.